WITHDRAWN

REVOLUTIONARY WARFARE AND COMMUNIST STRATEGY

Revolutionary Warfare and Communist Strategy

The Threat to South-East Asia

by

GEOFFREY FAIRBAIRN

FABER AND FABER
24 Russell Square
London

*First published in 1968
by Faber and Faber Limited
24 Russell Square London WC1
Printed in Great Britain by
Latimer Trend & Co Ltd Plymouth
All rights reserved*

SBN 571 08591 1

© *1968 by Geoffrey Fairbairn*

FOR MY CHILDREN
KATRINA, JAMES, AND CHARLES
AND
IN MEMORY OF
CHARLES RIDLEY FAIRBAIRN, D.F.C., WHO LIES IN EUROPE
TREVOR SEWARD WHO WAS DROWNED IN NORMAN WATERS
JOHN CLIVE CURRIE WHO LIES IN THAILAND
FRIENDS
WHO DIED YOUNG FOR THE FREEDOM OF OTHERS

ACKNOWLEDGEMENTS

I owe what little I have been able to learn about Communist revolutionary guerrilla warfare and Communist politics as a guerrilla mode of behaviour to a large number of people. Some of them cannot be mentioned by name because of their professional calling, both military and diplomatic; and some of them, chiefly 'Asians', because mention of their names might occasion them embarrassment in these troubled times. But should they chance across this book, I hope they will know that they have my gratitude.

I owe much in various ways to: Freddy Spencer Chapman D.S.O. author of *The Jungle is Neutral*, who first interested me in the subject while I was still a schoolboy during World War II; Vladamir Lezak-Borin, former partisan and French Foreign Legionnaire, perhaps the last surviving member of the Bukharin opposition group; Tran Van Dinh, former Chief-of-Staff of the Pathet Lao in its early days; James Murray Taylor M.M., former Sergeant in 'Z Special' Force and foreign correspondent; Denis Warner of *The Reporter* and other newspapers; E. F. Serong D.S.O., one of the most profound counter-insurgent experts; and Richard and Elsa Leach, formerly of the Burma Corporation.

Certain valuable insights have been offered by Brian Crozier, Patrick Honey, Brother Mortensen, John Coates, Frank Knopfelmacher and others too numerous to mention during conversations in all sorts of places across many years. They all share my gratitude, none my errors. I must add the name of a man I never knew who died of wounds in South Vietnam recently: Bernard Fall to whom every student of revolutionary warfare in Vietnam is very deeply indebted. I must also thank Masters Michael and Adam Body for advice on certain primitive techniques; and most of all my wife who helped throughout and went to see the war in South Vietnam as a journalist in order to make up her own mind whether the war is a just one or not.

CANBERRA, *23rd October, 1967*

CONTENTS

	Introduction	15
1.	The Battleground	29
2.	The South-East Asian Scene	63
3.	The Beginnings of Insurgency	88
4.	Nationalism at Bay	110
5.	Communist Revolutionary Doctrines	130
6.	The Nature of Revolutionary Guerrilla Warfare	143
7.	The Problems Confronting Counter-Insurgency	164
8.	The General Nature of the Struggle in Vietnam	184
9.	Vietnam: The Vietminh Revolution	211
10.	Vietnam: The Assault on South Vietnam	236
11.	Retrospect	264
	Bibliography	272
	Index	281

INTRODUCTION

The very fact that so many different terms have been coined or rediscovered in recent years to try to describe the kind of struggle which rages today at its most obvious in South Vietnam, suggests that a great deal more study remains to be done before its full implications are understood. What is altogether impermissible, though by no means wholly unlikely, is for Westerners to give up the attempt to define it and imagine that they will thereby escape its impact.

If the West chooses to withdraw from the struggle there is only one way in which it can be resolved; by vast totalitarian victories in the whole of the under-developed and, for the most part, uncommitted area that now lies between the territories that divide the Free from the Communist World, an area that is sometimes referred to as the third world. Only the West has the power to contain the expansion of Peking-based Communism which is now being pressed through revolutionary guerrilla warfare. The social and economic 'terrain' on which the struggle is being contested is very much a Western creation, for it was the West, through its world-wide colonial policies, that caused the upheaval that it could not control and which Peking believes it can.

The West cannot, in the long-run, escape involvement in the affairs of the third world, however much it may desire to do so, since effective Communist control of this vast area, coupled with a, by now, almost inevitable proliferation of nuclear weapons, would catastrophically alter the world balance of power in a fashion *permanently* unfavourable to the West.

As Mr. I. R. Sinai puts it, 'The outstanding and irreversible fact of contemporary history, then, is that Western civilization is now under concentrated attack on many fronts. It is being attacked not only by Communist imperialism, but also harassed and blackmailed by Afro-Asian nationalism and neutralism. . . . More and more a general impression is spreading that the Western countries lack that gener-

INTRODUCTION

osity of endeavour, that force of thrust and initiative, that sort of daring and faith in its own powers and that mercurial and buoyant spirit that are the true marks of a civilization at the height of its strength and energies. Western civilization may, therefore, if this is true, as it seems to be, increasingly become a small, gravely threatened numerical minority surrounded by millions upon millions who are either openly hostile to its ideas, beliefs and way of life or else contemptuously neutralist.'[1]

Mr. Sinai's chief remedy lies in revitalizing the West itself rather than trying to develop the 'slum countries of the world', though he sees that the West will have to remain militarily strong, 'ever ready to defend its crucial interests and to repudiate all threats; and at all times on guard against the danger of being dragged into a thermonuclear war.' It is easy to sympathize with this view, even if, in Australia, a little fearfully. It is easy to sympathize also with another Englishman, the historian Mr. F. H. Hinsley, when he writes, 'I groan again when I see us persisting in the existing forms of aid—in gifts of money which are wasted when unaccompanied by personnel; in military aid which only stokes the fires of violence by propping up rickety regimes or inciting people to premature revolt. . . . When I hear plans to put the British armed forces at the disposal of the United Nations to enable it to put out brushfires, I groan again. Not all the armies in the world could put out the brushfires we are going to witness.[2]

It will be the argument of this book that Communist revolutionary warfare campaigns are in no sense mere 'brush fires'. It is not the purpose of the writer to examine foreign aid to the under-developed world in detail. A single example and a moment's thought about it may, however, show that it just is not possible for the West to leave the 'slum countries of the world' to their own devices. Consider Pakistan, which in terms of poverty presumably belongs to this group: 'The Pakistani planners are the first to admit the vital importance of foreign aid. In 1964, it amounted to 40 per cent of total investment and covered the cost of 66 per cent of Pakistan's imports. Moreover it also played a crucial part in particular strategies. Releases of American grain reduced the risk of a wild inflation in food prices during the restoration of a free market to the farmers. Aid earmarked for commodities, not projects, enabled the government to dismantle import licensing without a crisis in the balance of payments.'[3]

[1] *The Challenge of Modernization*, Chatto & Windus, 1964.
[2] *The Listener*, 7th May 1964.
[3] Barbara Ward, *The Economist*, 5th June 1965.

INTRODUCTION

Quite apart from the question of deep-rooted Western values being lost through a refusal to afford aid to such countries, can it really be thought politically sane for the West irretrievably to lose all influence over a country as potentially significant as Pakistan? Moreover, one of the important reasons why the Pakistani-Indian war of 1965 was limited and professional, rather than protracted and 'tribal', was this very dependence upon the West, both in terms of economic aid and military equipment. 'Brushfire wars' are not all of a kind.

Anyway, even given a yardstick to determine the political decision of whether to continue giving aid or not to countries of the third world, the geographical spread would be very wide and quite clearly, unless the West is to abandon both its humanitarian tradition and its readiness to accept external challenge, there is no possibility of its making an overall disengagement from the problems of economic development in the world's most sensitive areas.

In fact there is not necessarily any direct relationship between a country's economic achievement and its freedom from Communist attack so far as the under-developed countries of the world are concerned, for even such established countries as Israel, Turkey, India, Thailand and Greece have at some time or other in the post-war world been threatened by Communist violence. Needless to say, Japan no longer belongs to this category of countries; nor perhaps does Taiwan, which has recently been able to dispense with U.S. economic assistance.

If Western support for the economic development of the vulnerable regions of Asia, Latin America, and Africa is to have any significance, it must take account of their position in the face of revolutionary guerrilla warfare. This involves first of all trying to understand the nature of this kind of organized and ideologized politico-military activity. It should be said immediately that this is not a specific problem that can easily be abstracted from the general problem of international relations and nuclear and 'conventional' defence. This is clearly put by Stanley Hoffman: 'The dimensions of international equilibrium have multiplied. The invention of nuclear weapons so complicates the military balance that one can now distinguish a strategic balance (the balance of terror, properly speaking), a tactical one (the balance of conventional forces), and what one could call the balance of subversion: guerrilla wars, which erupt both because of political conditions and because of a much lower risk of escalation. In addition, international politics must cope with economic development, with the promotion of social and political stability (or conformity), and

INTRODUCTION

with propaganda and cultural activities (so rich in political fall-out).'[1]

The interdependence of these distinguishable, but not always practicably separable, elements of the world struggle has been obvious since the beginning of large-scale U.S. involvement in Vietnam: the phasing of escalation of bombing targets and the promotion of social and political stability in South Vietnam alike affect, and are affected by, the actual ground operations against the Vietcong and the North Vietnamese armed forces in South Vietnam. In addition the 'balance of terror' affects the limits of U.S. escalation; and the promotion of stability through foreign aid affects not only the economy of South Vietnam but the economies and attitudes of surrounding countries such as Thailand and Cambodia, which are importantly related to the struggle within South Vietnam. Again, the predominately conventional make-up of U.S. forces affects their approach to counter-insurgency as a campaign involving much more than conventional weaponry and tactics.

'National security policy in the nuclear age thus goes far beyond the traditional concept of assembling overwhelming power,' as Mr. Henry Kissinger points out. 'It involves political, psychological, economic, and social factors. In its widest sense, it comprises every action by which a society seeks to assure its survival or to realize its aspirations internationally.'[2] If a quotation from a notable practitioner of insurgency and counter-insurgency is set alongside Mr. Kissinger's summary, an important clue to the nature of revolutionary guerrilla warfare is immediately revealed: 'Modern warfare moves at the same time in the military, political, psychological, and socio-economic fields, so that the nature of the attack is total . . . (it) is waged before as well as during hostilities. . . . War in this century has become a total people's war.'[3]

Nothing can be more damaging to the proper approach to the problem of countering revolutionary guerrilla warfare than the belief that, except on certain lower levels of the struggle which are often marked by the inflexibility of opposing guerrilla military tactics,[4] it can be abstracted from the totality of power relations and turned into a mere identifiable series of tactical and technical problems.

[1] Stanley Hoffmann, *The State of War*, Praeger, 1965.
[2] *Problems of National Strategy*, Praeger, 1965.
[3] General Abdul Haris Nasution, *Fundamentals of Guerrilla Warfare*, Pall Mall Press, 1965.
[4] 'With all their qualities as fighters, the Vietcong have this incredible inflexibility, which is their greatest weakness . . .' Major John Essex-Clark of the 1st Battalion, Royal Australian Regiment, *Sydney Morning Herald*, 22nd July 1966.

INTRODUCTION

Furthermore, the nature of the struggle is not simply total in the sense of being all-embracing; on the Communist side it is concerned with the destiny of mankind itself. It implies: 'the real or pretended subordination of public policy and military strategy to a stated and understandable purpose. . . . *Communism is important because ordinary Asians can give to it*, not because of what it may give them some day. It has the fanatic and religious appeal of a new system and its most formidable weapons are those which lie outside most of our own everyday thinking about politics and economics. Rights and wealth are not the issue. The destiny of humanity is.'[1]

On the Communist side, the struggle is total not only in point of totalitarian philosophy and organization but because the stake is the future of the under-developed world. *Revolutionary guerrilla warfare is simply the continuation of Bolshevik politics by means appropriate to under-developed countries.* This kind of struggle, the nature of which will be elaborated later, raises an issue of very great gravity for democratic societies which engage in it, once the war becomes prolonged and rises in intensity, which are the precise aims of the Vietnamese Communists in the present exemplary struggle. As Professor Paret points out, '. . . France after 1954 could have maintained her dominance over Algeria only if the political system and intent of the country had been re-shaped along totalitarian lines. . . . A totalitarian nation within the framework of an aggressively anti-Russian and anti-Chinese alliance might well have won the revolutionary war in Algeria.'[2]

There are no signs whatsoever of authoritarianism entering American political life as a result of the protracted struggle in Vietnam; and so the struggle remains an oddly uneven one in terms of social intensity. This is the price democracies must pay for their special kinds of dignity. But it is also a price that is paid willingly at present for a very ill-founded reason, which may be expressed in the sentence, 'If we win here, we shall win everywhere.' Certainly this attitude is in a sense a reply to General Vo Nguyen Giap's statement to the same effect on behalf of his side and his form of warfare. But it did not originate there: it was first importantly expressed by the archetype of the American liberal hero, Jordan, fighting international Fascism in Spain through the pen of Ernest Hemingway.[3] This attitude is part of

[1] Paul M. A. Linebarger, *South-East Asia in the Coming World*, The Johns Hopkins Press, 1954.
[2] *French Revolutionary Warfare from Indochina to Algeria*, Pall Mall Press, 1964.
[3] The writer owes this insight to His Excellency Dr. Ch'en Chi-Mai, Ambassador of China to Australia.

the American dream. (Of course it was a distinguished Frenchman, M. André Malraux, who saw the European as a man 'committed to the test of the act'; but history has permitted Americans, beyond all other Europeans, to believe in the efficacy of comparatively quick, decisive acts.)

Should the struggle in Vietnam become seemingly unduly protracted in the light of American attitudes, and especially should this form of warfare proliferate, then the greatest power on earth is going to have to take into account the very many levels at which modern warfare of the Bolshevik kind is fought. As M. Jules Monnerot was constrained to establish more than a decade ago, 'More than once in the twentieth century war has compelled the canalisation and transformation and concentration of energy by societies of the relaxed type in which energy enjoyed free play and could expend itself where it chose; and this energy brought victories to societies which, at the beginning of the war, had been less concentrated and were less equipped with "one-way" dynamism than their opponents.... We see here a sort of reversal of cause and effect: war has the effect of making a non-totalitarian society largely totalitarian, but a totalitarian dynamic was the cause of the war. Being by definition *turned outwards*, the totalitarian dynamic is essentially aggressive; and the result is that it stimulates energy in the outside world to resist it.'[1]

The built-in Communist aggressive dynamic has caused the war in Vietnam, but it was begun in such a slowly phased and camouflaged[2] manner that American resistance not only came very late in the day but with a severe division of national purpose beneath the level of executive government. This is regarded by Hanoi as being of supreme significance; General Giap has stated very explicitly how Hanoi foresaw such a struggle: 'The enemy will pass slowly from the offensive to the defensive. The blitzkrieg will transform itself into a war of long duration. Thus, the enemy will be caught in a dilemma: He has to drag out the war in order to win it and does not possess, on the other hand, the psychological and political means to fight a long-drawn-out war....'

Mr. Bernard Fall comments on this speech of Giap's: 'In all likelihood, Giap concludes, public opinion in the democracy will demand an end to the "useless bloodshed", or its legislature will insist on

[1] *Sociology of Communism*, George Allen and Unwin, 1953.
[2] Capt. B. H. Liddell Hart's Foreword to *Guerrilla Warfare* by Mao Tse-tung and Che Guevara, Cassell, 1962: 'Thus the concept of "cold war" is now out of date, and should be superseded by that of "camouflaged war".'

INTRODUCTION

knowing for how long it will have to vote astronomical credits without a clear-cut victory in sight. This is what eternally compels the military leaders of democratic armies to promise a quick end to the war—to "bring the boys back home by Christmas"—or forces democratic politicians to agree to almost any kind of humiliating compromise rather than to accept the idea of a semi-permanent anti-guerrilla operation. There is little indication in the 1960's that the logical conclusions have been drawn from earlier lessons.'[1]

But as one of the greatest counter-insurgency experts in the world, Sir Robert Thompson, has made clear: '... when the build-up phase, the insurgency itself and the continuing threat of subversion after the insurgency have been taken into account, the government and people of a threatened country, together with those members of the free world who support it, must be prepared to face a long, arduous and protracted struggle. The Emergency in Malaya lasted twelve years, and the insurgency in Vietnam has been going on for over six years with bitter intensity and no successful conclusion in sight.'[2]

Sir Robert goes on to write that 'in the life of a country it is a comparatively short span'; but the democratic countries which support governments abroad against insurgency are unlikely to think in such measured terms unless they have a very clear understanding of the international significance of revolutionary warfare. It is quite naturally one of the purposes of Communist propaganda, particularly the kind which is allowed to percolate through fellow-travelling and professional liberal circles in the West, to muddy the waters of such understanding as much as possible.

Part of the purpose of this book will be to examine this campaign of political obfuscation in the West, but what must be grasped immediately is this: that unless an insurgency is effectively dealt with locally at its subversive (or *potential*) stage—and insurgency is very carefully camouflaged to make this difficult to do—then a struggle commences so far as the patrons and allies of the affected country from the free world are concerned, that is not simply between armies and politico-military forces, but between *societies*. The arena of political struggle embraces an area vastly wider than the country in which the insurgency is being met, much wider indeed than the region in which this country is situated, in fact as wide as the world.

This happens not, of course, because of anything to do with the specific techniques and tactics of revolutionary guerrilla warfare as

[1] Bernard Fall, *The Two Vietnams*, Pall Mall Press, 1965.
[2] Robert Thompson, *Defeating Communist Insurgency*, Chatto & Windus, 1966.

INTRODUCTION

such, which *seem* to be localized in a fashion and to an extent that allows insouciance on the part of those Western countries which for various reasons are uncommitted, but simply because revolutionary guerrilla warfare is but *part* of a Communist attack on the free world, which *must* be backed in every available way by the rest of the Communist world.

And so on one side of the struggle there is a society which is totally engaged because of its very political nature and because it is seeking a victory which it believes is historically, definitively irreversible. It knows that supporting it in various ways are similar totalitarian societies moved by exactly the same belief in a world-wide consummation of history through organized violence. Now the writer is quite aware that both the nuclear balance of terror and the Sino-Soviet split have immensely complicated the task of predicting specifically how the Soviet Union will react to a major American counter-insurgency operation anywhere in the world, let alone one directed against an insurgency of which China wishes to pose as patron. But what North Vietnam knows, or at any rate believes (and soundly in the light of all past conflicts since World War II), is that neither the U.S.S.R. nor China will permit its Communist regime to be politically destroyed. The Russian anti-aircraft missiles provide the proof of this. The Hanoi government undoubtedly still entertains much higher hopes than this, of course, for it quite clearly believes that the will of the U.S.A. and its allies will not be strong enough to prevail even in *South* Vietnam.

But the *very worst* the North Vietnamese society can reasonably expect is to have its expansion temporarily halted and its economy severely damaged; and this is not only because of a belief in ultimate victory for historically 'revealed' reasons but because of the nature of its opponents. Its opponents are necessarily on the defensive throughout. Though the South Vietnamese society, as expressed through its various governments, formally makes claims to represent the whole country from time to time and some political leaders have talked about carrying the struggle to the North, it has never been organized or prepared for such activities. This is only partly because the Communists seized and held the political initiative; it is also because today only Communist societies are 'naturally' organized and prepared to expand.

The defensive commitment of South Vietnam is underlined by the incessantly proclaimed intention of its great patron, the U.S.A., to the effect that its war aims preclude any attempt to overthrow the regime

INTRODUCTION

in the North. This proclamation is the fruit of a civilized, non-aggressive mode of behaviour inherent in democracies, which obtains in all conditions short of outright, declared war. As a mode of behaviour it is admirable. But it has strategic consequences of a very exacting kind when it is opposed by Communist societies dedicated to an altogether different mode of behaviour.

If these consequences are going to be regarded as acceptable over a long period of time, then the meaning of revolutionary warfare must be understood in a much wider and deeper sense than that of jungle and paddy-field battles waged according to special politico-military techniques. Even to inflict limited defeats against Communist insurgency will very often require support from the free world; major insurgencies will necessitate considerable help to the governments under attack and will thus become international problems, as in the case of South Vietnam. It is not without significance that the only example of the 'roll-back' of Communist state power, the Soviet withdrawal from Iran in 1946, was brought about through Anglo-American pressure in the United Nations.[1]

In the field of international relations, Communist propaganda directed at the Western world is devoted to undermining sympathy for the U.S.A. and its allies on two quite different counts: first, this propaganda ceaselessly exacerbates fears of 'escalation' that might embroil uncommitted Western nations, while from time to time implying that negotiations are being sought by Hanoi.[2] Secondly, it incessantly attempts to particularize the Vietnamese struggle in a special way; to suggest that a Hanoi victory would anyway only be of Vietnamese significance, since Ho Chi Minh is really primarily a nationalist who at worst (for the West) would be a Titoist leader of a united Vietnam.

The thermo-nuclear 'balance of terror' does not always favour the side with the most powerful nuclear armoury, indeed it can have an inhibiting effect as the U.S.A. is finding in its attempts to regulate the level of hostilities in Vietnam. Moreover, compared with earlier confrontations such as the Berlin air-lift, the Korean War and the Cuban

[1] Angus Maude, *South Asia*, The Bodley Head, 1966.
[2] M. Monnerot delineates this feature of totalitarian diplomacy very nicely: 'Totalitarian diplomacy and propaganda frequently test the psychological resistance of the opponents they tend to disintegrate by suddenly switching from war talk to peace talk, in the hope of obtaining from "cowardly relief" what they were unable to achieve through menaces. Another of their objectives is to enable their friends to maintain, without too great implausibility, that "an agreement is possible" with the totalitarians. . . .' *Sociology of Communism*, op. cit.

missile crisis, the attitude of the West is altogether more muddled and diffused. This is because, over a number of years, Communist propaganda has fastened on the understandable European desire to free itself of overseas entanglements, on a latent distrust of U.S. global policy that it has found easy to manipulate, and above all on the fear of 'escalation' which, although rational, can become almost hysterical in the context of what, largely as a result of this propaganda, has become widely regarded as a 'dirty war'.

This is one of the purposes of the operation so far as Peking and Hanoi are concerned: to establish not only that revolutionary warfare cannot be defeated but that the very opposing of it involves the world in a situation of altogether unacceptable risks. It is not only, of course, a question of revolutionary warfare; it is a question of hemispheres. The Communists are aware that to the West risks which seem (just) acceptable in regard to Berlin or the Atlantic are not necessarily going to be regarded as acceptable in respect of Asia or the Pacific.

Some years back an Australian commentator described very succinctly the likely pattern of the future: 'The root of the matter is that the Communists are out for *total victory*: and we only want to avoid defeat by some sort of arrangement. It is no good to rely on "seeds of contradiction" in the Communist system to save the situation: nor can we hope to check the advance of their power and influence by our present methods. The end of the new phase of Western diplomacy, unbacked by *moral* as well as material strength, will, I believe, be a new set of small-scale retreats covered by a smokescreen of "realistic" arguments pitched in terms of the "nuclear menace" which paralyses *our* will, while leaving that of our enemies unaffected.'[1]

For certain special reasons this verdict is not applicable to the situation in Europe today; and the reasons are very relevant to an understanding of why the situation is quite different in Asia. From the beginning, Communist hopes in Europe have been centred on the conversion of the liberal capitalist and social democratic West into proletarian states. This has not occurred, and never will now occur. On the contrary, the Communist governments are faced with a gradual upsurge of liberalism towards a bourgeois society, a movement that is importantly related to an improvement in some living standards. As a result, the Communist regimes are increasingly hard put to justify Marx-Leninism as an ideology for a technological age. It is the ideology that is withering away rather than the state.

This is not to say that the U.S.S.R. has given up its attempts at

[1] Denis Jackson, *Twentieth Century*, Melbourne, Autumn 1960.

INTRODUCTION

subversion of the West; but it does mean that only subversion remains as a viable political weapon and the social 'terrain' is becoming less susceptible to such techniques with every year that passes. A combination of the thermo-nuclear balance of terror, the strains of liberalization within the U.S.S.R. and its bloc, and rising standards of living and opportunity in the West has indeed caused a stalemate that for the time being is apparently acceptable.

In Asia the situation is altogether different, as it is in Latin America and Africa. Revolutionary violence is increasing every year in the under-developed world. Of the more than one hundred and fifty important examples of it that have occurred since 1958 almost all have been in this area, which contains more than half the world's population. In 1958 twenty-three 'prolonged insurgencies' were recorded, in 1965 there were fifty-eight. Of the nations that have known serious violence an overwhelming majority are classified as 'poor'[1] and clearly there is a direct relationship between poverty and violence; but not between relative poverties and Communist attack. The latter depends upon a number of other factors which are not necessarily related to poverty as such at all, as will be shown later.

As Mr. Robert McNamara says, this area would be 'pregnant with violence' even if Communist subversion was absent from the scene. Most of it is not yet pregnant with true modernization; very little of it is about to give birth to a decent material life for the ordinary man and his wife and children. Such a situation can easily evoke one of two reactions on the part of Europeans; either to abandon the under-developed world to its presumedly hopeless future, while strengthening Europe itself and perhaps concentrating political attention upon the Middle East; or to continue with economic and technical aid, just hoping for the best so far as political developments are concerned.

The former reaction, though showing signs of becoming important, is not likely to prevail for reasons already touched upon. The latter might do so. If it does, it will of course be for a number of reasons; but primarily because there is a growing feeling in Europe, shared by men of exemplary mind and heart, that with Stalin and Dulles, the arch-supporters of intransigence, now both out of the way, intransigence itself is on the wane. The proponent of this argument, Professor R. C. Zaehner, for many of whose opinions the writer has the very highest regard, seems to see the present as a 'watershed between a dying civilization based on individualism, once arrogant, now abject,

[1] Robert S. McNamara, U.S. Secretary of Defence, *The Bulletin*, 11th June 1966.

that has shown itself bankrupt and stands self-condemned, and a collective civilization yet to be born in which the free development of each (will be) the condition for the free development of all'.[1]

To quarrel with this argument, framed by Marx and Engels, is in Professor Zaehner's opinion mortal sin. The trouble is that it is not really a question of quarrelling with an opinion but of opposing today in Asia those who would arrogate to themselves the right to define human relationships in a fashion taking no account whatsoever of 'free development'. Moreover, once one accepts that one's own European civilization is 'bankrupt and stands self-condemned', then there remains no right to act politically or militarily in its cause, except strictly in self-defence, and perhaps not even then. It is not very difficult to see how this individually deeply felt belief can help to paralyse the will of the West; or can be used with motives far from disinterested to rationalize and encourage more inward and self-centred policies. It is indeed very difficult to controvert this belief, in its application to events in Asia, unless it can be demonstrated that revolutionary warfare is something altogether different from, and more generally threatening than, mere localized guerrilla warfare.

Professor Herbert Butterfield, who, once again, is a writer for whom the author has the very greatest respect, can describe the present situation as simply 'the competition (and, in some respects the race) between Western Democracy and Eastern Communism as positive missionary ideals—alternative ways of producing what must now be regarded as inescapable changes in the world at large'.[2] Such an interpretation can pose a very real problem to the Christian.

If the world situation really is just a matter of competing missionary ideals; warfare merely an expression of this competition, and liberal capitalism, bankrupt beyond repair, can only decently be incorporated within the ideal Marx-Leninist society, then men of good will can but give their assent to such a 'convergence of the spirit', to use Professor Zaehner's phrase. But it is as well to understand what this will mean in practical terms: 'If (China) has, in addition to these power-assets (nuclear armament and very large conventional forces), control over the resources of South-East Asia, she will become an unmanageable heavy weight in the balance, rather in the way that Germany became an unmanageable heavy weight in the European balance.'[3]

[1] *The Convergent Spirit*, Routledge and Kegan Paul.
[2] *International Conflict in the Twentieth Century*, Routledge and Kegan Paul, 1960.
[3] Coral Bell, Congress of Cultural Freedom seminar, Sydney 1966. Mimeograph.

INTRODUCTION

And so it is perhaps at least worthwhile exploring the meaning and implications of revolutionary warfare for the world at large. What is happening in South Vietnam and probably beginning to happen in North-East Thailand; what was attempted in Malaya, Burma, and Indonesia from 1948-49 onwards; what was achieved in Cuba and perhaps nearly achieved in the Dominican Republic, and may be achieved next year or in a few years' time in Tanzania or Burma are events having singularly little to do with a convergence or divergence of the spirit, so far as the author can see. They have to do with the mode of behaviour, the organization, the tactics and strategy, the philosophy of history, and the hopes of small bodies of armed intellectuals who believe that they can exploit and later control the forces of disorder unleashed by the world-wide upheavals which have eroded the traditional patterns of behaviour in their own societies.

Such men operate according to a certain understanding of what history has been 'all about', a special understanding that has never freely won the allegiance of any society on earth, not even the very poorest; and so it is their intention to deny, through politico-military warfare (substituting political intensity of an armed kind for an intensity of weaponry denied to them at present) the exercise of free choice. In another book, Professor Butterfield wrote: 'We might almost say that the ideals of the French Revolution were realized over a long period in the nineteenth century in so far as they served the cause of power.'[1] The same may be said of the ideals of 1917 in the underdeveloped world today.

What is happening in places like South Vietnam is in no sense a missionary Olympic Games; nor is it part of an ineluctable process as Marx believed when he saw an electric locomotive on exhibition in Regent Street and exclaimed, 'Now the problem is solved! The consequences are incalculable. In the wake of the economic revolution the political must follow, for the latter is only the expression of the former.'[2] What is happening is the waging of totalitarian warfare adapted to special conditions. The present European distaste for the American effort to counter this kind of warfare is not at all the result of a more humane understanding of modern problems; rather it stems from the fact that 'A government that promises to do for its citizens what the social-service state promises to do, cannot, at the same time, take the risk of weakening the relative position of that worker in the

[1] *Christianity and History*, G. Bell, 1950.
[2] M. M. Bober, *Marl Marx's Interpretation of History*, Harvard University Press, 1927.

INTRODUCTION

world, even if, in the long run, the current policy fatally weakens his position absolutely, not relatively.'[1] The 'Peking-line' offensive is largely predicated upon that assumption; and only the extraordinary wealth of the U.S.A. permits its government to wage protracted war without relatively weakening the position of its working population to any significant extent.[2]

---

[1] Denis Brogan, *The Price of Revolution*, Hamish Hamilton, 1951.
[2] But in 1967 there is developing an important political argument to the effect that the struggle in Vietnam is beginning to erode domestic plans for 'The Great Society'.

Chapter 1
THE BATTLEGROUND

It may seem eccentric to begin an examination of revolutionary warfare in South-East Asia with a newspaper report about events in the U.S.A.; but by doing so it is in fact possible to go straight to the heart of the matter by giving a practical illustration of the worldwide scope of this kind of conflict. The report appeared in *The Australian* on 20th July 1965 under the heading: 'HO WAITS CONFIDENT OF REVOLT IN U.S.

It continued: 'A staggering assessment of the United States and its leadership—so unreal as to defy discussion—grips the Communist North Vietnamese regime as an article of faith. Not only does the party, run by the aged Ho Chi-minh, believe it will win, unconditionally, the war in South Vietnam. It is also certain that President Johnson will be overthrown.

'It forecasts a divided U.S.A. tearing itself apart over the war. These conclusions, reached by the top Vietnamese leaders, have dumbfounded a recent spate of visitors. How do the North Vietnamese account for their belief that revolution is around the corner in America? "Criticism in colleges and assorted debates always leads to revolution", is the collective reply.'

This belief is held partly because of the presumed effect of a protracted war upon democratic opinion and institutions, which has already been touched upon; and partly because the Communists see the present in the fashion described by a Chinese student: 'Our generation is given by history the task of eliminating imperialism from the world. For this the American people must overthrow U.S. imperialism and thus make possible world peace.'[1] Vietnam is to be the catalyst in this presumedly inevitable historical process.

The Maoist ideological foundations for this belief will be examined later. All that is being established at this point is that Peking and Hanoi see such protests and criticisms as a movement of great significance, and they regard the protesters as their allies in a struggle of worldwide dimensions. They can be made to serve a threefold pur-

[1] Anna Louise Strong, *The Australian*, 23rd July 1966.

pose; to undermine the determination of the Western powers directly involved in South Vietnam, to weaken the sympathy of uninvolved Western nations for the U.S. effort and to stiffen the resolve of Hanoi through producing apparently significant evidence of disaffection in the West—evidence that is of course hugely magnified by Peking and Hanoi propaganda agencies. It is perfectly clear to Peking and Hanoi that if the U.S.A. and its allies exert themselves over a considerable period of time, then the Communists cannot win in Vietnam. Therefore the indirect strategic approach, a traditional feature of Communist political warfare is resorted to. The intention is that Western Communists and particularly their fellow-travellers, by exploiting the 'contradictions' presumed to be inherent in capitalist societies, will slowly erode their purposefulness to the point where any kind of negotiations however disadvantageous to the West and to those they would protect, will appear more acceptable than persevering with the struggle.

The protest movement has from the beginning been made into a political operation directly analogous in certain all-important respects with the revolutionary warfare campaign being directed and led by the Communists in South Vietnam. The writer is quite aware that on the face of it such a statement sounds altogether bizarre, but the fact is that the type of revolutionary guerrilla warfare with which we are dealing is simply an application of Communist political warfare to special conditions and it cannot be properly understood unless it is studied in the general context of Bolshevik activism and organization. It cannot be comprehended merely in terms of panji sticks and fortified villages, terrorist attacks and ambushes, weaponry and mobility. Its essence lies in the manipulation or control of the population by the organizational weapon'[1] of the Communist party either through terror (or mere bullying), or by way of disguised objectives that appeal to large numbers or significant sections of the population whose acquiescence is required for the attainment of the ultimate, irreversible objective of the Communists: total power for the Party.

It is the skills inherent in Communist organization and methods of political activism, immeasurably more than fieldcraft and the like, that makes the revolutionary guerrilla cadres such formidable enemies. Wherever a Leninist party operates there is political guerrilla warfare being waged; and if necessary it can be just as protracted as the new guerrilla warfare proper that is expounded by Mao. The reason that it

[1] Philip Selznick, *The Organizational Weapon*, The Rand Corporation, 1952.

can be so protracted lies in the definitive nature of the victory being striven after; definitive in the sense that it is irrevocable, though not that the objective can be defined in detail. This is the source of the deeply impressive 'motivation' of trained Communist militants: 'The legitimate ends of action in the Communist image of the militant are the seizure of power by the party and the ultimate values to which the seizure is supposed to lead.'[1]

On the one hand any and all methods are permissible because of the nature of the objective. 'There will be a change comparable to the change one likes to imagine (but it is only an optical illusion) between history and pre-history . . . For these believers the idea that impersonal, omnipresent and ineluctable forces might come to nothing is the very essence of the absurd.'[2] On the other hand the objective is so vaguely formulated that its manner of achievement, however horrifying to non-Communists, can in no way degrade it. So the Communists quite clearly believe. This permits them to use any means available for the seizure of power. Lenin is very explicit about this: 'We repudiate all morality that is taken outside of human class concepts. . . . We say that our morality is entirely subordinated to the interest of the class struggle of the proletariat. Our morality is derived from the interests of the class struggle of the proletariat.'[3] Or again: 'We must be able to withstand all this, to agree to any sacrifices, and even—if need be—all sorts of stratagems, artifices, illegal methods, to evasions and subterfuges, only so as to get into the trade unions, to remain in them, and to carry out Communist work within them at all costs.'[4]

Thus the Communists declare their outlaw position at the deepest level; and yet, in order to be able to act effectively, every Communist party of course strives unceasingly for legitimacy within the society it intends to subvert. So does the National Liberation Front, the political arm of the Vietcong, which is now fighting precisely for its own recognition as a legal party. The aim is always a *political one*, to be achieved by whatever methods seem most appropriate to given conditions, with no holds barred.

[1] Gabriel A. Almond, *The Appeals of Communism*, Princeton University Press, 1954.
[2] Monnerot, op. cit. Compare Almond op. cit. In Lenin's *'What is to be Done'*, only six out of a total of 801 references to the traits and actions of militants, etc. deal with the ultimate constructive aims of the movement. In Lenin's *Left-Wing Communism*, less than 4 per cent of a total of 764 references relate to ultimate aims.
[3] Collected Works, Vol. XVII, David Shub, *Lenin*, Mentor Books, 1948.
[4] Philip Selznick, op. cit. An appeal to Western democrats, 1920.

However, while preparing to gain a position within the enemy bourgeois society from which to destroy it, the Communists use all the available institutions and organizations of that society in order to broaden their influence or control.[1] In just the same way, the revolutionary guerrilla uses all available existing organizations *before* an insurgency, insurgency being usually, though not always, embarked upon only after a Communist failure to achieve power by other means or, as in the case of the Franco-Vietminh struggle, when other means are thought unlikely to be offered. Moreover because, during an insurgency access to government institutions is denied to the insurgents, they are normally willing to give it up in order to be accepted once again as a 'legal' party belonging to a coalition government which they estimate they can dominate through political subversion. For the Communists, the difference is simply one of methods and tactics: 'Politics is war without bloodshed. War is politics with bloodshed,' as Mao Tse-tung put it.

During an insurgency, the revolutionary guerrillas attempt to set up a parallel administration—a kind of alternative government apparatus—while seeking violently to smash the legitimate administration. But there is nothing new about this. As Lenin explained, 'The Communists can have no confidence in bourgeois legality . . . They must everywhere create a duplicate illegal apparatus which, at the decisive moment, could help the Party perform its duty to the revolution. . . . The absolute necessity in principle of combining illegal work with legal work is determined not only by the specific features of the present period . . . the eve of the proletarian dictatorship . . . but also by the necessity of proving to the bourgeoisie that there is not, nor can there be, a sphere or field of work that cannot be won by the Communists.'[2]

For this kind of total political or total politico-military warfare, as the case may be, two things above all are required, a special kind of political organization and the ability of this organization to manipulate significant sections of the population towards the achievement of Communist ends, these being always camouflaged.

The organization is itself a political weapon of a quasi-military kind, composed of cadres comprising 'a very special kind of person, sharing

---

[1] ". . . Leninist political doctrine rests upon a broad interpretation of the nature of power. In particular, Bolshevik theory and practice recognize that power is *social*, generated in the course of all types of action (not simply the narrowly 'political') and latent in all institutions." Selznick op. cit.

[2] Selected Works X, William R. Kintner, *The Front is Everywhere: Militant Communism in Action*, University of Oklahoma Press, 1950.

in an esoteric knowledge not assimilable by the average proletarian during the era of the bourgeois dictatorship'[1] and highly disciplined in a wholly centralized, military fashion. The qualities of a cadre member were outlined by the great Bulgarian agitation and propaganda (agitprop) expert, Dimitrov, as follows: '(i) Absolute devotion to the cause of the working class, loyalty to the Party, tested in the face of the enemy—in battle, in prison, in court. (ii) Closest possible contact with the masses. (iii) Ability independently to find one's bearings and not to be afraid of assuming responsibility in making decisions. (iv) Discipline and Bolshevik hardening in the struggle against the class enemy as well as in irreconcilable opposition to all deviations from the Bolshevik line.'[2]

Since the cadre members are the directing operatives in a trade union or on a university campus as well as in a revolutionary guerrilla movement, it is as well to consider in more detail just what is involved in the formation of this kind of 'politician'. Philip Selznick provides a brilliant summary of those features of the cadre that are applicable to both communist fields of endeavour, the 'merely' political and the revolutionary guerrilla. 'It has a meaning consistent with but not limited to military usage . . . Each member has special training and ideally should be able to lead non-party groups as they may from time to time become accessible. The movement is expected to change in response to events but . . . ideally, the cadre represents a permanent hard core prepared to take advantage of opportunities as they may arise or be created. In sum, the cadre party is a highly manipulable organization of trained agents; it is sustained by political combat and is linked with mass movements as its members become leaders of wider groups in the community.

'The formation of cadres is a basic task of Communist organization. The expenditure of years of effort on the gathering and development of basic cadres is not begrudged, for they constitute the precious and indispensable vanguard of the revolution . . . Bolshevik cadres cannot be created simply through indoctrination; they are trained and tested *in* the struggle for power . . . Hence Communist infiltration tactics are valuable not only for the strategic objectives they win, but for building the party.' In the same way, a protracted guerrilla war is seen sometimes not only as a means of discouraging the enemy but also of inuring Communist-controlled guerrillas to warfare.[3]

---

[1] Gabriel A. Almond op. cit.
[2] *United Front*, International Publishers, 1938.
[3] e.g. Truong Chinh (*Long March*), the theoretician of the Indo-Chinese

In order to underline the similarity between the political guerrilla in the West and his politico-military counterpart in South-East Asia (or Africa or Latin America) it is worth quoting a definition of the latter offered by an Australian student of the Vietnam struggle: 'A guerrilla cadre is not merely a soldier toting a rifle, knife or grenade. He is the permanent nucleus of a force around whom its expansion must be built. He must be superbly trained in all aspects of guerrilla warfare—military, psychological, political, and sociological. He must learn to 'live among the population as fishes live in the sea' . . . direct the recruitment of support from the local population, lecture on guerrilla strategy and tactics, give weapons instructions, personally lead terrorist campaigns, plan day to day military operations, collate and interpret intelligence information, administer captured districts and collect taxes. He must be completely dedicated to the cause he is serving, engendering in his colleagues and followers the will to continue, whatever the hardships and handicaps. He is at once soldier, psychologist, propagandist, terrorist, lecturer, politician, administrator, disciplinarian and leader. When one speaks of thousands of guerrilla cadres entering South Vietnam, one is speaking of a tremendously formidable force.'[1]

And so is any Communist party very formidable; and always for the same reasons: the possession of a thoroughly efficient organization, and an ability to manipulate social groups. The two factors are inseparable in assessing the efficacy of individual parties in different situations: it is not only the guerrilla but the member of *any* Communist cadre who must exist in the population 'as a fish in the sea'. If there are insufficient 'contradictions' to exploit within a society or if the institutions and organizations in a society are fully aware of Communist methods, then the Communists quite clearly cannot win out. In such a case they must look to the power of the 'Socialist bloc' or blocs outside the national borders to install them in power, as was the case with the East European Communists after World War II: Communists in nearly all liberal societies are spiritual and doctrinal irridentists. The significance of the established Communist bases for the export of revolution will be discussed later. As a result of a Western self-denying ordinance, assisted at times by the fear of escalation

---

Communist party: 'Why must the war be protracted? . . . The enemy has planes, tanks, etc. . . . The enemy troops are well-trained, our are not inured to war. . . .' *The Resistance Will Win*, Foreign Languages Publishing House, Hanoi, 1947.

[1] Frank Mount, *Vietnam*, National Civic Council Publication, Melbourne, June 1966.

beyond the nuclear threshold, these privileged sanctuaries of Communist subversive expansion are never directly assaulted.

What is to the point here is the similarity of approach adopted by Communists throughout the world towards the winning of absolute political power and the similarity of the organization that is always used. This can never be properly understood unless the quasi-military nature of all Communist parties is firmly grasped, and this involves first understanding the Leninist conception of leadership: 'Classes are led by parties and parties are led by individuals who are called leaders ... This is the ABC. The will of a class is sometimes fulfilled by a dictator.... Soviet socialist democracy is not in the least incompatible with individual rule and dictatorship. ... All phrases about equal rights are nonsense.'[1]

This in itself is not obviously militaristic but it does reveal a rather curious notion of democracy, socialist or otherwise. When it is linked with self-proclaimed ethical outlawry, the limitless (and hence nihilistic) aims of Communism[2] and the *language* of Communist activism, then the militarized nature of Communist behaviour and organization becomes clear. As Kintner remarks, 'The ultimate objective of all military operations is the destruction of the enemy's will to resist. The consistent aim of all Communist operations is not to reform existing institutions "but to smash them" (Lenin). The smashing, the destruction of the existing system of states, is a purely military objective.'

Indeed the language of Communism is altogether militaristic. This extremely important fact is too often ignored in western assessments of Communism. It is central to understanding what Communism is all about. Virtually all Communists since Marx and Engels have been almost obsessively attracted by military methods and a militaristic approach to politics. Lenin's admiration for the modern army knew no bounds: 'Let us take a modern army, here is a good example of organization. This organization is good simply because it is flexible, because it knows how to impart a single will to millions of people. Today, these millions sit in their homes at the different ends of the country. Tomorrow a mobilization order is issued and they gather at appointed places. Today, they lie in trenches sometimes for months at a stretch. Tomorrow, in a pre-arranged order, they march forward to storm the enemy. Today, they perform miracles in evading bullets

---

[1] Lenin in 1920. Quoted in David Shub, op. cit.
[2] An element of Communist thinking today was prefigured by the nineteenth-century 'Communist', Babeuf, to whom Lenin refers: 'Let everything return to chaos, and from chaos let there arise a new and regenerated world.'

and shrapnel. Tomorrow they perform miracles in open battles . . . That is what you call organization, *when in the name of one object, inspired by a single will, millions of people change the form of their intercourse and their action, the place and methods of their activity, their weapons and their arms, in accordance with the changing circumstances and demands of the struggle.*'[1]

But it is not at all a matter of mere admiration for the totalitarian aspects of military organization. Simply because the Communists since Lenin have opted for a necessarily small élite organization that eschews all democratic methods (though seeking to penetrate democratic institutions) and that even rejects propaganda unless it is linked with agitation, they have had to adopt quasi-military methods in order to constitute a truly effective 'organizational weapon'. As Lenin put it, 'In its struggle for power the proletariat has no other weapon but its organization. . . . International capital will not be able to withstand this army . . . (But) Unless such an organizing and leading staff (the Communist party) exists the victory of the proletariat and the maintenance of its power is impossible. Hence the enormous importance of Party organization, unity of view and singleness of will, the strictest Party discipline with expulsion from its ranks of all opportunist and alien elements.' The command structure of the Communist Party is essentially military[2] and its objective . . . the destruction of the 'enemy' society within which it operates . . . is in effect a quasi-military objective (that is, a definitive defeat of the 'enemy' society which cannot be described in terms simply of politics as understood in the West). Moreover, this defeat is to be brought about through the application of militarized politics by the methods of irregular warfare: guerrilla politics.

Again and again in recent years pronouncements by the leaders of revolutionary warfare in Asia have been quoted in the Western press as though they represented something new and specific to revolutionary guerrilla warfare proper. Whereas on closer examination they are revealed as nothing but orthodox Leninist doctrines. When, for example, Mao Tse-tung speaks of war as 'the highest form of struggle' he is only echoing the Programme of the Communist International of yesteryear: 'The highest form of struggle follows the rules of warfare and necessitates a preliminary campaign, an offensive character in

---

[1] Kintner, op. cit.
[2] This is clearly established in Kintner, op. cit., in the form of a tabular comparison of the essential components of a military apparatus and their parallels in the Communist movement.

the fighting and unlimited heroism and devotion on the part of the proletariat. When General Giap writes of 'Each person a soldier, each village a fortress, and each Party branch a resistance committee staff' he simply parallels an old Communist saying, 'every shop and factory our fortress.'

When Lozovsky praised Lenin he praised him in terms that would gladden the heart of any revolutionary warfare leader in South-East Asia today: 'In the whole of Lenin's activities the following passes like a red thread: Initiative, determination, ruthlessness, the pursuit of the enemy until he is destroyed, quick action and the concentration of proletarian forces at the weakest spot of the enemy's front.'[1] A number of the essentials of revolutionary guerrilla warfare are contained in that appraisal of Lenin's political activism.

The nature of the Communist party and of its methods of operation is not only basically militaristic; Communists throughout their history have been preoccupied with the problem of insurrection as such, which is simply a form or a stage of revolutionary guerrilla warfare. Marx himself wrote: 'Insurrection is an art quite as much as war or any other, and subject to certain rules of proceeding which, when neglected, will produce the ruin of the party neglecting them.' But it was Lenin with his altogether more conspiratorial cast of mind who refined the principles of insurrection with special attention to 'camouflaged warfare': the meticulous preparation of forms of agitation designed to win over at least a proportion of 'the masses' under slogans that hid the real aims of the Bolsheviks, and to neutralize other groups in society which, if they had known armed insurrection was being planned, would have opposed it.

One more general point should be made here about Communist methods as they relate to guerrilla politics and warfare: 'Unlike the citizen of a democratic country, the guerrilla does not feel ill at ease in the presence of violence.'[2] The violence is not only actual but potential; not only physical but moral as well. Everywhere the Communists, whether revolutionary guerrilla fighters in South Vietnam or political activists in the West, are committed to doing violence to their enemies, physically or morally; to *destroying* their enemies either with a bullet or through character assassination. ('Politics is war without bloodshed. War is politics with bloodshed'.). Since Communism has nowhere come to power except through violence, quite

---

[1] *Lenin—The Great Strategist of the Class War.* qu. in Kintner, op. cit.
[2] Colonel Wilkins, F. M. Osanka (Editor), *Modern Guerrilla Warfare,* Free Press of Glencoe, 1964.

clearly the democratic practice of intellectual and emotional persuasion is for Communists only subsiduary to a quite different kind of activity.

All Communists are committeed to a belief in violence, overt or covert, as an integral part of their political behaviour; to political activity conceived as warfare; and to a kind of warfare which is necessarily chiefly covert. Given this understanding and the mode of behaviour that flows from it, then 'Guerrilla warfare may be waged in the Malayan jungle, in the rear areas of Korea, or on a college campus or in the councils of a labour union.[1] But this kind of political behaviour is so foreign to democratic politics that it remains difficult for most democrats quite to accept the reality of it. It was Fidel Castro who said of the Americans that they were not guerrilla minded[2] and he might well have said it of the West in general. For example, the following quotation from Lenin describes a kind of behaviour which a number of espionage investigations and other detailed reports on Communist activity have revealed to be quite typical; and yet it reads grotesquely to the average citizen of a democracy: 'A resistance group should be formed from men living near each other who meet regularly. The first duty of the combat group is to ensure constant liaison with each other and specially with neighbouring groups. Special recognition signs should be agreed on in advance, such as signals from windows, whistling, and peculiar call sounds . . .'[3] Put like that it sounds absurd; and yet every Communist party cell feels itself to be operating in enemy territory and knows itself to be using the methods of irregular combat.

This is not only because of the nature of Communist organization and methods; it is also because Communists, far from being the missionary servants of a Higher Idea as their admiring intellectual fellow travellers like to represent them, are men and women owing allegiance to a *source of power* which *determines* their behaviour, their 'ideas', and their doctrine.[4] It may seem as though the Sino-Soviet split and the growth of what has come to be called polycentrism alters this 'irridentist' role of Communist parties. However this is not yet

[1] Colonel Wilkins, op. cit.
[2] Often as a result of sheer ignorance. Theodore Draper's *Castro's Revolution: Myths and Realities*, Praeger, 1962, shows how this supposed 'peasant revolution' arising out of poverty occurred in fact in a society 57 per cent urban with the fourth highest living standard in Latin America and a per capita income almost as high as Italy's.
[3] F. O. Miksche: *Secret Forces*, Faber & Faber 1950.
[4] M. Vyvyan: *The Language of cold political warfare*, *Twentieth Century*, February 1951.

generally the case. In Australia the General Secretary of one Communist party may visit Moscow and the other Peking, but although this has undoubtedly weakened the Australian Communist movement in some ways, it has in no way altered the essential Communist political behaviour. For example, it has been the Moscow party that has played the biggest part in regard to Vietnam, though on the theoretical plane it was Peking's insistence on revolutionary warfare as the prime form of struggle for the times that led to the Sino-Soviet split. Again, whatever its theoretical reservations about Peking may be, the Moscow party was certainly hoping for—and would most graciously have welcomed—a Peking-orientated Communist victory in Indonesia.[1] What is quite certain is that neither the Sino-Soviet split nor the development of polycentrism has altered Communist modes of political behaviour nor the quasi-military nature of the 'organizational weapon'. Its direction, based on a kind of élite party-cum-revolutionary general staff, necessarily has to make use of comparatively large numbers of people who are neither effectively indoctrinated nor, in many cases, in any way sympathetic to the idea of the dictatorship of the proletariat as Communist totalitarian rule is called by Communists. Still less would they approve of the conspiratorial techniques, the outlaw morality, and a commitment to violence that are all part of the Communists' stock in trade.

Despite much talk about 'the masses'—'the raw material of history', as Stalin so charmingly called them—the Communist parties in fact, exploiting the 'contradictions' within society, concentrate on certain groupings of people which they seek to transform into 'front' organizations for the party. This technique is precisely the same whether it is used to form a guerrilla 'resistance movement' in South-East Asia or an 'anti-war movement' (bogusly called a 'Peace Movement' by Communists and fellow travellers) in order to hamstring Western policies towards Communist expansion. In Vietnam a number of political parties and organizations constituted the Communist controlled Vietminh 'resistance movement'; in Australia a significant section of the Labour Party and various organizations have been used to form a 'front' directed against Australian commitment in Vietnam. The Communist party in neither country has operated during the 'resistance' phase other than in a clandestine manner and by way of camou-

---

[1] It is rumoured that an Australian Communist leader was 'worried' to find that the Indonesian Communist party regarded Australia as a future target area. But this naturally did not affect party policy, since the 'compatriots' of Australian Communists are foreign Communists, not non-Communist Australians.

flaged objectives. Both have exploited 'contradictions' and both, as good guerrilla parties, have operated on the basis of a profound understanding of the human 'terrain'. The tactics of the Communist Party of Indo-China will be examined in detail later; the recent tactics of Australian Communism will be examined in the light of what has so far been established about the guerrilla nature of Communist activity throughout the world.

The Australian example is interesting and relevant on a number of counts. Australia is a society with some specific 'contradictions', psychological rather than social or economic, and yet in many ways intellectually imitative of the U.S.A. and Great Britain, symbolized by the fact that at the beginning of the so-called 'Vietnam debate' the Government supporters nearly all relied wholly on British and U.S. White Papers, the protesters on a U.S. journal, *I. F. Stone's Weekly*. Moreover, as one of the only two Western allies of the U.S.A. whose leadership is notably disinclined to 'go it alone'—for reasons of international solidarity rather than any lack of courage—Australian popular reaction to the Vietnamese war is obviously psychologically important far beyond its general national significance in the world.[1]

What was the social 'terrain' like in Australia at the time (the end of April 1965) when the committal of Australian troops to Vietnam was announced? How did the political guerrilla leaders of the Australian Communist party (Moscow) see the 'objective conditions' obtaining in the country? It is along these lines that a Communist party thinks, in tactical, quasi-military terms. (The *strategy* to get the Americans out of South-East Asia, had been clear for many years, but it was something the Australian Communist party could do little about.) Communist parties are not at all concerned with broad issues of national policy in democratic countries in the way democrats are, simply because they are not nationalists in this sense; they are solely concerned with the ultimate achievement of absolute political power, which may well depend—and certainly does in Australia—upon events far away beyond the national frontiers. The specific significance of this for the Australian 'Vietnam debate' will be touched upon below.

The way in which Communist parties think politically is peculiarly well put by Mr. Doak A. Barnett: 'Almost all Communist parties . . . are confronted by a number of crucial questions, most of them concerning strategy and tactics, that demand answers. What is the nature

[1] Hence, amongst other things, an otherwise inconceivable visit from President Johnson in 1966.

of the local society and what are the special features of the "class-struggle" presumed to be operating in it? Who should be defined as the main targets—the primary enemies of the revolution at any given time? Who, at any particular stage, are potential allies whom the Communists should try to bring into a united front under their control, and what sort of united front should it be? What "stages" must the revolutionary process go through, and what should be the minimum programme—the immediate goals—at each stage?'[1]

The Australian Communist party should have seen the situation in the following terms, and the nature of the protest movements suggests that it did. As a *party*, an 'organizational weapon', its numbers had shrunk over the years, partly as a result of general affluence, partly because of Moscow's repression in Hungary, partly as a result of the local division which mirrored the Sino-Soviet split, and partly because Marx-Leninism was increasingly being revealed (as elsewhere in the West) as utterly irrelevant to the problems of modern societies. Nevertheless it had a firm power *base*, a secure base being a pre-requisite of *all* kinds of guerrilla activity. In the Trade Union movement it had an irreducible minimum of 200 out of 550 votes in the A.C.T.U. (all-union) Congress and it enjoyed the support of the powerful Left Wing of the Labour party machine, the chief aims of which, particularly in the field of foreign politics, were effectively the same as the Communists.

Their travellers and 'Stalinoid'[2] liberal sympathizers were well represented in television, broadcasting, and the Press, but their greatest advantage lay in the nature of the Australian social 'terrain'. Unlike the physical terrain on which guerrilla fighting proper is waged, the social terrain can be subtly changed over a period of time. Probably the Communists' greatest success in this regard—a success owing more to the efforts over many years of fellow-travellers and liberal progressives than to open Communists—was the slow sapping of anti-Communist will in the 'intellectual world', ranging from academic circles to newspaper offices. The test of being progressive came, in the course of time, to be a person's attitude to Communism. He might stand for the abolition of hanging, or for the legal ameliora-

---

[1] A. Doak Barnett, *Communist Strategies in Asia*, Praeger, 1963.

[2] *The Organizational Weapon*, op. cit. Philip Selznick cites a number of the essential characteristics of the Stalinoid. For example, 'The Stalinoid is distinguished from the traditional liberal by his search for release from anxiety ... (he) is regarded by those who use him as well as by those who oppose him as being essentially weak and dependent, ultimately unreliable, capitulating easily to power ...' cp. Monnerot, op. cit., on what he calls 'contemporary nihilism.'

tion of the situation of homosexuals, he might be a fierce opponent of censorship and a courageous advocate of liberalizing the immigration laws affecting coloured people, but these are not the tests of being progressive. There was and is only one test: acquiescence to Communism or active opposition to anti-Communism (sometimes called anti-anti-Communism).

This is not of course a phenomenon peculiar to Australia. As a French student of political warfare puts it: 'The highest form of abuse perpetrated by the (crypto-Communist) apparatus is to call someone a systematic anti-Communist. Unhappily, many democrats have long since become convinced that there is something reprehensible about being a systematic anti-Communist . . . forgetting that they take pride in being systematic anti-Fascists themselves. This is precisely the kind of double standard which the crypto-Communist apparatus sedulously cultivates. Its success can be measured by the fact that in many quarters anti-Communism has come to be regarded as a greater evil than Communism.'[1]

A large number of sensitive democrats accept this state of affairs, simply because they know that any trenchant and consistent criticism of Communist activities will immediately make them the targets of crypto-Communist warfare and involve them in public debate, often of peculiarly disagreeable kind. The tendency towards acquiescence in a state of affairs—or psychologically prepared 'terrain'—such as this is exacerbated in Australian intellectual life, which is marked in general by an extreme reluctance to offend anyone by severe criticism in public. It is a very small 'intellectual world' in which most people know each other personally; and it is permeated by the admirable everyday tradition of good-fellowship at all costs. (When debating with the Secretary General of the Australian Communist party (Moscow), the author found himself almost unnerved by the sweet friendliness of the man!). In this environment a 'good chap', if he wants to go on living an agreeably sun-baked life, does not go out of his way to draw attention to the fact that all sorts of other good fellows, albeit more definitely progressive than himself, are in fact hoping the Vietcong will win and acting politically according to that hope.

When a highly respected professor at the Australian National University, who is himself an intellectual luminary of the Labour party, wrote in a students' magazine, 'The point I now want to stress is that it is primarily if not wholly because, on balance, they want Commun-

[1] Suzanne Labin, *The Unrelenting War*, The American–Asian Educational Exchange, n.d.

ism to win in Vietnam that all the Government's most active critics
... oppose the present policy,' it was not long before Professor Heinz
Arndt's German ancestry was being brought to the attention of all
progressive 'good fellows'. Here one comes to the reverse side of the
progressive environment. On the one hand, Communists and their
allies enjoy complete freedom of activity and a measure of remote
control because of the crashing good fellowship that abounds; on the
other hand, anyone who would be prepared to lead a less agreeable
life as a result of systematically opposing Communism and crypto-
Communist activities is singled out for exceedingly rough treatment
and even on occasion condign social and professional punishment.
This is what is known in the language of guerrilla warfare proper as
'pinpoint coercion'. Here is an example of it from the battlefield: 'But
the Vietminh success has also resulted from pinpoint coercion. The
French apply their force almost indiscriminately to the whole community. The Vietminh know accurately who in each village has what
influence—who is for them, who is against them. The French and
their Vietnamese partners have much less precise information. ... It
is as though two men were trying to force a third to do contrary things.
One stands at the victim's back with a pistol pressed against his spine,
the other stands half a block away with a shotgun. There is no question
which one the man will obey. ... Even when the pistol is withdrawn,
because of the temporary arrival of the French, the villager knows
that it will return with precision. While it is away, the feel of that
pistol remains at his spine.'[1]

In the case of Dr. Knopfelmacher only the terrain and the weapons
were different from those employed in guerrilla warfare proper;
otherwise the procedure was exactly the same. Dr. Frank Knopfelmacher, a lecturer in psychology at the University of Melbourne, a
man with very high academic qualifications from London and Bristol
universities, had learned about Communism the hard way in his
native Czechoslovokia. He became easily the most articulate and
sociologically best-equipped analyst of Communist tactics in Australia; and through force of personality and incisiveness of mind began
substantially to erode the carefully prepared progressive liberal terrain
on which the Communist party and its crypto-Communist allies had
been operating so successfully. It was successful not in terms of
recruitment (though since the really effective side of Communist
activity in democracies is undercover work, recruitment is difficult to

[1] Gerald Winfield in C. Groves Haines (Editor), *The Threat of Soviet Imperialism*, The Johns Hopkins Press 1954.

assess)¹ nor of attaining significant prestige as an organization; but it was very successful indeed from the point of view of creating an 'anti-anti-Communist' climate of opinion that could easily be manipulated (as was shown in the case of Vietnam) against firm government policies overseas. It is this which is crucial for Australian Communist leaders, since they know that only an American withdrawal across the Pacific and the threat of Asian bayonets can ever bring them to power and the seizure of power is the sole aim of Communist parties.

Knopfelmacher was singled out for 'pinpoint coercion' because he was altering the terrain; he was enabling students and other young people to think their way through to *firm* democratic values, which of their nature were explicitly anti-Communist. And so political energies were concentrated against him in true guerrilla style. Just as in the case of a village headman marked down for Communist assassination in South Vietnam, the first move was to try to make Dr. Knopfelmacher unpopular.² This was done over a period of years by a subtle playing upon the carefully observed weaknesses of various types of academics. There was an element of pragmatism about the campaign but this again can be found on the guerrilla battlefield too. As a profound French student of Vietnam, M. Laul Mus, recently remarked: 'The Vietnamese Communists are pragmatists too in a way. They want to give the villagers as many reasons as possible for hating the French colonialists and the American capitalists. . . .'³ In situations of Communist warfare, wherever it is waged, every 'contradiction' is exploited.

All that is required for the Knopfelmacher kind of political operation is the acquiescence of the majority of the people whose attitudes are relevant. (In a guerrilla war one per cent of the population at most actively works for the insurgents; what is required of the 'masses' is no more than acquiescence.) Though the terrain had long been prepared, the occasion for the operation did not arise until Dr. Knopfel-

[1] The aim of Communist indoctrination of recruits is, as Comrade F. Brown, writing in *The Communist* in 1933, candidly admitted, to transform them 'from mere fighters for better conditions into Communists.' Quoted in Kintner, op. cit., Lenin laughed at those who saw in the eight-hour day an aim in itself worthwhile.

[2] Robert Thompson, *Defeating Communist Insurgency*, op. cit. 'The Communists are normally careful, however, not to murder a popular person until he has been discredited. This discrediting can be done in several ways: perhaps by associating him with an unpopular aspect of government policy, or by accusing him of corruption, or, better still, of rape. There is no shortage of keen female workers who are prepared to engineer a situation which will justify a charge of this nature. It does not have to be proved.'

[3] *Asia* No. 4 Winter 1966, Asia Society Inc., New York.

macher applied for a job at Sydney University. With one abstention, the selection sub-committee approved of his appointment; in the case of other academics throughout the country (provided they had not been labelled systematic anti-Communists), the approval of the appointment at that level would have meant automatic acceptance by the Professorial Board. Instead Dr. Knopfelmacher's appointment was rejected. This happened in the middle of April, 1965, shortly before the Prime Minister of Australia announced the commitment of Australian troops to South Vietnam. The case became a *cause célèbre* since it was obvious to a large section of the educated public that something most unusual was happening, and that a man was being denied natural justice... or 'a fair go', as non-intellectual Australians would call it. But nothing done on Dr. Knopfelmacher's behalf could reverse the verdict. He remained in Melbourne.

The details of the university procedures are not germane to the argument here; what is germane is the manner in which Dr. Knopfelmacher's character was successfully assassinated. The campaign was brilliantly executed. The self-consciously Anglo-Saxon graduate was led to believe that Knopfelmacher had been tainted or disordered by his European background; the easy-going academic learned that Knopfelmacher was a 'trouble-maker' (which as a determined anti-Communist of course he was) and given the environment described above, this was probably the most powerful explosive charge laid under his application—though it says more about Australian intellectual life than about Dr. Knopfelmacher.

Some academic Jews who, for most understandable reasons, fear slights and are ever eager to reduce the likelihood of them, were reminded that Knopfelmacher was a Jew and that trouble from him might make trouble for them all. Intellectual anti-Semites were informed that he had a 'ghetto mentality' inappropriate to sunny Australian camaraderie. The psychiatrically inclined found that he was a man 'bent on self-destruction' whose writings showed 'paranoid' tendencies. The 'Stalinoids' quickly attached themselves to the assassination forces simply because these forces seemed to be already strong and growing in the intellectual world... such people always being humanly predisposed towards backing the winning side[1]... but just

---

[1] It has been noticeable ever since the Soviet trials of the 1930's that the Stalinoid intellectual supports totalitarianism *because* of its naked displays of absolute power, not *despite* them. They rallied then to 'an omnipotent state and its firing squads rather than to its victims', as Eugene Lyons put it in *Assignment Utopia*, Harrap, 1938, just as today they are much more attracted by the total political violence of Peking and Hanoi than by the partially humanized policies

in case they weakened, sounds like 'Goldwaterite' and 'McCarthyite' were rung out in their vicinity. Anti-religious academics were told that Dr. Knopfelmacher, an agnostic Social Democrat, was a slavish follower of the predominantly Catholic and consistently anti-Communist Democratic Labour party; libertarians learned that his political vehemence arose out of a frustrated sexual life while puritans were regaled with lies about his promiscuity. No depths of ignobility were left unplumbed by his political enemies; but because he was a systematic anti-Communist who had on occasion used very intemperate language this was a successful campaign.

The purpose of the operation was to show through one act of exemplary vengeance that steady and articulate opposition to Communist activities just did not pay. What happened was in no way a a case of individuals being *directly* manipulated in any fashion; it was the result of a decade long camouflaged campaign to discredit a man, the end result of which was a poisonous cloud of prejudice in which sound judgements became lost. And this is how T. E. Lawrence in his *Seven Pillars of Wisdom* described an effective guerrilla movement: 'an influence, an idea, a thing intangible, invulnerable, without front or back, drifting about like gas.'

The Communists and their allies operated in exactly the same fashion in the so-called 'Vietnam debate', which quickly followed the Knopfelmacher affair. The debate was never really about Vietnam at all and the protest movement that quickly grew up campaigned under the banner of 'Peace', never with slogans directly supporting the Vietcong or Hanoi, just as the Communist directors of the Vietcong never campaign in terms of Communism but always by exploiting 'contradictions' and offering a superficially unexceptional programme directed at the 'broad masses'. The Knopfelmacher affair was relevant to the Vietnam protest movement in two ways: first, whereas hundreds of academics (nearly all of them wholly unequipped to discuss Vietnam itself in any informed way) were quickly persuaded to sign a petition opposing Government policy, and some were emboldened immediately to step on to the public platform in this interest, only a handful were prepared to support Government policy; secondly, Vietnam became almost imperceptibly yet another test of progressivism on the crypto-Communist and pro-Communist

of Moscow. They are akin to Ch'en, the onanist-terrorist in André Malraux's *Man's Fate*: 'The only thing which his present state of mind did not transform into nothingness was the idea of creating those doomed Executioners, that race of avengers.'

dominated intellectual terrain. This Vietnam was not a geographical and social entity but simply an image, a slogan, a banner; those who by their silence or the repetition of gross canards had acquiesced in a deep injustice to Knopfelmacher found him prominent amongst supporters of the Vietnam commitment, and knew they had been right all along. Their manipulation in this vileness was strictly analogous to the revolutionary guerrilla leaders' tactic of involving recruits in an atrocity so that they may have blood on their hand and are thus committed psychologically to all that follows.

The point is that there were very serious, though not (to the author) ultimately compelling reasons, against the commitment of Western troops en masse to South Vietnam in the first half of 1965. But those reasons were scarcely ever offered up to the public, except in the form of ignorantly expressed caricatures of the most unfortunately *phrased* 'domino' theory about South-East Asia, a theory that held that were South Vietnam to be seized by the armed might of the Communist Party of Indo-China, then the whole region would fall, country by country, like dominoes. If the visually absurd image is set aside, there is much truth in the theory which was very ably defended by Dr. Knopfelmacher in the following terms: 'After World War I the French were instrumental in setting up a number of dependent States in Central and Eastern Europe. Those states were viable only in so far as they could be protected by effective French military action against Germany. The demilitarization of the Rhineland had as its chief purpose to make the interior of Germany accessible to the French Army in case of an emergency. Yet when Germany was allowed to remilitarize the Rhineland in 1936, with the connivance of the Western Powers, it became obvious that the fate of the East European 'successor states' (which the French had been instrumental in setting up) was sealed.

'By allowing the Germans to occupy the Rhineland the Western Powers had given de facto notice that they did not intend to take offensive action against Germany under any circumstances. Germany was, thereby, granted a free hand in Central and Eastern Europe and in the Balkans. Yet it took another three years for the consequences to become apparent to the peoples of the target regions . . . The three years 1935-38 were years of an invisible crisis; the tiger, released from his cage in 1935, was stalking his victims, who were still conducting themselves as though no tigers were about.

'I have not yet heard any convincing argument against the domino theory in relation to Vietnam. If Vietnam falls, the American system of alliances will crumble. If it does, Australia will be faced by the full power of Communist China, probably without allies ... yet China's future victims, like the nations of Central and Eastern Europe in the thirties, are not yet aware of the fact that they are cast for the role of victims. Accustomed to the status of a safe dependency of the British Empire, Australia has been flung into a civil war belt in which Communist China is gradually asserting her dominance.'[1]

The Communists and their allies could not on any account afford to have the debate argued in these terms; but in view of the intellectual terrain, softened and muddled and subverted by that form of *trahison de clercs* known today as the 'double standard',[2] they did not *have* to have the debate argued that way at all. They obeyed the maxim of good guerrilla fighters anywhere and immediately *seized the initiative*, through the agency, of course, of various brands of near-Communist fellow-travellers.

The protest movement in its beginnings *was* in a sense spontaneous —as, in a special sense, all guerrilla struggles are; it was begun by the intellectual and emotional victims of Communist manipulation rather than by the Party itself. None of these people knew much, if anything, about the realities of South Vietnam's agonies but they did know that the frustrations that they experienced themselves through the defeat in Vietnam of the political nihilism with which they had been indoctrinated could be laid at the door of the United States and the civilization that it represented.

Once they believed this there was enough for the Communists to work on, just as the general frustration of intellectuals can, for different reasons and at certain levels, be exploited by the revolutionary Communist guerrillas of the world's under-developed territories.

The most important thing about an organization or a movement, as Lord Russell has observed is not, however, the private motives of the individuals, but the purpose for which those individuals are in fact organized. Organization was imposed on the initially unorganized body of the protesters by the introduction of the Communist party

---

[1] *Sydney Morning Herald*, 13th August 1965.

[2] This term will be referred to again later. At this point Philip Selznick's comment must suffice: 'Another symptom of alienation, further identifying the mass character of the Stalinoid liberal, is the devaluation of means and ends ... what matters is to be on the winning side ... A ... devaluation is reflected in the Stalinoid application of a double standard when appraising, say, imperialism as practised by Russia or a western power. There is applied a doctrinaire interpretation of imperialism that loses sight of the human factor, the actual consequences for human life and dignity in the dominated countries.'

into their midst. It made its first impact by arranging for messages of congratulation to be sent to the centres where the movement was making headway; where political conditioning was in progress although political control had not yet been established. These messages purported to come quite spontaneously from other centres of opposition to the Australian (disguised as the American) commitment in Vietnam. It is of the *utmost* importance to the Communists, whether in South Vietnam, Australia or anywhere else, always to represent revolutionary warfare campaigns as being quite *spontaneous* and *indigenous* forms of popular protest or revolt; a natural *response* to presumedly intolerable conditions, *never* a planned campaign for the seizure of power.

The next step for the Communists is to unite, in a clandestine fashion, the various movements of protest (whether it be against the committal of Australian troops to South Vietnam or against a resolutely counter-insurgent government like Ngo Dinh Diem's in South Vietnam) under the banner of a Cause that has nothing at all obviously to do with Communist party purposes. The Communist 'organizational weapon' is in itself very formidable indeed; but without a generalized Cause it cannot be successful. The Cause has usually been found in the aftermath of war or in the despairing sense of shame attendant upon the last phase of defeat. As Georges Bernanos once put it, 'The French Revolution issued out of the sunlight of the Enlightenment, the Russian Revolution out of the blood and mud of a military rout.' Sometimes the Cause has taken the form of a sense of identification with an historically determined élite of war leaders whose political victory has been frustrated by the post-war activities of Western Powers, for example the Malayan Communist Party in 1945–48. A Cause there must be; and it must always be part of the camouflage necessary to the achievement of total, irreversible political power for the Communist party. This is an axiom of revolutionary guerrilla warfare, and part, if not the essential part, of the axiom is to make the Cause as *nationalist* in as widely general a sense as possible. There is a psychologically deep-seated reason for this: to gain the widest support—in order, stated more bluntly to be able to exploit the whole depth and weight of a society—it is always desirable to represent the struggle as being one of *resistance*, rather than one of revolution: the easiest way of dynamically manipulating the greatest number of people, most of whom will inevitably be psychologically conservative, is to persuade them that the movement is resisting something (foreign if possible) that threatens the generality of their beliefs and lives. Only the cadres must know what it is all about.

Communists are manipulators but not conjurers. Or as Marx put it, 'Men make their own history, but not out of the whole cloth.' There is an element of truth in the endlessly reiterated Communist claim that a resolution cannot arise except out of 'existing conditions'. The point is that Communist revolutionary activity depends upon the Communists' ability to 'interpret' (as Mao Tse-tung would argue) these conditions in a fashion—this is where *camouflaged* warfare comes in—that suits the long-term ambitions of the Communist party.

The necessity for a clearly understood Cause is, of course, much more necessary in the case of guerrilla warfare proper, since this is an altogether more exacting kind of activity than carrying placards or mouthing slogans in a democratic society. As Paret and Shy explain most judiciously, 'Social pressure, at times even terror, plays a role; but it requires an element of individual conviction to compel men to take part in this most punishing kind of combat. Undoubtedly, this conviction can be created; yet even sophisticated processes of indoctrination are ineffective unless they can exploit real problems, real hopes and fears.'[1]

But the problem of involving the masses remains: 'The best cause for the insurgents' purpose is one that, by definition, can attract the largest number of supporters and repel the minimum of opponents. . . . To be perfectly sound, the cause must be such that the counter-insurgent cannot espouse it too, or can do so only at the risk of losing his power, which is, after all, what he is fighting for. Land reform looked like a promising cause to the Hukbalahaps after the defeat of Japan and the accession of the Philippines to independence; but when the government offered land to the Huks' actual and potential supporters, the insurgents lost their cause and the game.[2]

A Communist political campaign does not, however, depend *just* on finding a suitable all-embracing Cause, since the Communists also aim at winning total political power through the exploitation of 'contradictions' within society, and these are by definition specific, even localized, seeds of discontent.

The campaign is thus in fact two-tiered (as will be shown in detail

[1] Peter Paret and John W. Shy, *Guerrillas in the 1960's*, Praeger, 1964.
[2] David Galula, *Counterinsurgency Warfare*, Pall Mall Press, 1964. Mr. Galula's description of the putting down of the Hukbalahap insurgency is, in fact, as will be shown, greatly over-simplified. His initial generalization is sound, though it is by no means clear in 1967 that the Huks have yet 'lost the game'.

in the case of Vietnam): a generalized Cause has superimposed on it all manner of subversive and propaganda operations designed to disintegrate the actual society over which the Communist party is endeavouring to assert political control. The disintegrative aspect of Communist tactics working in conjunction with the 'creative' generalized Cause is of enormous importance, particularly in the third world where societies have already been started upon a process of cultural disintegration, by the enormous intangible but overpowering forces of capitalist colonialism. J. S. Furnivall, a Burma Civil Servant deeply affected by the humanly deleterious effects of western colonialism once wrote: 'The Communist solution is even less practical than the capitalist solution, and no less certain to intensify social disintegration. In this respect, however, it starts with a tactical advantage over capitalism. For it deliberately aims at completing the destruction of the older order of society based on nationalism and religion.'[1]

And so, in South-East Asia, 'given a basic cause, many other issues can be tacked on to it, such as land for the landless, exploitation of labour on estates and mines, regional autonomy for ethnic minorities and political equality for immigrant races with the indigenous races.'[2] The list of 'contradictions' is of course much longer than that and to some extent varies throughout the region, though only within limits. While all these 'contradictions' are being exploited, thereby contributing to a general disintegration of the society at large, the chief aim in this part of the world is to seize control of the nationalist movement in order to manipulate it according to Communist purposes. This aim does not, as is sometimes supposed, end with political independence; rather, an attempt is made to represent the Communist party as the most 'truly' nationalist political group in society.

This was the case with the Indonesian Communist party (PKI) when accepted by President Sukarno as one of the pillars of his regime. The PKI hastened the disintegration of Indonesian society through its activities as the most perfervid advocate of 'Confrontation' with Malaysia, a policy that was economically ruinous and yet permitted the PKI to pose as a predominately nationalist party with an apparently unexceptional broad 'reformist' programme and a sure claim to 'legal status'. It linked these with such activities as the subversion of armed service personnel, the civil service, para-military units, and manipulable political leaders like Dr. Subandrio (whose role was to have been similar to that of Fierlinger in Czechoslovakia).

[1] *Australian Outlook*, June 1953.
[2] *Defeating Communist Insurgency*, op. cit.

THE BATTLEGROUND

There followed the steady build-up of control over the largest labour confederation (SOBSI) and later, the arming of certain reliable sectors of workers in factory and other working-class 'militias'. Something very similar to the Prague coup of 1948 was being attempted; while apparently accepting non-Communist *forms* of government and administration, the *substance* of power relations within Indonesian society was being slowly changed. But while there is no dichotomy between Communist 'legal' and 'illegal' activities being carried on at the same time, psychologically the attempt to marry the two kinds of activity on a grand scale can on occasion, as seems to have been the case in Indonesia, result in a failure of last-minute preparations for armed insurrection.

In general, the approach of Communist parties to a situation of recently achieved political independence, unless their country is geographically contiguous with a Communist country that can provide a 'privileged sanctuary' for the training, arming, and supplying of guerrilla forces, must be like that of the Philippines Communist party in 1946-47: 'The Communist Party of the Philippines as the vanguard of the proletariat must set itself at the head of the Philippines national emancipation movement. It must be the most energetic and consistent fighter for the establishment of a democratic republic of a new type at the present stage.... The carrying out of the bourgeois revolution—establishment of a democratic republic—is the task to be accomplished during the whole stage and this will not change until the whole task has been accomplished. But conditions within the whole stage may change and have changed and because of this, our programmes do change corresponding to the changes that have taken place and will take place.'[1] When the extraordinarily tortuous language is translated, it reveals that since there was a bourgeois republic already in existence, what was really being attempted—in disguised fashion as always—was the political dictatorship of the 'vanguard' in conditions continually being changed to the detriment of bourgeois interests. In the Philippines too, armed revolutionary warfare was only part of the broad assault upon the Philippines society.

What is required by Communist parties, even when conditions of insurrection exist in the countryside, are footholds of politically strategic significance within the institutions of the country to be overthrown, above all acceptance in a coalition government, which they believe their military-type organization and special tactics will enable

[1] Part of a statement by the Sec. General of the Philippines Communist Party made late in 1946 or early in 1947. Quoted by Selznick, op. cit.

them to turn into a monolithic 'front' government directed by the 'vanguard party'.[1]

Sometimes it seems possible to infiltrate an existing party within the country's body politic. This was the case with the Communist Party of China's infiltration in the 1920's of the Kuomintang which at that time had not made its future policies clear, seemed potentially revolutionary, and was declared by the Communists to be 'not a bourgeois party but a coalition of all classes.' In theory, Communists entered the Kuomintang as individuals but in fact, according to the principles of Bolshevik revolutionary organization hammered out by Lenin as long ago as 1904, the party never lost its identity.[2]

This consideration of the elements of Communist activity in the under-developed countries of South-East Asia may seem a far cry from a valid consideration of Communist activities in Australia in 1965, but on the contrary, they are essential for an adequate understanding of these activities, which differ only because the operational 'terrain' is altogether different. They differ in form, not in substance. The Communists needed in the so-called 'Vietnam debate' a generalized Cause to which large numbers of non-Communists could decently attach themselves. As a result of long preparations for an eventuality such as Vietnam, the Communists had the so-called 'Peace Movement' at hand. The Cause was to be 'Peace in Vietnam'. People were invited to oppose the Australian commitment, not on the ground that the Vietcong should not be opposed but on the ground that the fighting should be ended. The Communists made no secret in their own journals of how they saw their role in the organized protest movement: 'The Communist Party . . . has been a driving force in the whole struggle (i.e. Vietnam protests). . . . There was 'unity of action around the common points in ALP (Australian Labour Party), Communist party, and ACTU (Australian Council of Trade Unions) policy on Vietnam . . . at all stages in broad organizations or more advanced forms of action against the Vietnam war the Communist party publicly took its stand on the principle of helping and participating in the broad movement.'[3]

At first sight this kind of claim may read simply as a form of

[1] The use of coalitions in post-War Eastern Europe is lucidly analysed by Professor Hugh Seton-Watson in his *Neither Peace Nor War*, Methuen, 1960.
[2] 'There is no evidence that the party represented other than a unified, disciplined caucus within the KMT during the whole period of KMT–Communist collaboration.' Benjamin I. Schwartz: *Chinese Communism and the Rise of Mao*, Harvard University Press.
[3] *Communist Review*, January 1966.

boasting but it was clearly established in an expert analysis that 'No "broad front" demonstration had been held where at least one of the key organizations taking part was not open to direct Communist control.'¹ Moreover, an article in *Communist Review*, complaining that 'Very seldom are (the demonstrators' placards) framed to convey the protest in the most vital and fundamental terms, that what the Governments of Australia and the USA are doing in Vietnam is wrong because it is morally wrong. . . . The seeds of victory lie in the solution of the moral question,'² was immediately followed by an appropriate change of emphasis in the protesters' slogans. This kind of evidence is never in itself compelling, nor does it throw a great deal of light upon the intentions and hopes of the Communist party in general. Obviously the Australian Communist party is to be expected to take a leading part—though in a disguised fashion—in a movement whose only objective effect can be to strengthen Hanoi's will to resist, and to weaken the Australian commitment. Communist activity on this level is to be found throughout the western world.

Because of certain features of Australian politics, the Australian Communist party (CPA), however, is in a position altogether different from, say, that of the Communist party of Great Britain, which has no hope whatsoever of coming to power in foreseeable circumstances. Odd as it may seem, especially to those who know what an intellectually risible party the CPA is, it *does* see itself as having a very significant role to play in circumstances that are not wholly inconceivable. Apart from the activities referred to above, relating to the 'softening up' of the social 'terrain', chiefly by fellow-travellers, the CPA cannot claim much credit for these presumedly favourable circumstances. It can only think in terms of appropriately using them for its own ends.

Communist tactics were clarified by an intellectually outstanding and generally respected Labour Member of Parliament, Mr. Kim Beazley in this way: 'The Communist party has a tripartite strategy, every point of which involves the Labour Party in a dilemma of extrication . . . (1) To make Marx-Leninism the thinking of the Labour Movement. The alienation of Catholics is essential in this.

¹ *The Bulletin*, 26th March 1966.
² Endel Niit, *Communist Review*, November 1965. It is perhaps not without significance that this writer also wrote in that issue—quite clearly *à propos* of the Knopfelmacher affair—about the reluctance of 'right wing intellectuals' to rally to the Government side: 'The cause is endemic in the ideology of the right-wing intellectuals, who are motivated by personal interest for their careers which might be damaged by them defending anaemic (i.e. anti-Communist) policies . . .' Such was the presumed result—and the presumption has truth in it—of the application of 'pinpoint coercion' against Dr. Knopfelmacher.

By the withdrawal of Catholics to the D.L.P. in Victoria[1] the Marx-Leninist ideology has been enabled to occupy the vacuum ... (2) To have the Vietcong accepted as the negotiating authority in Vietnam ... the seal of approval on the strategy of war by subversion ... (3) to ensure that at every significant political meeting in Australia on Vietnam and conscription there is a trained core of professional Communist demonstrators. This is to counterfeit indignant public opinion.... The Labour Party is always being invited to follow these political master minds, whom some in the Party seem to accept as mirrors of opinion.... The Communists have sought to implement their policy through Labour. But, after all, seats are not their aim. Their aim is the nationwide acceptance, beginning with the Labour Movement, of Communist-inspired issues. These issues are mostly on foreign policy, for Communist power can only be advanced by foreign power. The (Communist) party is unacceptable in Australia.'[2]

This of course is the crux of the matter. The Communists are very powerful in one-third of the trade union movement ... including the Amalgamated Engineers' Union, the Waterside Workers' Federation, the Australian Railways Union, and the Seamen's Union (Communists always select the *militarily* significant unions). Moreover they have been skilful in creating, influencing, or infiltrating a large and growing number of organizations protesting against the Australian commitment in Vietnam, ranging from Greek and Italian migrant organizations and anti-conscription groups to church, women's and youth groups (the Communists call this 'politicalizing the moral issue'; others would describe it as 'front' activity). Marx-Leninist thinking has penetrated the dominant left wing of the Labour party to the extent that that party now regards the Vietnamese war as an unjust one, from which, if elected to power, it promises to extricate Australian forces at the earliest opportunity.

Now *of course* this extraordinary situation has not come about simply through conspiratorial methods; much of it is the result of the successful exploitation of psychological 'contradictions', that is, in this case attitudes out of tune with social realities, by fellow-travellers and by left-wingers afraid that affluence will render their ideas permanently unacceptable to the electorate, rather than by open Communists. The English Secretary of the Labour party, Mr. Cyril Wyndham, described these kinds of people within the Labour Party

[1] The anti-Communist Democratic Labour party commands 230,000 votes in that state.
[2] *Australian Outlook*, August 1966.

as follows: 'Some people claim that capitalism has not changed in any respect since the nineteenth century and that the problems of 1965 are precisely the same as those of 1901. . . . There is yet another group which accepts quite readily that a democratic socialist party is only successful when there is an economic or other national crisis . . . they always appear to be looking for an economic depression or a national calamity as our salvation. . . . There are those who still cling to the belief that there is some magic in Marxism. . . . They are not Communists but they accept quaintly that there is a common purpose or an affinity between the Communists and the social democrats. . . . It is the height of futility to advocate the expenditure of more moneys on aiding the under-privileged of the world without at the same time expressing our intention to defend their right to develop a democratic society, if they so desire, and if they want our help. . . . Some speak glibly of "armed neutrality" as the role for the Australian Labour party to play in the larger world scene. . . . Nowadays, it is fashionable in certain quarters to knock the United States of America, to belittle everything that great country tries to do. . . . Anyone who puts a contrary view or endeavours to be a little more objective is immediately dubbed a reactionary. . . .'[1]

The clearest expression of Communist party attitudes to the Labour party in recent years appeared in the memoirs of a veteran Communist, Mr. Ralph Gibson, published in mid-1966: 'Whatever I have said critically about some Labour party leaders, or about the Labour party in some periods, is nowhere intended to be destructive. It is part of an effort to win a clear understanding and a common purpose on the part of all sections of the Labour movement alike. This end should be sought by free and honest debate and mutual criticism between Labour party and Communist party members, and by unity of both in common action for the many purposes they can immediately agree upon.'[2]

The chief of these is, as it is for Peking and Hanoi, the removal of the U.S. presence from South Vietnam and then, as a result of a nation-wide sense of frustration in the USA with revolutionary guerrilla wars, from South-East Asia altogether. The Communist party is solely concerned with the attainment of absolute political power, and it knows that this can only be achieved through the manipulation

---

[1] Seminar of the Queensland Young Labour Association, 5th December 1965. B. A. Santamaris: *The Politics of 1966*, The Hawthorne Press, Melbourne, 1966.

[2] Ralph Gibson, *My Years in the Communist Party*, International Bookshop, 1966.

of the left wing of the Labour party, which in turn could only possibly achieve political office as the result of a catastrophe in South-East Asia. Its set purpose is therefore to induce effective opposition in Australia to the commitment in Vietnam through the activities of its various Vietnam front organizations and the exploitation of psychological contradictions, and thereby to make a maximum psychological impact upon a U.S. public opinion only too well aware of their country's isolation in the West so far as the Vietnam campaign is concerned.

Late in 1967 such Communist activities, and the hopes they are based upon, seem doubtful; but when the camouflaged operation, 'The Peace in Vietnam' campaign, was launched in April 1965 the most important component in Communist tactical thinking was its appraisal of the South-East Asian situation. It was a situation of apparently quite rapid deterioration. Laos, diplomatically neutralized in 1962 under Great Power agreement, provided the necessary protected supply and reinforcement route for the intensification of revolutionary guerrilla warfare in South Vietnam.

The degree of escalation and the apparent extent of political demoralization in South Vietnam suggested that U.S. intervention might be too late to avert a complete collapse in that country. The development of subversion in North-East Thailand into insurgency and the reactivation of Malayan Communist party guerrilla violence in South Thailand was apparently getting under way. Indonesia's 'confrontation' policy was not only permitting the Indonesian Communist party to initiate guerrilla warfare in Malaysian Borneo (and in the Malayan-Thai border area) but the alignment of political forces underpinning the general policy of 'Confrontation' seemed likely to offer the Indonesian Communist party the opportunity of coming to power by way of a Prague-type coup.[1] There was in effect a pincers movement directed against the stability of the South-East Asian region from Hanoi and Djakarta. The fortunes of South-East Asian Communism hinged upon the outcome of the South Vietnamese struggle and the Indonesian Communist party's bid for power. However much sophisticated academics in the West might pour scorn on the 'Domino Theory', Communists throughout the area, including

[1] 'The state is dissected rather than smashed. By purging and indoctrinating the captured organizations, the Communists change them in a fundamental way: they destroy the *role* and the *loyalties* of these institutions while keeping them organizationally intact. They then cease to be normal participants in a constitutional order but become, on the contrary, prepared bastions for a revolutionary coup.' Philip Selznick, op. cit., describing the 1948 Communist coup in Prague.

Australia, were wholly convinced of its validity, and they were right.

And so in Australia, the CPA, like Communist parties everywhere, thought on politico-military lines on two levels: internationally, it was concerned to undermine Western morale in order to help bring about the collapse of regional anti-Communist stability, on which its own whole future depended. In the event of a regional collapse into revolutionary warfare, marked by significant Communist victories, there were plenty of psychological 'contradictions' in Australian society, among their, at times, almost overwhelming concern with parochial affluence, a long history of protection by the British Empire and the disguised isolationism that such protection allowed, the old gormless belief in Australia as a privileged New Jerusalem for white men whose memories of Europe were unhappy and humiliating, and a deep naïveté about the nature of Communist expansionism. If these could be exploited under favourable conditions the Labour party, already dominated by the left wing and by its Communist mentors, could quite easily come to power in an atmosphere highly conducive to Left Wing Communist party plans for the neutralization of Australia. A U.S. withdrawal to Hawaii, which was by no means inconceivable in the event of political disaster in South Vietnam, would have isolated Australia geographically to such an extent that under a Government of this complexion she might very easily have been drawn in as a satellite to the orbit of a Peking-dominated South-East Asia.

It is not to the point here to develop such considerations in detail. All that is being established is this: the political component of Communist warfare is the same everywhere: the pursuit of absolute power under cover of camouflaged objectives (a Cause or causes, which can gain general acceptance and appropriate the energies that flow from many different motives), through the exploitation of 'contradictions' and the manipulation of social groups in front organizations. This kind of activity is not only denied to democratic parties; it is psychologically opposed to their manner of ordering affairs, since their mode of behaviour is civic and constitutional, whereas the Communists' is quasi-militaristic and fundamentally extra-constitutional: in fact that of the outlaw or guerrilla.

If the documents relating to the early days of the Communist-dominated Vietminh movement (1945) are examined, as they will be later, the political component of its planning will be found to bear striking similarities to that of the Australian Communists. There is the camouflaged bourgeois nationalist Cause (couched in the language of Jefferson for the benefit of world opinion); the attention paid to the international situation; the front organizations; the pinpoint coercion of enemies, including co-operation with the French in the destruction of rival nationalist groups; the exploitation of contradictions (between French and Japanese and between segments of French opinion as well as between Vietnamese groups); the willingness in certain circumstances to join the French Union as a transitional step (equivalent to the acceptance of isolated neutrality in ACP terms); the softening up of the intelligentsia through double-talk; and the use of all available forms of social power, from trade unions and youth groups to market suppliers,[1] by an organization essentially military, thinking tactically and strategically in terms of gaining absolute power.

Naturally, the differences were great too; but these arose out of different circumstances only, not out of a different approach to the problem of power. The intentions of French colonialism in the end forced the Communist party of Indo-China (CPI) to engage in an armed struggle; and circumstances, for instance the use of base areas in South China and North Vietnam, and the Japanese decision, in the face of defeat, to aid in some areas the new liberators of Asia from the white man rather than surrender to their Western conquerors, provided the C.P.I.-dominated Vietminh with the opportunity to arm and prepare for this insurgency. Once insurgency was begun, then all manner of other military factors came into play and the peculiar geographical and social terrain was politically and militarily exploited in ways that were strange to urbanized Western thinking and arose out of time-honoured, technologically primitive guerrilla methods, ranging from fieldcraft to animal traps.

Nevertheless, the efficacy of Communist revolutionary warfare can never be understood simply in these terms, since it primarily lies in the 'organizational weapon' and its political applications. The methods of application vary according to the terrain, naturally; but the nature of Communist guerrilla warfare simply cannot be understood without first understanding Communist tactics. Even so, a caveat must be entered here. The social terrain of a free Western country makes it extraordinary difficult for a Communist party and its camouflaged

[1] e.g. 'We must establish Liberation Committees in factories, villages, on the properties of landlords, in city streets, military barracks, schools, etc. These Committees will acquire the character of a broad United Anti-Japanese Front; on the other hand, they will be a sort of 'provisional local administrative organ' in each factory village, etc.' Rima Rathausky (Editor), *Documents of the August 1945 Revolution in Vietnam*, Department of International Relations, The Australian National University, 1963.

allies to translate an initiative seized in a particular instance into a truly significant increase in political power, let alone into the establishment of 'dual power'[1] within the democratic society. There are a number of obvious reasons for this, which do not concern a study of revolutionary guerrilla warfare; but nearly all the reasons relate to the *openness* and *pluralism* of such a society. This is the one political and social terrain on which revolutionary political warfare can seldom successfully be waged, since a totalitarian initiative cannot be *sustained* and a fraudulent Cause cannot indefinitely be 'pushed' in an open society.

Guerrilla warfare of any kind depends upon keeping the initiative throughout the struggle and this depends basically upon the *control* of the population. In a revolutionary guerrilla war such as the Vietnamese one, 'as the struggle grows in momentum, freedom of choice increasingly contracts. The individual is plunged into a thicket of confusion and conflicting fears and possibilities of deep betrayal. His family structure is eroded; his village structure crumbles under violent pressures; new dreams are introduced into this new environment that has unnerved his whole personality. Slowly the pressures close in upon him until at the height of the struggle his "choice" is virtually restricted . . . by the very intensity of the struggle, it being a chief aim of the Communist revolutionary guerrillas continually to increase the intensity since this quite clearly favours a totalitarian organization against any non-Communist government it has engaged.'[2] In such conditions a totalitarian armed 'society' is locked in battle with a society much less adequately equipped for total politico-military warfare. Only when the initiative in intensifying the struggle according to revolutionary rhythm—or phasing it, if it is preferred—has been significantly blunted, can the government under attack have the opportunity to start the long haul back known as pacification or rural reconstruction. Here one is obviously dealing with dimensions of political warfare that can scarcely ever be mounted in a fully modernized free society.

Even so, the revolutionary guerrilla strategy of building up what

[1] This is fundamental to Communist revolutionary warfare of *any* kind. 'The historic preparation of a revolution brings about in the pre-revolutionary period a situation in which the class (read C.P. and allies) which is called upon to realize the new social system, although not yet the master of the country, has actually concentrated in its hands a significant share of the state power, while the official apparatus of the government is still in the hands of the old lords.' Leon Trotsky qu. in Selznick, op. cit.

[2] The quotation is from the author's Chapter in Sibnarayan Ray (Editor), *Vietnam: Seen from East and West*, Thomas Nelson, 1966.

Bernard Fall calls 'parallel hierarchies' is simply an example of creating 'dual power', which was the method adopted in Czechoslovakia. In this case a fully modernized, democratic society, admittedly under great external pressures, was taken over by the Communists through a method of 'dissecting' rather than 'smashing' the state while the Communist party formally existed simply as a member of a coalition government: 'The building of this dual power within the government received tactical support from the mass organizations under Communist party control outside the government. And throughout, the Communist party was the integrating cement of the complex and informal pro-Communist movement in the government, in the factories, and among the peasantry. Unlike any other political party, the Communist party was in a position to prepare an entire system of social control which could be automatically instituted at the time of the coup. . . . Organizational preparation can largely eliminate the element of mass upheaval without sacrificing a fundamental transformation of the social order.'[1]

So far (mid-1967), the guerrilla initiative in South Vietnam has only been blunted even by the massive intervention of U.S. and allied power. General Giap has been able to trade manpower for time and by poising at least three divisions of North Vietnamese regulars on North Vietnam's southern border, an area which remains a 'privileged sanctuary' so far as ground force operations are concerned, he has been able to impose the detachment of substantial U.S. forces from the anti-guerrilla task. But even if the guerrilla initiative has been blunted, Hanoi still has the option at any time to enter into negotiations which would in turn be used as a political guerrilla operation designed to exploit 'contradictions' in the allied camp and indeed within the allied societies.

The intention would be to secure the recognition of the National Liberation Front (Vietcong) as the major negotiating party on the Communist side. The moment that that recognition was granted the guerrillas of yesterday would become the Prague-type politicians of the day, using their newly acquired 'legal status' and mass organizations to win through conspiratorial coups what they had failed to win on the battlefield. If the Allies agreed to negotiate before hostilities were terminated, as was the case in Korea, then the public of the U.S.A. and its allies would still daily be confronted with figures of heavy casualties predisposing them to accept conditions of negotiation more and more favourable to the Communists. In such a case nothing

[1] Selznick, op. cit.

would have altered in the revolutionary guerrilla campaign, except that emphasis would be placed more heavily on the political aspect of the total 'terrain'. To see the Vietcong as mere guerrilla fighters, skilled in fieldcraft, sowing panji sticks, and the like, is totally to misconstrue the true nature of revolutionary warfare.[1]

---

[1] In revolutionary guerrilla warfare the state is liable to be both 'dissected' *and* 'smashed' according to the stage of the struggle and its intensity. The intention is to destroy the substance of all that is open and civic in the target society, though not necessarily all existing state forms, during the struggle for power.

Chapter 2

THE SOUTH-EAST ASIAN SCENE

Since Communists and their fellow-travellers throughout the world have taken immense pains, for obvious enough reasons, to represent the Vietnamese kind of Communist revolutionary war as an activity arising out of special conditions, poverty and 'feudalism' in particular, it is necessary briefly to examine these underlying influences. Unless the West understands with some sympathetic insight the various facets of nationalist resurgence within the area known as Asia,[1] then it will come to resemble that class of which Chekhov wrote, 'while we intellectuals are rummaging among old rags, and according to the Russian custom, biting one another, there is boiling up around us a life which we neither know nor notice. ... And I also thought that before the dawn of a new life has broken, we shall turn into sinister old men and women, and we shall be the first who in our hatred of that dawn, will calumniate it.'

In the quite recent past it was very difficult for Westerners belonging to imperialist countries to be objective about Asian problems. They were ruling Asian countries on the ground that their civilization was superior to that of the countries they ruled. It was very seldom understood that such an assumption was necessary for civilized imperial rule; if it had not been held, then that rule would not only have been onerous for Asian nationalists to bear (as it was) but an altogether monstrous affair (which it was not). But in the course of time it brought to the fore a real denigrating kind of arrogance as in Kipling's 'And when your goal is nearest (the end for others sought) Watch sloth and heathen folly Bring all your hopes to nought!'

Another Englishman, G. K. Chesterton could write, on the one hand, 'And if we do not know that the whole civilized world sees Ireland with Poland as a typical oppressed nation, it is time we did';

---

[1] The author is unaware why the name of a meadow by a Greek stream was conferred upon a continent embracing a number of very different great civilizations; he is wholly aware of the way professional progressives use the term as though it were a monolithic entity in order to sap the West's will to act. Only a concern for the printer prevents him using the term between inverted commas throughout.

and on the other hand, 'Men of the Far East will submit to very low wages for the same reason that they will submit to "the punishment known as Li, or Slicing"; for the same reason that they will praise polygamy and suicide, for the same reason that they serve their temples with prostitutes for priests; for the same reason that they seem to make no distinction between sexual passion and sexual perversion. They do it, that is, because they are Heathens; men with different traditions from ours about the limits of human endurance and the gestures of self-respect.'

And it was not only the apologist for Christendom's golden age who wrote in such a manner. The gentle pagan from Cambridge, Goldsworthy Lowes Dickinson, wrote: 'I believe everything in India will have to be and ought to be swept away—except their beautiful dress and beautiful brown bodies.' Even D. H. Lawrence donned an intellectual topee at the entrance to Singhalese Buddhist monasteries: 'Those ratholes . . . Better Christ than Budda.' Curiously, even today an unconscious and gentle denigration is sometimes reflected in the writings of impeccably progressive minds. For example, 'Those features of Communist theory and practice that repel so many Westerners—the suppression of political and civic freedoms, the ruthless liquidation of class enemies and "deviationists" do not repel the people of East Asia in the same way. This is partly because . . . these rights seem less important to them than food. It is partly because the liberalism of the West, with its central emphasis on the rights of the individual citizen, is alien to the thought of most Easterners.'[1]

Given this stance of cultural superiority, it is not really very surprising that the West, while its scholars were reconstructing the often long forgotten histories of these peoples, permitted where it did not actively assist in the disintegration of the living Asian societies. Some Europeans foresaw the erosion of the Asian cultures. 'I see the East troubled within itself,' the former Abbé Lamennais wrote in 1833, 'It watches its ancient palaces crumbling, its age-old temples falling in powder, and lifts its eyes as if to seek other grandeurs and another God.'[2] That was the year in which a very different kind of European,

---

[1] W. McMahon Ball, *Nationalism and Communism in East Asia*. Cheshires, 1952. Cp. a Filipino progressive liberal, Ramon Magsaysay: 'Our freedom is the fruit of the efforts, the sacrifices, and the blood of our people. We won it by rising against Spain, by persuading America, and by resisting the Japanese. That is why our people love our freedom so much.' Qu. in Claude A. Buss, *Southeast Asia and the World Today*, Van Nostrand, 1958.

[2] Progressives who see in Communism a missionary faith may like the title: *The People's Prophecy*.

T. B. Macaulay, laid the Parliamentary groundwork for the introduction of English education into India, the aim of which he stated later was the creation of 'a class of persons, Indian in blood and colour, but English in taste, in opinions, in morals, and in intellect.'[1]

This was, of course, a task never undertaken in a thoroughgoing fashion—that is, accompanied by wholehearted legislative destruction of the old societies—anywhere in the colonial territories of the nineteenth and twentieth century, since the metropolitan powers during this heyday of overseas rule were not moved by a single, packageable 'ideology', as had been the case with Spain and Portugal earlier. Nevertheless the assumption remained that the outcome of imperial rule would be Asian societies gratefully (even if not comprehensively) informed by democratic ideas, Western-style civic behaviour, liberal progressive hopes for the future and foreign policies agreeable to the West, all these things being expressed through democratic parliaments and under the rule of Western law. The task of religious conversion, never effectively backed by metropolitan state power, had long since ceased to appear other than vulgar; but it was generally assumed that the traditional native religions would either wither away under the attrition of a rationalism backed by the natural sciences or would transform themselves out of recognition by a generalized acceptance of the Christian ethic.[2]

There were indeed violent outbreaks on the part of the traditional orders of Asia, designed to halt the slow but deadly erosion of the old cultures, the most famous being the 'Indian Mutiny' of 1857, the last of which were the Achinese War in Indonesia and the Boxer rebellion in China at the turn of the twentieth century. But all such outbreaks were not only militarily unsuccessful in the face of technologically more advanced societies, they seemed to demonstrate that if any anti-Western political movement were to be successful, it would have to

---

[1] Macaulay's successors came to regret this when they found themselves assailed by the Indian National Congress's political guerrilla warfare campaigns they found English-educated Indian *men* behaving like those dreadful home-grown suffragettes!

[2] Not always of course. General Ludendorff lamented in his *Totalitarian War:* 'The people which have been christianized no longer find themselves in the happy position, like the Japanese people, of possessing a specifically racial religion such as Shintoism, founded in the cohesion of government and people, of people and army, and of the whole of ethnic life.' And long after Macaulay, the African missionary, Charles de Foucauld could optimistically argue: 'The Touaregs should not be taught Arabic, which brings them nearer the Koran ... They must be taught Tamashek, an excellent, very easy language: gradually the words indispensable to expressing religious ideas, Christian virtues should be introduced ...' qu. in Anne Fremantle, *Desert Calling*.

come to terms with the very modes of thought and behaviour and organization against which the traditionalist risings had been directed.

That the general outcome of Western imperialism (and economic penetration of China and Thailand) was not to be parliamentary democracy and the untrammelled rule of Western law did not become apparent until very recently indeed. The year 1958 may reasonably be selected as the first high-water mark of neo-authoritarianism, chiefly by way of military government, in the non-Communist countries of Asia. This now widespread political development throughout most of South and South-East Asia came as a saddening surprise to the West for a number of reasons that are central to an understanding of why the intellectual 'terrain' of the area would in theory greatly favour the working out of Communist polities.

There was another Western hope, most persuasively argued by Professor Arnold Toynbee, to the effect that Western technology was but the 'entering wedge' of a Western civilization that was not only to erode the traditional societies but also build the scaffolding of a unified world society. The West was to be responsible not only for an upheaval on a world-wide scale—an argument which few Asians would have disputed—but also for creating the framework of a single Great Society. Certainly he was not arguing that it would at all necessarily be dominated by the old Western seats of metropolitan power, the greatest of which he clearly finds increasingly unadventurous.[1] Nevertheless the presumption is there throughout that technology is basically an attribute of a single definable society.

It is interesting to compare this vision with Señor del Corral who sees the technology of Western Europe being expropriated, yet conquering the minds (and judgement) of its expropriators: 'Politics, philosophy, science, art, religion, are all fused in the crucible of a deified technology. Its production is not immediately directed towards well being, but towards political power, but in the background there is always the ideal of a human paradise identified with technology. It is an ideal that Communism has communicated to the ancient peoples of Asia, who are suddenly disposed to break with static traditions and to bow down (or break into an orgiastic dance) before European technology, the herald and architect of an unsuspected Kingdom of God.'[2]

---

[1] 'It is her revolution; it was she who launched it by firing that shot heard round the world . . . Can America rejoin her own revolution? . . . (Can she give up) Metternich's dreary part?' *America and World Revolution*, OUP 1962.
[2] Luis Diez del Corral *The Rape of Europe*, George Allen and Unwin, 1959.

Now there is no doubt whatsoever that technology, particularly in the form of large-scale industry, has an attraction for the new Asian élites—for the non-Communists quite as much as the Communists—which is not only related to solving population problems through rapid urbanization or trying to lessen the dependence of a primary producing country upon a Western-dominated world market, let alone an attraction basically founded upon a desire for general human betterment.

Independent Asia is an area of *régimes* rather than governments in the Western parliamentary sense; and the *régimes* seek to identify the factories with themselves in the minds of the people—which, incidentally, is the most cogent reason for bombing the industrial complex of North Vietnam, provided it can be politically exploited through propaganda designed to separate the rulers from the people.[1] It can therefore immediately be seen that technology does not necessarily induce recognizably Western democratic modes of thought. Of course, without industrialization and modernization of agricultural technology, the people of the undeveloped countries cannot even *opt* for Western ways of thinking, which are based on a considerable freedom from physical servitude to seasonal vagaries and a means of livelihood significantly raised above subsistence level. It can even be argued that 'when the essence of economic development is probed it is revealed to offer benefits of the same character as those being sought in the development of liberal-democratic political forms'[2] even where those political forms do not obtain. This is what is undermining the whole Leninist ideology in the U.S.S.R. Doubtless one day it will undermine this now utterly irrelevant ideology throughout the world.

In this sense, perhaps Toynbee is right: 'The truth seems to be . . . if one abandons one's own traditional technology and adopts a foreign technology instead, the effect of this change on the technological surface of life will not remain confined to the surface, but will gradually work its way down to the depths till the whole of one's traditional culture has been undermined. . . .'[3] But this is a very long-term process, involving great anguish, terrible perplexities, large-scale alienations, and all manner of disguised reactions. Moreover,

---

[1] This is not easy to do, since the U.S.A. has consistently undertaken not to overthrow the regime in the north.
[2] Peter Samuel, *Quadrant*, May–June 1966, op. cit.
[3] *The World and the West*, O.U.P., 1953 (II).

the process of erosion, except in the very generalized sense mentioned above, bears no built-in creative component at all capable of universal application that could be recognized as comprising part of a new Great Society—let alone one recognizably Western or even, through recognition of commonly shared aspirations friendly towards the West.[1]

This is a factor of very great importance in understanding the intellectual and social terrain upon which the Communist revolutionaries are operating: 'A Christian in a southern Indian village is not a Westerner, nor is a 'mission African' who, apart from attending vernacular religious services, belongs to a football team. Still less is a Mongol soldier a Westerner because he is taken into battle in a truck built on the upper Volga with a machine carbine manufactured near Irkutsk. The Mongol's technical equipment may be even more pervasive of his immediate experience than the African's religious observances, but it is even further removed from any spiritual origin in the West. . . . The truth surely is that insofar as modern *technology* is to be considered historically as an attribute or a single definable society, then it is one of the attributes which can be diffused in segregation from the others.'[2]

Technology is neutral (as the jungle is in guerrilla warfare). M. Paul Mus provides chastening examples of this in Vietnam of a kind very relevant to the morale of the Vietcong today. He describes how even the French-made bus is adapted to a different kind of society and shows how the Vietnamese would say to the Frenchman, 'Yes, you press the button on your camera, but who has the secret of developing the film? The Vietnamese photographic expert in the town nearby . . . Your motor cars? Oh yes, but who knows how to drive and repair them? You or your Vietnamese chauffeurs?'[3]

The chief reason why nearly all the Asian nationalist movements at first adopted democratic systems was not so much that such systems were already to some degree 'going concerns' in which many of the leaders had already participated but because industrialization seemed to have been immeasurably most effectively achieved by Western

---

[1] The great French soldier–administrator, Marshall Lyautey, argued: 'Show force in order to avoid using it . . . One factory is worth a battalion.' The Algerian nationalists were politically unimpressed.
[2] Michael Vyvyan, *Cambridge Journal*, June 1950 (13)F. Spencer Chapman, *The Jungle is Neutral*, Chatto & Windus, 1949, contains very fine descriptions of how different human beings react to a new environment, besides providing an excellent account of guerrilla warfare.
[3] *Vietnam: Sociologie d'une guerre*, Editions du Seuil, 1952.

democracies. Despite all the nationalist arguments about exploitation and the economically retarding effects of imperial rule (there was the specious corollary to the effect that the Great Powers of the West were rich because of this exploitation of foreigners, although most nationalist leaders were aware of countries like Sweden and Switzerland),[1] democracy seemed to most of them to be a precondition for effective industrialization, whereas in fact, except for countries peculiarly favoured in the relationship between population and natural resources, like the U.S.A. and Australia, a high level of industrialization had been the enabling condition of real, adult franchise democracy.

True, there was the rise of Nazism and Fascism but these were seldom regarded as other than temporary aberrations. There was Japanese militarism but though the early Japanese naval victory over Russia in the Straits of Tshushima was of great psychological significance to the other Asian élites, the Asians who attempted to use Japanese expansionism as a means of freeing their countries from Western rule appear to have been little impressed, even at the time, by the ideology accompanying it.[2] There was of course the U.S.S.R. 'In view of the extreme poverty of the masses in Asian countries . . .' Mr. Geoffrey Hudson remarked, 'it is astonishing *how little* success Communism had in Asia . . . during the first two decades after the Russian Revolution.'[3] He goes on to point out, 'But it must be remembered that the Soviet Union in those years did not appear to Asian eyes the irresistible power that it seemed to be by 1945 . . .' Nevertheless all the Asian countries opted for democracy at the time they won their political independence, with the sole exception of the Vietnamese nationalist movement which had come under Communist control by 1945 *before* the issue of independence arose and under very special circumstances.

The early period of political independence 'streamed with the pomp of a too-credulous day.' Gone was the arid 'despotism of despatch-boxes tempered by loss of keys';[4] gone the old complaints of a

---

[1] It is one of the delightful ironies of history that Lenin should have written his *Imperialiam: The Highest Stage of Capitalism* in Switzerland.

[2] Such is the impression gained from talking with a man like General Ne Win and from reading the work of Subhas Chandra Bose, e.g. *The Indian Struggle 1920–42*, Asia Publishing House, 1964. Bose, incidentally, saw in Indian independence the *economic* liberation of the *English* working class! See also Leonard Barnes, *Empire* and *Democracy*, Left Book Club, Gollancz, 1939.

[3] *Questions of East and West*, Odhams Press, 1953.

[4] Guy Wint, *The British in Asia*, Faber, 1947.

Western administration 'too expensive, and too complicated for the Eastern nations';[1] gone the vicarious revenges;[2] and gone, of course, the old excuses—or most of them[3]—until President Sukarno and others were to invent, not *altogether* fictitiously, the slogan of Neo-colonialism. An optimism, that in retrospect seems fantastic, ruled the minds of the new rulers. Democracy and political independence promised far, far more than they could really produce in the foreseeable future.

The Premier of Burma, U Nu, representing a London School of Economics type of Marxist (he was later to pin his hopes on a Buddhist revival and end up incarcerated by a more determined modernizer) reached the heights of confident expectation; 'Therefore, many branches of knowledge such as relativity, eugenics, quantum theory, laissez-faire, surplus value, utilitarianism, geo-politics and so on . . . will be within easy reach of our cowherds, cultivators, hewers of wood and drawers of water. . . .'[4] An Indian Marxist, as late as 1956, could write, '(India) does not have to go through the harrowing experiences of early industrial revolutions. She need not repeat the errors made by others. She can look forward to substantial, lightning advances, for she has begun her journey into the atomic age, made possible by the achievements of world science.'[5]

Within a decade or so of the achievement of political independence, a new authoritarianism was established, largely as a popularly acclaimed alternative to a democratic and economic mess, in Pakistan, Burma, Thailand, and Indonesia; and by that time (the end of the '50s) confidence was nothing like so high in India, nor were Western democratic friends of India so eagerly disposed to proclaim that society as a model for Asia. As the Indian M. N. Roy had warned

[1] Anon, *Letters of an Indian Judge to an English Gentlewoman*, Peter Davies, 1934.
[2] '(Moderates) and Extremists alike learned with satisfaction of German victories. There was no love for Germany, of course, only the desire to see our own rulers humbled. It was the weak and helpless man's idea of vicarious revenge.' Jawaharlal Nehru in Dorothy Norman (Editor): Nehru, *The First Sixty Years*, The Bodley Head, 1965.
[3] Some nationalist leaders who spent their lives arguing that their nations were ready for independence, spent the aftermath negatively concentrating attention on the very points the imperialists had used as excuses or reasons for remaining: lack of technicians, university graduates, etc.
[4] Qu. in Richard Butwel, *U Nu of Burma*, Stanford University Press, 1965.
[5] Romesh Thapar, *India in Transition*, Current Book House, 1956, cp. S. C. Bose, op. cit.; 'In Free India, the standard of living will rise rapidly and, in consequence thereof, consumption will increase by leaps and bounds. Free India will thereby become one of the biggest markets for manufactured goods. This should be of interest to all industrially advanced countries.' (1942)

Lenin many years before, there were two kinds of nationalist struggle going on in Asia, the bourgeois democratic and 'the mass struggle of the poor and ignorant peasants and workers for their liberation from various forms of exploitation'; and there was no guarantee that the latter would win. However, the disabilities and failures of the bourgeois nationalists, coupled with the presumed exemplary modernization of China, should in theory have made Communism seem very attractive by the early '60s. Instead Communists are prescribed in Pakistan, gaoled in India, hunted down in the Burmese countryside, executed in Thailand, outlawed in Malaya and Singapore, ever more firmly combatted in Laos, opposed in Cambodia, and decimated in Indonesia. Only in Indonesia (Vietnam is a special case which will be treated in detail later) did the Communists at any time establish a mass base or a focus of attraction for significant groupings within the ruling classes of South and South-East Asia.

Despite the fact that the aftermath of political independence under bourgeois nationalist leadership was marked not only by the political failure, in most places, of that leadership, but by an ever widening economic gap between the developed world and these backward regions, Communism has never significantly advanced except through revolutionary guerrilla warfare; that is to say through organized violence. The reasons for this are important in understanding the precise nature of Communist policy in South-East Asia.

The most obvious, and certainly not least important reason is the fact that Communism in a starkly Leninist form is today the ideology of China, a power which most Asian leaders have come to believe—unwillingly and slowly in some cases—is politically expansionist or at the very least an ungainly large bully evoking a sharpened historical recollection of various kinds of subservience (even if often only in the form of a symbolic 'tribute') which the Middle Kingdom had imposed upon areas of South-East Asia in the past.

On the plane of theory, probably many Asian leaders would accept Sir Denis Brogan's suggestion that, 'A patriotic Chinese, faced with the poverty of that country, with what may be its increasing poverty and seeing no way out except a rapid increase in industrialization and a rapid increase in the output of land may conclude, in no selfish or vulgar intention, that only a vigorous, rigorous, modern power in China can do both and provide the necessary political authority without which the best schemes of industrial technicians and agronomists will come to nothing. And to that end, he may put up with a great deal of mendacity, a great deal of intellectual isolation and coercion, even with the shedding of a great deal of blood. He may be willing to pay the price of revolution.'[1]

However, this acceptance of the theoretical *bona fides* of the Chinese Communists, so far as China's own development alone is concerned, has become less and less willing, even on the theoretical plane, as evidence accumulates of Chinese agricultural failures, the fiasco of 'The Great Leap Forward', the actual suffering involved in such a process of modernization[2] and the dramatically increasing anti-intellectualism of the regime. There is too a febrile insistence upon revolutionary war and subversion as the only correct form of Communist struggle, not to speak of clear Peking moral support, when physical support is rendered impossible by geography, for actual campaigns of subversion aimed as much against 'progressive' governments like Burma's as against the 'reactionary' government of Thailand.[3]

It is not only Moscow which finds it '. . . impossible not to note the fact that instead of the internationalist approach expressed in "Workers of the world unite" the Chinese comrades stubbornly propagate the slogan deprived of any class meaning: "the wind from the east prevails over the wind from the west".'[4] Professional progressives in the West may think and talk of 'Asia'; the countries of the region are quite unwilling to identify themselves with such a monolithic concept. Nationalism remains a very potent force, detrimental to regional defence and economic development, on the one hand, and to the hopes of Peking-line Communist expansionism on the other.

But this is by no means the sole reason why Communism has advanced only through revolutionary warfare. There is another reason that is seldom noticed: over the past century China has known warfare to an extent quite foreign to all the other recently independent Asian nations. Whereas it was possible to report of China as early as the first decade of this century that 'the most noticeable change is the growth of a military spirit and the improvement in the training and equipment of the troops'[5], the experience of the other nationalist movements was almost entirely non-military.

[1] *The Price of Revolution*, op. cit.
[2] Guy Wint, *Spotlight on Asia*, Penguin, 1955: 'But the way I saw these Chinese labourers being driven to work evoked a stronger emotion than desire for emulation or pity; I was plainly horrified. After all a human being is not a beast.' (An Indian view)
[3] Only in Pakistan does one find any notable enthusiasm amongst the élite for revolutionary war in Vietnam; and that because of nationalist feelings about the use of this technique in Kashmir.
[4] Michael Field, *The Prevailing Wind*, Methuen, 1965.
[5] Sir Charles Eliot, *Letters from the Far East*, 1906.

THE SOUTH-EAST ASIAN SCENE

Even where military régimes have taken over from failed democratic politicians, there has been no attempt to inculcate a militaristic caste of thought amongst the population. This in itself creates a gulf between China (and North Vietnam) and all the other independent states of Asia. The Chinese experience has been altogether different and almost certainly more psychically damaging; the nihilism of Old China Hands was much more destructive of human dignity than the rule of the Indian Civil Service and so, together with decades of internecine and international war, evoked a much more terrible reaction.[1]

The only equivalent reaction is to be found in North Vietnam: 'The terrible hostility of the Asian Communist towards the Westerner, particularly towards the American, is something which has, perhaps, to be personally experienced to be understood in all its virulence. The people I saw in North Vietnam are, like their Chinese allies, emaciated through inadequate nutrition. They automatically fulfil the dictates of their fanatical leaders who are themselves obsessed with their own vision of 'the truth'. They aim to destroy all that the West stands for. To spread the poison with which they have been inoculated, they will kill, torture and deceive. They will accept untold privations. They have learnt to hate their adversaries absolutely. There can, at present, be no reasonable discourse with them, for they are the homunculi of the phantasmagorical world issued from the 'scientific socialism' of Marx.'[2]

There are also much more subtle reasons why there has been no sign of any Asian country freely opting for the Communist 'solution' to the problem of modernization. They relate to the kind of revolution that is acceptable to non-Communist leaders and the masses which they necessarily have to influence rather than coerce. The moment the word revolution is inserted into the discussion is the moment when the writer must pause, since it is a privileged word[3] which today is being used as an intellectual weapon in the West by progressives who are arguing that to oppose Communist revolutionary warfare in South Vietnam is simply to oppose a localized form of a generalized

[1] 'When the (Kuomintang) government attempted to ban child labour from factory employment and to establish minimum conditions of work, it was unable to secure the co-operation of those who controlled the greatest portion of the industry and who were protected by concessions and extra-territoriality —the foreign investors.' F. L. K. Hsu, *Chinese and Americans*, 1955.
[2] *The Prevailing Wind*, op. cit.
[3] 'The word Revolution has many meanings. When it is used in a certain sense it is not rigidly confined to that sense, but still partakes of an affective and motive force derived from all the other meanings. Certain kinds of words are privileged in this way.' *Sociology of Communism*, op. cit.

Asian revolution. The presumption underlying this argument is that whereas Indians have chosen a diluted form of social democracy (or mixed economy, if it is preferred), North Vietnamese (and a majority of South Vietnamese) have chosen *in the same way, and within the same area of choice*, the Communist system of government.

This kind of reasoning is nicely compressed in the following extract from a review of *Living with Asia* (Lansdowne Press, 1966) by Dr. J. F. Cairns which adumbrates such a theory; 'However, these deficiencies do not seriously weaken the central theme of Dr. Cairns' book: that Australians should try to understand, and even to sympathize with, the struggles by Asian peoples for national identity, self-respect and economic progress, problems which are infinitely more challenging than any faced by European societies. Such understanding should be present even in cases where Communist influence may be found to exist. "While the challenge of Communism must be met effectively and resolutely", we should not oppose those forces who are most likely to bring about social and economic change simply because they may have Communist tendencies or associations. Our response should not be one of opposition, certainly not in a military form. Foreign intervention, he believes, has tended to strengthen rather than weaken Communist influence. In fact, in the absence of such intervention, it has been extremely difficult for Communists to gain a predominant role in nationalist movements in Asia.'[1]

This is liberal-progressive wishful thinking at its most vividly absurd. The only significant Communist movements in South-East Asia *are* militarized groups which cannot be opposed 'resolutely and effectively' except by arms. There *are* no governments in Asia with 'Communist *tendencies* or *associations*' (except until recently in Indonesia, which was certainly unopposed by the West, except in its military manifestations in the form of 'Confrontation'—and then with Asian allies). The only Communist party in power, in North Vietnam, assumed control of the nationalist movement *before* the French returned. Lastly, as will be shown, a major reason why Communists today find it 'extremely difficult to gain a predominant role in nationalist movements in Asia' is because, having been defeated by arms, the Communist parties are proscribed or hunted down or kept on a short leash, as in India. The intervention of the British Army in the Malayan insurgency can scarcely be said to have strengthened Communist influence there.

[1] Ian Ward, *Australian Outlook*, Journal of the Australian Institute of International Affairs, August 1966.

The situation in South and South-East Asia bears no resemblance to these simplistic wish-dreams '. . . the real issue lies between libertarian revolutionaries and others who can envisage the transformation of Society only in terms of the Soviet experience since 1917 (in 1967, read: the Chinese experience).'[1] This is not to say for a moment that in the event some non-Communist nationalist leaders have not behaved in a repressive and reactionary way but usually this has been the result of very special circumstances or has not really affected the trend towards modernization (as in Thailand, for example). 'All disputes (within the nationalist movements) are at bottom differences about the degree and form of centralization requisite for the task of building a modern nation.'[2] But of course when it comes to defining the appropriate attributes of a modern nation the problem becomes much more complex than it might seem at first sight.

From the cultural point of view the Asian nations have for a very long time been engaged in a situation of dilemma which may be simplified by posing the stark question: What can be retained of the old culture while trying to catch up with the West economically and socially? This is not at all a drawing-room question; it is a question of identity, a question of pride and belief. There is a great sadness in listening to a certain kind of 'Asian' explaining, for example, how the Pali Canon contains an adumbration of nuclear physics made 2,000 years before Rutherford or another arguing that the Chinese were so civilized that they could bear to use gunpowder only for fireworks. It is not a matter of whether these beliefs are true or false (though it appears the Chinese could bear to apply hydraulics to torture); it is a matter of where national pride can rest in a world changing rapidly as a result always of discoveries and advances made in the West. Technology is neutral and easily universalized in theory but in practice its effective use depends upon certain social factors that are not easily or *willingly* assimilated by Asian societies. As Mr. Maurice Zinkin puts it: 'Getting rich must be a major objective, for which people are prepared to sacrifice old habits as well as present consumption. They must save instead of hoarding, or spending on festivals or ceremonies. . . . If wealth is the aim, wealth must be the criterion, not power, or autarchy, or even fairness.'[3] Or as Mr. Eugene Staley writes: 'The will to develop is in essence a matter of what individuals and

[1] G. L. Arnold, *The Pattern of World Conflict*, Dial Press, 1955.
[2] G. L. Arnold, op. cit.
[3] Maurice Zinkin, *Development for Free Asia*, Chatto & Windus, 1963.

social groups *want*, and *whether they want it badly enough to be willing to change their old ways of doing things* and to work hard at installing the new.'[1]

This may seem obvious enough to Westerners, since they are heirs to a long and unique historical development culminating in this untrammelled willingness to concentrate upon development and increasing national wealth. The beginnings of the European mind that brought off the scientific and cultural revolution can be traced back to the Middle Ages: 'The study of medieval technology is therefore more than an aspect of economic history: it reveals a chapter in the conquest of freedom. . . . The labour-saving power-machines of the later Middle Ages were produced by the implicit theological assumption of the infinite worth of even the most degraded human personality, by an instinctive repugnance towards subjecting any man to a monotonous drudgery which seems less than human in that it requires the exercise neither of intelligence nor of choice.'[2] The significance of this interpretation may of course be disputed, as the thesis to the effect that there was a special, identifiable 'protestant ethic' engendering capitalism may be disputed. What cannot be disputed is that over centuries Europe went through an intellectual, economic, and social experience which created that 'pervasive spirit of the West' (as Dr. Perceval Spear calls it) which is regarded with a mixture of longing and loathing by many Asians.

There are a number of reasons for this ambivalent attitude. There is the very recent discovery that political independence and democratic institutions do not in themselves close the gap between West and East. There is the slow realization that a whole culture and not simply a number of machines has made the West what it is. There are sudden glimpses of the enormity of the task of modernization[3] and there is the sense of being prisoners not only of a myth of foreign provenance that cannot be lived out locally in a spiritually meaningful way, but also of a resurgent nationalism which demands thoroughgoing economic and social modernization of a kind likely to exhaust the well-springs of national pride. Aware of already being cultural

[1] Eugene Staley, *The Future of Underdeveloped Countries*, Praeger, 1961.
[2] Lynn White in Alfred F. Havinghurst (Editor), *The Pirenne Thesis*, D. C. Heath and Co, 1958. See also John U. Nef, *Cultural Foundations of Industrial Civilisation* and I. R. Sinai, *The Challenge of Modernisation* op cit.
[3] 'But by all the relevant tests of history and sociology these regions approximate more closely to the European world of 1,200 years ago . . . We might as well ask why William the Conqueror did not achieve the industrial revolution as expect present-day Indonesia to achieve it in our time.' F. H. Hinsley, *The Listener* op. cit.

mosaics,[1] and that far from dividing and ruling, the imperial powers often in fact created political nations, the integration of which they could sustain immeasurably more easily than their successors have been able to do, the nations of Asia are deeply concerned to try to fashion modernized societies bearing a specific nationalist imprint. Hence labels like Arab socialism and the Burmese Way to Socialism. The most heartening examples of a recovery of indigenous nerve are to be found in the growth of various community development concepts, most eminently associated with the Indian Jayaprakash Narayan, a man of great intellect and great nobility of spirit. He very significantly, has *thought his way through* from Western-style extremism to an understanding based upon certain elements of the local tradition and, equally important, upon a calmly critical rejection of certain elements of Western civilization, particularly its imprisonment in the fetters of urban growth and the pursuit of mere size in industry.[2]

The Communist alternative to this groping, tentative search after a new kind of national society—with all its dangers of going too slowly as a result of vested interests exploiting genuine moderation—is to smash completely the old order of society by engendering as much hatred for it as for the capitalist West. The human mind as well as industrial and agricultural organization is to be smashed and then reconstructed, and out of this catastrophic reversal and transformation, characterized in literally apocalyptic terms by Mao Tse-Tung,[3] a new kind of human being is presumed to emerge. Apart from sinicized Vietnam, for reasons which will be touched upon later, this

---

[1] The result of this lack of integration by the dialectic of need is the existence in all colonial countries of what can only be termed a cultural mosaic. By this I mean that in all colonial countries the cultural features are juxtaposed but not harmonised . . .' Aimé Cesaire, *Culture and Colonisation* in Hans Kohn and Wallace Sokolsky (Editors), *African Nationalism in the Twentieth Century*, Van Nostrand, 1965.

[2] Hugh Tinker, *Ballot Boxes and Bayonets*, OUP, 1964 and *Cultural Freedom in Asia*, Congress for Cultural Freedom, Charles E. Tuttle, 1956. In Latin America, the preservation of the culture has often seemed more important than technological advance: '(The intellectuals) have almost unanimously expressed the conviction that the values of Hispanic and Anglo-American culture are in conflict . . . they are an obstacle to the development of a successful foreign aid programme . . .' Lewis Hanke: *Mexico and the Caribbean* (Van Nostrand, 1959). There are, of course, other reasons, importantly the existence of pre-industrial urbanization. Claudio Veliz, *Obstacles to Change in Latin America*, OUP, 1965.

[3] 'Once man has reached the age of peace (once man has eliminated capitalism), he will never again desire war . . . At this moment will begin the third epoch in the history of humanity . . . Throughout all eternity our sons and grandsons will never know war again . . .' Stuart R. Schram, *The Political Thought of Mao Tse-Tung*, Praeger, 1963

kind of thinking has no wide appeal whatsoever in South-East Asia, not least because every nation in the area is plagued with minority and border problems which evoke, often unwisely, a rigorous nationalistic outlook on the part of the modernizing élite, which is necessarily predominantly drawn from members of the majority race or, as in Java, the most populous region. Moreover since, throughout South-East Asia, these ruling élites of society are more often to be found forming the single party that governs the state than in leading rival political parties offering alternative programmes, the one party-programme of the day is used to reinforce the nationalist claims of the governing body.

As a result, despite all failures and shortcomings in the economic and social fields, the régimes impress upon their societies such a weight of slogans and programmatic activities that the Communists have little chance of offering an alternative 'solution' to the people. Since the Communist parties of the region have all either committed insurgent violence or made explicit their intention to use it, there is understandably little disposition on the part of the rulers to offer 'legal' opportunities for agitation and propaganda of any kind.[1] It might be added, in passing, that this fact increases the attraction, from the Communist point of view, of initiating and slowly expanding the techniques of revolutionary warfare on the periphery of such countries, launched preferably from a 'privileged sanctuary' across the border.

In this way, if the phasing is appropriately protracted, the insurgency may not be identified and effectively met until dangerously late. It is poor administration in the outlying areas, caused as much by an urbanized hatred of rural service as by technical deficiencies, which

[1] Of course, some of the political élites (as in Burma, for example) regard many other groups besides the Communists as subversive. Though offering a very much larger area of intellectual (and so, *potential* political) activity, all the ideologised authoritarian élites have an in-built tendency towards self-satisfied stagnation. 'It is no more than a doctrinaire belief of political élites that they embody completely all the interests of the people whom they rule and that they care for them all equally. But the fact that it is only a belief does not make it less real or less effective. In many cases it probably is a sincerely held belief.' Edward Shils in *Government and Opposition* (Vol. I no 2 January 1966) cp. U Ba Swe, a former leader of the Burmese Socialist regime, who believes that 'Marxist theory is not antagonistic to Buddhist philosophy. The two are, frankly speaking, not merely similar. In fact they are the same in concept.' Nevertheless: 'In as much as Russian methods are not conducive to success in China, Chinese methods are out of place in Burma. Only a revolutionary movement which is entirely Burmese, conforming to Burmese methods and principles can achieve any kind of success . . .' Frank Trager (Editor) *Marxism in Southeast Asia*, Stanford University Press, 1960.

permits attempts at subversion to develop into first-phase, 'pinpoint coercion' insurgency. Besides, slow escalation in outlying areas permits the creation of the myth of spontaneity, which is so important in influencing public opinion in the protecting Power against the government under insurgent threat. Democrats, as a result of their own experiences at home, are naturally psychologically prone to see in such peripheral beginnings of revolutionary warfare a political protest locally engendered rather than a politico-military organization at work exploiting 'contradictions'.[1]

The minority and border problems of South-East Asia are central to an understanding of the nationalisms of the area. Known in the past as Further India or Indo-China, South-East Asia is one of those originally military terms that can be very misleading politically. It may be said to begin on the Naaf River dividing East Pakistan from the Arakan Division of Burma. Immediately the minority problems begin. After independence a vociferous if not very determined movement was established to secure statehood for the minority within the Union of Burma and an able group of politicians were sent to Rangoon. Arakan itself was for a time plagued by 'Mujahids' (in fact Muslim bandits) from across the border in Pakistan and has long resented the support offered by its own Muslim minority in Akyab district to governments bent on unification in Rangoon, 'The Centre' as it is ominously called in the minority areas. There was also Communist insurgency in the Arakan Division, cut off from Burma proper by the rugged Arakan Yomas.[2] In the North the Kachins and Shans have both mounted insurgencies, which are in operation today; in the South-East, the Karens for more than a decade waged guerrilla war-

[1] This in itself is obviously a healthy reaction in Western democracies; but it also reflects the kind of popular ignorance that vitiates the claim for 'popular participation in foreign policy decision-making' e.g. Marvin Gettleman, *Vietnam: History, Documents, and Opinions,* Penguin Special, 1965. It also points up the validity of Charles W. Thayer's remark that 'Mao's three-phase rule omits what is often the most decisive phase of all—the pre-combat, organizational or conspiratorial phase.' *Guerrilla,* Michael Joseph, 1964

[2] Apart from its conservative leadership, which includes a number of Cambridge men, Arakan is rather analagous with North East Thailand: aware of a separate historical past and different dialect, deeply conscious of economic neglect by 'the Centre' (British as well as Burman). In 1931 Arakanese leaders presented a memorial to the British Government asking for certain safeguards, failing which 'Arakan should become an autonomous state, either federated to Burma or completely left to herself as in the days of her kings.' See the author's article in *Australia's Neighbours,* June 1957. But unlike the Thai North-Easterners who can look to their 'compatriots' across the Mekong in Laos, the Arakanese, though prone to speak of their 'Bengali physiognomy', know they are Buddhists next door to a Muslim state.

fare in the hope of winning statehood. Kachins and Shans (Thais, in fact) are to be found in significant numbers in China's southernmost province; and only the Burmese Thais' conservative social structure, sometimes quite incorrectly described as feudalism, prevent their being susceptible to the propaganda put out by the 'Thai capital' of Che-li in China's Yunnan. Kuomintang remnants established themselves in the South Shan State and their opium-running network straddles the Burma-Thai border. General Ne Win settled his country's northern border issue with China at small territorial cost to Burma at a time when emphasis in Peking was being placed on the 'Bandung spirit' and 'Panch sila' in order to keep Burma out of any SEATO-type alliance with the West. A rigorous and penurious neutralism has been the price required of Burma. Though there are political exiles in Bangkok from the various minority states and regions, the Thai Government, worried about its Cambodian and Laotian frontiers, has behaved correctly towards Rangoon in this matter: even the Shan insurgents, camped quite close to the Thai border, do not appear to receive help from Thailand.

A very great part of Burman political energies since independence in 1947 has been devoted to blunting Communist and minority insurgencies; to keeping the Union of Burma in being as a political entity. The confident economic and social aspirations have had to be subordinated to the sheer effort of maintaining control over a territory given artificial unity by imperial overlords. In the event, the dictum of a great colonial authority to the effect that 'a colonial government has to be much more careful not to offend the traditions and authorities of the groups than a national government, because it lacks the sacred character of the latter'[1] did not prove true of the nation states actually created by Western technological and administrative excellence, since these states involved a kind of *modernizing* intensity of control unthinkable in the old states of South-East Asia.

Like all the other countries of the region, Burma had important foreign minorities, Indian, Pakistani, and Chinese, which under imperial aegis had come to control the middle level of commerce and to own, as absentees, a great deal of the agricultural land of Burma. For the most part, the 'Indian moneylenders', who in fact included a large, very poor urban coolie force, have been repatriated under harsh conditions; and the Chinese minority is under strict surveillance and suffers social disabilities, which are by no means only politically motivated, such a minority being regarded as subversive of centrally-dir-

[1] A. D. A. de Kat Angelino, *Colonial Policy*, Martinus Nijhoff, 1931.

ected modernization, irrespective of its presumed political allegiance. As a result of this situation, the Burman 'overlords' (or 'chauvinists' as the minority people call them) who make up about two-thirds of Burma's population (about 25 millions) have a leadership primarily devoted to establishing the necessary power structure for modernization and an armed services command and organization wholly directed towards internal security. It is made difficult for men of the other races to ride high in the government services, and Burmans are infiltrated into the machinery of government in the minority states. This very great emphasis upon translating national ethos into appropriate political forms through the steady application of force, whether by arms or through propaganda, against all recalcitrants, combined with what to Westerners is an astonishing lack of interest in the affairs of neighbours like Thailand, makes the appeals of Communism exceedingly difficult to implement; while it contributes to making South-East Asia a very 'friable' area to use Dr. Don Kennedy's happy expression[1] from the point of view of any kind of regional collective defence. The Communists, committed to revolutionary guerrilla warfare since 1948, still lack a sanctuary for the arming, supplying and training of their cadres, a problem that will be referred to again later. Moreover the fact that individual Communists have been accepted as advisers and that General Ne Win's economic and social policies are far to the left can offer no comfort to the Party, which is solely concerned with the seizure of power for itself and is not interested in certain local emulations of its policy unencumbered by the ideology that alone keeps the Communist on his arduous path.[2]

Thailand gives the impression of being one of the most homogeneous and 'natural' societies of the region but in fact, as has been made clear during the recrudescence of 1966 insurgency in the Muslim Malay south and its appearance in the Lao-speaking North-East her borders are susceptible of challenge by her neighbours should they be so minded. This former buffer state between British and French spheres of influence has also had border disputes with Cam-

[1] D. E. Kennedy, *The Security of Southern Asia*, Chatto & Windus, for the Institute of Strategic Studies, 1965.
[2] The Burma Communist party, being very much a Burman organization, has for the most part eschewed significant operations in the minority areas, where it is intensely disliked for racial reasons. Its main areas of operation have been 400 miles or more from China, whereas the motor distance between a Vietnamese–China border town like Langson and Hanoi itself was half this during the Vietnamese French struggle, the distances between the border and the Viet Bac base areas very short indeed—and traversing country dominated by the Communists from before the end of World War II.

bodia. The interests of the ruling classes became dangerously centred around Bangkok, at the expense of the more outlying districts, during the untroubled and, for most of the country, prosperous years since 1949, when potentially subversive opposition was put down at the centre, to be replaced only very gradually by subversion on the periphery of the North-East Region abutting Laos. But it has throughout had a very large Chinese minority problem (perhaps $3\frac{1}{2}$ millions) to cope with; and the fact that it has tackled it through a firm policy of assimilation through Thai education, backed by the imposition of certain financial disabilities on foreigners in general, has greatly strengthened the kind of perfervid nationalism that emasculates Communist opportunities of penetrating the ruling classes with their ideas. In Thailand the disaffected intellectual, upon whom the Communists rely throughout the region for leadership, does not suffer from a sufficiently deep discontent to move him into the Communist camp.[1] Only the Vietnamese minority in the North-East presents a permanently committed minority threat, should conditions deteriorate seriously in Laos and the Hanoi-controlled Pathet Lao actually come to power there. North-East Thailand lacks a disaffected intelligentsia and a real sense of being a self-identifiable minority group; its peasantry have real grounds for discontent with past Bangkok neglect but no abiding Cause behind which to rally. There is a particular reason for this. Laos across the Mekong is so far in no sense a nation state capable of appealing to would-be irridentists in Thailand: 'Laos is less a nation state than a conglomeration of tribes and languages (eighteen major dialects are spoken in Phong Saly Province alone), less a unified society than a multiplicity of feudal societies. The family clan is all-important.[2]

This does not mean that if Hanoi were granted victory throughout Vietnam the Hanoi controlled Pathet Lao could not, as a result of protracted struggle, smash the old societies and incorporate North-East Thailand into a Thai Democratic Republic based on Vientiane or perhaps Dien-Bien-Phu.[3] But that is to speculate. All that is being

[1] '... it is evident that in Buddhism the Thai intellectual has a *Weltanschauung* which is both satisfactory and comfortable... Moreover, the vitality of Buddhist ethics most certainly discounts the particularities of Marxian theory. The emphasis upon violent revolution and social conflict, on materialist values, and on group loyalty runs counter to Buddhist concepts.' Frank N. Trager, *Marxism in Southeast Asia*, op. cit.

[2] Arthur J. Dommen, *Conflict in Laos*, Pall Mall Press, 1964.

[3] One of the oddest of many reasons adduced to support the French decision to garrison the fore-doomed basin in N.W. Vietnam was that Dien-Bien-Phu was the 'natural centre' of 'the Thai Empire'.

argued here is that, as in Burma, the consensus of articulate representatives of the major racial group has reached a clear understanding that Communism threatens the very existence of Thailand as an historical society. It is only out of concern for Thailand's national integrity that Thais welcome the alliance with the U.S.A.; they are quite as independent-minded by natural disposition as the Burmese. The decision in the mid-fifties to opt for a close relationship with the West was a very hard-headed one; an American withdrawal from South Vietnam in circumstances offering political opportunities to the National Liberation Front would very quickly result in an 'agonized reappraisal' in Bangkok. In the meantime Thailand is becoming one of the most prosperous states in the region and this can only be fundamentally altered by the application of Communist violence or a collapse of anti-Communist effort in Laos and South Vietnam.[1] Laos's opportunity to forge its disparate social elements into a non-Communist nation-state depends, in turn, altogether on the outcome of the struggle in South Vietnam.

The national future of Cambodia also depends upon the outcome of that struggle. Cambodia provides a peculiarly interesting example in support of the argument being offered here, that Communism has no appeal whatsoever to the countries of the region, and has only advanced through revolutionary violence and camouflaged aims. Its government wholly accepts the derided 'domino theory', yet refers to South Vietnam as a 'Yankee protectorate, even a Yankee Colony'. 'Between 1955–65, Providence left us free to choose between adhering to the "free world"—a choice which would have exposed us to the fate of South Vietnam and Laos—and to adopting a policy of neutrality, which has hitherto enabled us to live in peace, and to follow the path of progress . . . YOU (AMERICANS) WOULD HAVE PREFERRED—IF YOU HAD ANY SAY IN THE MATTER—THAT, BEFORE WE FELL WITH OUR FACES TO THE FOE, WE SHOULD HAVE EXPOSED OUR COUNTRY TO TEN YEARS OF MISERY, STRIFE, QUARRELS, HATRED, CRISES OF EVERY SORT . . . you would like to have deprived us of ten years of happiness . . . What I am aiming at is to ensure that my beloved Kampuchea is granted the maximum of UNTROUBLED years, months and days, before the advent of Communism, and that my Country is able to preserve intact all achievements, together with all the advances, made during this lapse of time. . . . It is my wish that, when the inevitable

---

[1] Which explains Thailand's fundamental rejection of a de Gaulle-style neutralization of S.E. Asia. As the former Prime Minister, Sarit Thanarat put it in 1961, 'As for Laos, it cannot stand on its own feet.'

change in regime comes about, the transition is made with the MINIMUM of ruin and destruction.'¹

Cambodia is little concerned with minority problems but very much concerned with border ones: its arguments with Bangkok and Saigon in this regard are really about Cambodia's right to exist as a racial society, since for several centuries past Cambodians have faced what they believe in retrospect to have been the possibility of extinction at the hands of their expansionist Thai and Vietnamese neighbours. According to Cambodian sources, their race which now numbers about six millions, was reduced to little more than a million by the end of the nineteenth century.² How to persist into the future as a race is the great question for the modernizing patriots grouped around Prince Norodom, the hereditary, charismatic, and 'Cambodian socialist' leader.

As in Burma, the modernizing élite sees itself as developing a specifically Cambodian kind of society; as Norodom has put it, '... although we have rejected the Western type of parliamentary democracy, which is not only inoperable in our country, but even presents certain dangers, we have none the less remained faithful to the democratic spirit and have evolved ... an original formula for the institution of a semi-direct régime which invests the people with control over public affairs.'³ Clearly there are inherent ambiguities in a policy which on the one hand seeks to create a uniquely appropriate society for the Cambodian people while, on the other hand, helping on the inevitable (as Norodom believes) spread of Chinese Communist influence by opposing and indeed undermining U.S. intervention in South Vietnam. At times Norodom's foreign policy seems suicidal: 'I concede again that after the disappearance of the U.S.A. and the victory of the Communist camp, I myself and the People's Socialist Community that I have created would inevitably disappear from the scene.'⁴ Nevertheless what is perfectly clear is that there is no legitimate role for the Communists to play in Cambodia; and they exist only as a 'sleeper' group within the Hanoi-based Communist party of Indo-China.

[1] These quotations are extracted from issues of Prince Norodom Sihanhouk's personal publication 'Kambuja', a monthly journal published in Phnom Penh.

[2] At the Geneva Conference on Indo-China in 1954, Cambodia refused to sign until its special concern for Cambodians resident in South Vietnam was recognized. Against this hopefulness there should be placed the (private) Vietnamese joke that 'There is only one Cambodian—Prince Norodom.'

[3] *Kambuja* 15th February 1966, quoted in B. McFarlane and S. Cooper, The Asiatic Mode of Production, *Australian Quarterly*, September 1966.

[4] Letter to the *New York Times* 5–6th June 1965.

THE SOUTH-EAST ASIAN SCENE

In Malaya very great efforts have constantly to be made to hold the multi-racial society together. Very early on, the political leader Tungku Abdul Rahman recognized that 'The real danger facing the (all-races) Alliance coalition is not from the opposition. I do not fear their challenge and their manœuvres. The real danger comes from the Alliance itself.'[1] He was referring to the sharing out of offices of power between the Malayan Chinese Association and the United Malays' National Organization. The attempt to sublimate this problem in the creative activity involved in building a Malaysia that included Singapore and Malay states in Borneo, failed chiefly because the rate of modernization favoured by Singapore's socialist People's Action party was unacceptable in Malaya; but the fact of Singapore's leaving Malaysia in this fashion simply emphasized the plural society problems of Malaya itself. Again, as in Burma, Thailand, Laos and Cambodia, though in a more acute form, the régime is overwhelmingly concerned with holding together a political society within imperially demarcated frontiers. In both Malaya and Singapore the Communists are proscribed;[2] they exist solely as underground subversive organizations waiting for opportunities to be provided for them by events outside Malaya and Singapore.[3]

Only in Indonesia did the Communists gain acceptance, until the attempted coup of October 1965, as a constitutional party sharing a measure of power at the centre of affairs. There were a number of reasons for this, some of which cannot be discussed here. But it is relevant to notice that part of the Communist party of Indonesia's (PKI) success may be attributed to its flair for representing itself as a perfervidly nationalistic group, forcing the pace of chauvinism through a typically Communist ability to seize initiatives as opportunities arose[4] and *apparently* accepting the wide-ranging (and spuri-

[1] *Straits Budget* 20th May 1959.
[2] In Singapore the public security ordinance was broadened to include in subversion activity on behalf of any foreign power, Communist or Western. *The Observer* 7th June 1959.
[3] e.g. The Chief Minister of Singapore, Lee Kuan Yew, informed a group of Australian Labour Party M.P.s in 1966 that a Communist victory in South Vietnam would be catastrophic for Singapore. This was revealed in the Australian Federal Parliament in September 1966.
[4] e.g. 'With the trade unions under SOBSI (the PKI federation) and most the towns and villages in east and central Java under their control, the Communists were well set to anticipate events when the U.N. predictably threw West Irian back in Indonesia's lap . . . Overnight the Communist party seized the initiative. Under their skilful direction, what began as a snowball ended as an avalanche, with workers seizing, one by one, all the major Dutch installations and, later, even the minor ones, including chemist shops and bakeries . . . Since

ous) synthesis of nationalism, Communism and religion, which President Sukarno foisted on the intelligentsia and to some degree upon the educational system of the Indonesian society. This search for an 'ideology' which could attract the other natural and historical regions within Indonesia, Sumatra, the Celebes and the rest, was doomed to failure for a number of reasons, not the least being the belief in these regions that all Sukarno's 'ideological' formulations were only a sophisticated manner of disguising 'Javanese chauvinism', which, in some measure, it was.

Yet a remarkably able Western economist like Benjamin Higgins in a sense missed the point when he wrote in 1958: 'Much of the unrest in Indonesia reflects the wide and deep disappointment that Merdeka (political independence) failed to bring prosperity in its wake; and the struggle between Java and the outer islands reflects a feeling that the central government has not done what it could to build on the 'growing points and leading sectors' in the outer islands.'[1]

Economic neglect did indeed cause risings against the Centre, Djakarta; but it was eight years before the régime responsible for this neglect was brought down. Then it was brought down at the centre, not as a result of revolt in the peripheral regions, but for quite different reasons. The regionalists and the federalists were powerless against a régime dedicated to create a unified modern nation state, based upon the overwhelmingly majority population of privileged Java. The relations between Java and the rest of Indonesia were analagous with those between Burma proper and the Burmese minority states; and to some extent they are likely to remain so, since the Indonesian élite of modernizers will always be conscious of the dangers of diluting nationalism to the point of national disintegration if the regions are given what might seem to Western federalists their proper due. Nationalism in South-East Asia is not an assumption binding citizens together in the common pursuit of economic and

(the government) did not have the capacity to oppose (this policy), it had to make the best of a bad job. Things certainly went according to plan—but it was the Communists' plan, not the government's. 'Denis Warner, *The Straits Budget*, 13th December 1957.

[1] '*The Annals of the American Academy of Political and Social Science*, July 1958. There is a dilemma built into the modernizing minority ridden underdeveloped areas. Central control feeds majority appetites and exacerbates minority resentments. And '... in an under-developed country ... the spread effects are weak. This means that as a rule the free play of the market forces in a poor country will work more powerfully to create regional inequalities and to widen those which already exist.' Gunnar Myrdal, *Economic Theory and Underdeveloped Regions*, Gerald Duckworth, 1957.

social progress; it is something yet to be adequately forged, and this is a necessary *condition* of economic and social progress. The South-East Asian nationalist cannot of his political nature share the universalist optimism of Communism's Vo Nguyen Giap with his cry 'If we win here, we shall win everywhere.' If he is a Burmese, he is scarcely concerned about, or even aware of, what is happening in Bangkok; if he comes from Singapore he is ignorant of Burmese affairs, and so on. There is no awareness whatsoever of regionally shared problems and hopes but simply a concentration upon strictly national development. This makes for enormous difficulties so far as regional defence agreements are concerned.[1] But it also makes the appeal of Communism, a system altogether foreign and derivative, not to speak of its relationship with Peking foreign policy, seem quite as irrelevant as the liberal capitalist faith of the U.S.A.'s Middle West. It is not an accident that the two most obviously socialist and neutralist states of the region, Burma and Cambodia, like quasi-neutralist India, show the clearest signs of trying to build according to some indigenous political understandings and even perhaps vaguely according to an old and special kind of economy. This search for specific indigenous adaptations in order to establish[2] a feeling of national identity that makes sense in the modern age is not confined to those countries and provides the best hopes for the region. Only the half-political, half-military form of Communist violence known as revolutionary guerrilla warfare stands in the way of this course being pursued in the future. There is no competition between missionary faiths. There is warfare.

---

[1] 'This general weakness . . . invites intervention by super-powers and blocs to fill the "power vacuum", a penetration that is resented and feared by many states . . . Indeed, it is the low level of power in Southern Asia that gives China, an extra-area actor, virtual *carte blanche* access to the system, as well as *de facto* membership in it.' Michael Brecher, *The New States* of Asia, O.U.P., 1963.

[2] McFarlane and Cooper, *The Australian Quarterly* op cit. for a discussion of the *Asiatic Mode of Production*.

Chapter 3

THE BEGINNINGS OF INSURGENCY

As early as 1920 Lenin was arguing that 'in as much as you have in these (Asian) countries the exploitation of the people by mercantile capital, and semi-feudal relations in agriculture ... in such countries it is quite possible to establish Soviet power'[1] and by 1921 Stalin had spelt out the strategic significance of South-East Asia for world revolution.[2] Yet it was not until 1948 that a widespread Communist attempt was made to conquer the region through revolutionary guerrilla warfare. This series of insurgencies involving India, Malaya, and Indonesia—insurgencies were already under way in Vietnam and the Philippines—was engendered by Moscow, not Peking, but within a very short time indeed after the Communist conquest of China the Peking Communists were laying claim to being able to offer a specially relevant understanding of this kind of struggle.

There are a number of reasons why Communist violence and subversion had been very unsuccessful indeed up to the Second World War. One which is central to the problem of revolutionary insurgency is this: eschewing the kinds of modernization likely to appear to threaten the traditional customs of the people, the imperial overlords concentrated upon perfecting the kind of administration that lent itself to remarkable achievements in hygiene, irrigation, rail and road communications and agricultural productivity *without* much altering the social relationships between the various indigenous classes, and without greatly encouraging the development of socially dislocating large-scale industry. The motives for this policy are not to the point here. The author is only concerned to establish the fact that both the policy of acute gradualism (if the Irishism be forgiven) and the sheer administrative skills of the imperial government made them far more adept at

[1] In that year the Council of Propaganda and Action of the Peoples of the East was founded in Baku; a journal called *The Peoples of the East* was published in Russian, Turkish, Persian, and Arabic; and the 'University of the Toilers of the East' was established.

[2] 'If Europe and America may be called the front . . . the non-sovereign nations and colonies, with their raw materials, fuel, food, and vast stores of human material, should be regarded as the rear, the reserve of imperialism. In order to win a war one must not only triumph at the front but also revolutionize the enemy's rear, his reserves.'

detecting and effectively dealing with political subversion *in the early stage* than independent South-East Asian governments have shown themselves to be. It is very much easier for a colonial administration to detect *potential* subversion, since to quite an important extent the administration's existence depends upon first-class intelligence and because its antennae are constantly tuned to discern any extra-constitutional content in any nationalist political manifestation. The members of a nationalist government, on the other hand, have often discovered the subversive intentions of their supposedly nationalist colleagues only when the subversion is under way, as was the case in Burma and Indonesia, for example. Moreover, once independence comes, then members of the administration itself are intellectually and morally drawn towards political leaders who may prove subversive in a way that was not possible while a colonial administration was in power, even if a quite large degree of self-government had been granted and political parties vied with each other in a parliament. Most nationalist ruling groups realize this today and therefore take enormous pains to represent themselves as the one fit *régime*, to the point often of representing all opposition, however mild, as *ipso facto* potentially subversive of the nation's interests which the ruling group claims accurately and comprehensively to reflect in its own organization and programme.

Independence found truncated administrations, aware for the first time of political pressures and infiltrated by political appointees, facing a war-wrought breakdown of civic order throughout most of the countryside and asked to implement modernizing programmes of a grandiosity which no colonial régime would have attempted in the most piping times of peace. The Communists were much better equipped to swim in a sea of shambles and violence than administrators brought up in conditions of peace imposed by a power they knew was much more powerful than anything that could erupt from out of the countryside. It was this transitional period which should have afforded the Communists their great opportunity since as Mr. Walt Rostow puts it, 'The Communists are the scavengers of the modernization process. They believe that the techniques of political centralization under dictatorship control—and the projected image of Soviet and Chinese Communist economic progress—will persuade hesitant men, faced by great transitional problems. . . .'[1]

But it was not to be matter of persuasion in South-East Asia, it was

[1] Guerrilla warfare in under-developed areas in Marcus G. Raskin and Bernard F. Fall (Editors), *The Viet-Nam Reader*, Random House, 1965.

to be a matter of revolutionary war—once it became clear that 'legal' activity within nationalist coalitions was not winning power for the Communists. It cannot be reiterated too often that Communists in South-East Asia do not wage guerrilla warfare as a *first and only choice* of methods; they wage it when it is necessary and appropriate according to their understanding of a given situation. This understanding has has always been part of a general line laid down in Moscow (and more recently Peking), the source of doctrine, except where events— as in Vietnam—force the issue. And even *during* an insurgency efforts are continually being made to gain legal status' for the Party and widen the purely political aspects of the struggle.[1]

Until quite recently the Communist parties of South and South-East Asia acted perfectly orthodoxly in line with general Moscow policy. Wherever possible they followed, immediately after World War II, the tactic of entering, or trying to enter, coalition governments; operating in terms of liberal democratic slogans and within a 'legal' framework. As in Eastern Europe, Communists showed considerable skill in representing themselves as democratically minded and pleased to accommodate themselves to the programmes of widely-based nationalist governments. But there was one great difference between the situation of the East European and South-East Asian Communist parties. After paying tribute to the inherent tactical skills of the East European Communist parties, Professor Hugh Seton-Watson wrote, 'Yet it was not this skill, but the might of the Soviet Union, which gave power to the Communists. Soviet force was used most crudely in the case of Poland . . . they set up their puppets as the government of 'liberated' Poland . . . In Roumania direct Soviet intervention in February 1945 caused the appointment of a Communist-controlled government . . . Similar intervention in Bulgaria in the spring and summer of 1945 produced similar results. In Hungary the crisis came in the spring of 1947, when the Soviet police broke the resistance of the Smallholders' Party by directly arrresting its outstanding leader, Bela Kovacs. . . .'[2]

---

[1] e.g. the Malayan Communist party directive published in part in *The Straits Budget*, 8th November 1957: 'To counter this organization (the constitutional Alliance coalition) we should not attack them face to face but from the flank . . . Any political party or group of individuals so long as they accept our party's main patriotic slogan (end the counter-insurgency and abolish the Emergency Regulations) should become an object for union and should be won over by us . . . the work of winning support from school children and organizing them to struggle is more important than military struggle.' The Emergency Regulations outlawed the MCP.

[2] *Neither Peace, Nor War.* op. cit.

THE BEGINNINGS OF INSURGENCY

No such assistance was available in South-East Asia where, apart from Vietnam, none of the Communist parties was in a position to make a bid for power. Yet in 1948 a number of them did make a bid by way of revolutionary insurgency. Why? The answer lies in the commencement of the 'Cold War' in Europe. In September 1947 the Cominform was founded; on 5th October there appeared a Moscow statement, described by the *New York Times* as a 'clear declaration of political war', attacking the Marshall Plan as 'only the European part of a general plan of world expansion being carried out by the U.S.A.'; and on 22nd October the Cominform chief, Zhdanov, spoke of 'American imperialism' replacing the old imperialisms and of 'the crisis of the colonial system'—Stalin's 'capitalist rear'—which was causing 'a powerful movement for national liberation in the colonies and dependencies.' He specifically mentioned Indonesia and Indo-China as countries which 'were joining the anti-imperialist camp' and argued that 'the chief danger to the working class at the present juncture lies in underrating its own strength and overrating the strength of the enemy'.

As the author of the standard work on Communism in South-East Asia remarks, 'This, then, was the first move in the new Russian offensive, soon to be known as the cold war. It was a matter of expanding Russian power through the manipulating of Western Europe's economic and political difficulties. The next step was to intensify these difficulties by action in South and South-East Asia. Preparations for this were completed by the beginning of 1948.'[1]

Preparations having been made in Prague, a conference of various front organizations was called in Calcutta in February 1948. There were over 900 delegates, besides a number of observers. There were representatives from Vietnam (where the struggle against the French had commenced), Indonesia (where the Dutch were still holding on), Burma, Pakistan, China (where the Kuomintang was still fighting), Nepal, the Philippines (where there was an interval in guerrilla fighting), Malaya, and of course the host country, India. There were 'observers' from the Soviet Central Asian Republics, Australia, (Mr. Lance Sharkey, then Secretary-General of the Australian Communist party), Korea, Mongolia, Yugoslavia, France, Canada, and Czechoslovakia. It was in theory a conference of Democratic Youth.

At Calcutta, a thesis was presented and accepted, which laid down that the 'correct' form of struggle at that juncture was 'armed struggle'; revolutionary guerrilla warfare. Thus what is today des-

[1] J. H. Brimmell, *Communism in South-East Asia*, O.U.P.

cribed by many in the West as 'an indigenous and spontaneous response to existing political and economic conditions' arose in independent Burma, and in colonial Malaya within a short time of the Calcutta Conference. Since it was necessary to launch these campaigns under cover of political disguise, the meaning of the Calcutta Conference has remained shrouded in mystery so far as details are concerned.[1] But most observers would agree with Mr. Denis Warner when he writes, 'Specific proof that instructions were also given at this time to Asian Communist parties to initiate and lead violent risings throughout the area is lacking but there is no dearth of convincing circumstantial evidence.'[2]

It is important to notice the very great importance attributed to the coming struggle by the Communists. For example, the veteran Mr. Rajani Palme Dutt of the Communist party of Great Britain wrote: 'The whole region of South-East Asia is today the *central arena* of the struggle for national liberation against imperialism. The approaching victory of democratic China heralds a new era in Asia. ... The example of the courageous and vigorous fight of Vietnam and the Indonesian Republic is an inspiration to the youth of Asia. The war plans of Anglo-American imperialism, which seek to make South-East Asia a main strategic centre, arsenal and base of exploitation, can and must be defeated.'[3]

The Chinese delegation at Calcutta also drew attention to the strategic significance of 'liberation warfare' for Communist revolution in Asia: 'The Chinese people are on the eve of victory, but they are struggling for an earlier realization of it and the guarantee of its outcome. This requires the assistance of and association with the *liberation campaigns*[4] of the peoples of South-East Asia. On the other hand, the victory of the Chinese people would facilitate the struggle of South-East Asia and would greatly encourage the fight. The liberation

---

[1] e.g. 'Writers holding the theory that it was (there) that the decision was taken to launch Communist uprisings throughout South-East Asia, admit there is no hard evidence of Soviet instigation . . . In regard to Malaya those writers disagree whether it was the Communists of the U.S.S.R., China, or Australia who were most influential . . .' V. Thompson and R. Adloff, *The Left Wing in Southeast Asia*, William Sloane for I.P.R., 1950. Joseph Frankel in Max Beloff, *Soviet Foreign Policy in the Far East*, O.U.P. 1953 quotes Soviet delegate A. Kharlamov as writing: 'The Conference unanimously adopted a resolution supporting national liberation struggle against imperialism,' which is simply the Communist name for revolutionary warfare'.
[2] Denis Warner, *Out of the Gun*, Hutchinson, 1956.
[3] Madhu Limaye, *The Indian Communist Party: Fact and Fiction*, 1950.
[4] Author's italics.

campaign of the Chinese people cannot be separated from the liberation campaign of the peoples of South-East Asia.'

In other words, a decade and a half before the U.S.A. became engaged in South-East Asia on a large scale, the international Communist world regarded the area as one of very great importance. Its appreciation was couched in terms relating to world-wide political and strategic issues, and had nothing to do with 'spontaneous and indigenous responses to existing conditions'—which quite clearly differed greatly from country to country. Moreover, even before the Communist victory had been attained in China, there was being laid down what Mr. Brimmel called 'the concept of a Chinese sphere of influence, embracing the whole of South-East Asia. . . .'

Given this expectation of a major clash with the new imperialism, it has throughout been of the utmost importance for the Communists to try to disguise the nature of revolutionary warfare precisely in order to avoid direct confrontation with the immense power of the U.S.A. As a result, the Australian Communist leader Mr. Lance Sharkey argued that it was *impossible* for Malayan problems to have been discussed at Calcutta because there was no representative of the Malayan Communist party present; that the armed uprising of a section of the Chinese population in Malaya was 'of a pattern . . . with that of Burma against British imperialism . . . as well as the great struggle of the Indian masses for liberation'; and that 'wars of national independence cannot be conjured up by "instructions" from anyone but arise out of existing conditions'.[1] That the British had granted Burma political independence and that conditions varied widely had to be ignored in order to sustain the necessary fiction that the coinciding bids for power in 1948 were simply 'spontaneous' expressions of discontent. This disguising of policy was later even more carefully carried out in Vietnam where a direct confrontation with the U.S.A. was a very present danger from 1961 onwards. At this time it involved the rather extraordinary device of establishing that some independent countries were more independent than others: India and Burma, both led by socialist premiers, were dubbed 'quasi-

---

[1] Walter Blaschke, *Freedom for Malaya*, Pamphlet, no date. Foreword by L. L. Sharkey. Mr. Denis Warner *op. cit.* writes that Mr. Sharkey and Mr. Lee Soong of the Malayan Communist party both reported back to the Malayan Communist party. A defector from the Australian Communist party, Mr. Cecil Sharpley, writes that Mr. Sharkey informed the National Congress of the Australian C.P. that he was commissioned by Cominform representatives at Calcutta to convey the decisions to the M.C.P. *The Great Delusion*, p. iii, Heinemann 1952.

colonies'; their true 'independence' only came when the Communist line changed from 'illegal' to 'legal' struggle—after the armed uprisings had clearly failed of their purpose. In Burma, the new form of struggle was carried out through the parliamentary National United Front, even while the insurgency continued.

It is necessary now to look at these post-Calcutta 'responses to economic and political conditions' more closely. For a number of reasons, the situation in Burma in 1948 should be examined first. It had only just received its independence under a left wing Socialist-dominated coalition known as the Anti-Fascist People's Freedom League (AFPFL); and so there was no possibility of the Communist rising being a response to 'reactionary' mistakes or injustices committed by the Government against which the Communists rose. Indeed, as was normal Communist practice during the pre-Calcutta phase, the Burma Communist party had been a member of the AFPFL coalition until it was expelled.

Moreover, this AFPFL Government was from the very beginning committed to policies which it carried out and which altogether removed the possibility of the Communist rising being directed against a socially reactionary policy. Amongst the central policy measures of the AFPFL were complete neutrality in the cold war, an extensive land reform—a large scale redistribution of lands (many of them formerly belonging to the Indian Chettiar money-lending minority) in the interests of the small peasant tiller, and the nationalization (sometimes, temporarily, government control) of all significant foreign investments: the Burma Corporation, the Bombay-Burma agency house, the Irrawaddy Flotilla Company, and so on.

And yet the Burma Communist party rose in arms. Why? First of all, Thakin Than Tun, its Secretary-General had failed to use participation in the AFPFL coalition as a means of conquering it from within—one of the rare examples in Communist political annals of this kind of failure. Secondly (as in Malaya) the B.C.P. tried and failed to gain power through fomenting unrest amongst the labourers of the city proletariat. Thirdly, Thakin Than Tun banked on a British refusal to grant independence, believing that his party would then assume leadership of the 'resistance' movement, which on the surface would be a purely nationalist movement. (It was just such a nationalist movement that the Communist party of Indo-China controlled against the French with such success.) Thakin Than Tun seemed to be stymied.

But then his lieutenant, H. N. Goshal, an Indian Communist

educated in Burma, brought in from India 'a thesis inspired by the Communist party of India, known as "the Revolutionary Possibilities for 1948".[1] As non-Communist Burmese put it to the author in 1951, 'Thakin Than Tun moved to the beat of the big drum beaten in Calcutta.' It is perhaps most satisfactory at this point to quote outright the left wing Burmese Government's White Paper, published in 1948 under the title of *Burma and the Insurrections*. It is an important document not easily obtainable today.

The gist of the B.C.P. directive states the Communist case as follows: 'independence (of Burma) is a sham and under cover of this sham British Imperialists would work a stranglehold on the defence and the economic life of the country. The AFPFL by accepting and acquiescing in this sham is lending itself as a tool of the British Imperialists, in fact AFPFL is itself promoting British Imperialist hold on the economic life of the country. . . . It should be clear that our (B.C.P.) position *vis-à-vis* the present Provisional Government (AFPFL) is, no support to it, exposure and fight against its anti-people policies. That Government cannot be a "strategic weapon" in the hands of the people. On the other hand, it is acting as a weapon in the hands of Imperialism against the people . . . To sum up, our central slogans become the following: No support to the present Government . . . National Rising . . . Set up a People's Government.' In March 1948 the armed uprising of the B.C.P. began.

The nature of the campaign of revolutionary guerrilla warfare was described as follows in the Government White Paper: 'When the insurrection started, the White Flag Communists' (that is, the B.C.P.) Organization had hardly 25,000 active followers and sympathizers throughout the country. Unlike the rival group of Red Flags ("Trotskyites" who had rebelled earlier), they draw their recruits from all classes of labourers and cultivators and command a considerable following amongst the middle class landowners, cultivators and workers, in short the petty bourgeoisie. Without being extremely harsh in their methods like the Red Flags, they have the knack of expanding their sphere of influence by absorption, peaceful penetration and intimidation. They keep themselves on the best of terms with other disruptive forces and exploit them to their advantage against the Government. Like the Reds (Red Flags), pamphleteering is the major weapon they use against the Government and they keep up a continuous flow of propaganda leaflets and pamphlets from their underground headquarters. Their policy is to seize power by force of arms; and when

[1] *Burma and the Insurrections*, Rangoon, 1948, Government White Paper.

power is seized to denounce the Anglo-Burmese Treaty (that is, a treaty allowing a small, insignificant British Military Mission to remain, and granting certain rights to the British—the B.C.P. had to be able to protest against *something*); to expropriate all foreign concerns (that is, without compensation; the left wing AFPFL did pay compensation, though it was naturally regarded as inequitable, on occasion, in London); distribute agricultural lands to cultivators (part of the AFPFL programme) and to set up a People's Democratic Republic (that is, Communist dictatorship). Seizure of power is, however, the prime objective. *They analyse the situation in Burma in exactly the same pattern as the conditions in Russia or the Chinese Communists.*[1]

'They sometimes mouth the dictum that the peculiarities of a country must be given special importance in analysing a situation and formulating a programme; but they lack the intellectual capacity either to distinguish the peculiarities or to suit a patterned programme to the peculiarities.' In fact, it was not a lack of 'intellectual capacity', but an obedience to the source of doctrine (then the Soviet Union alone), that dictated B.C.P. policy at this time.

The White Paper continues: 'In Prome area where the Communists had taken control for some time, Communist partisans armed with rifles, Sten guns, etc. called for meetings of villagers, killed the previous Land Committee members if found, ordered the villagers to elect new Land Committees and brandishing their guns challenged if this was not true Democracy.'

The decision to wage guerrilla warfare was made in March 1948; it emanated from the then sole source of doctrine and obedience, Moscow; it bore no relationship whatsoever to 'economic and political conditions' in Burma, yet it had to be carried out. And so under the pretence that the Government had not carried out its programme (a few *months* only after the Government had attained complete freedom of action through the granting of independence to Burma) the Burma Communist party's operatives began to do what the operatives of the Indo-Chinese Communist party began to do in South Vietnam some twelve years later: through force of arms in the peasant countryside dismiss the representatives of the Government (and kill them where dismissal was not sufficiently effective) and put in their place the Communist party's own nominees. This was warfare, as politics *always* are for Communists, and the objective striven for was carefully to create an administrative vacuum and place in it an *alternative*

[1] Author's italics.

THE BEGINNINGS OF INSURGENCY

government apparatus controlled by the Communists—what, in the case of Vietnam, Bernard Fall called 'parallel hierarchies'. It was unsuccessful in Burma in the long run, but a very long run it proved to be.

But the pattern is everywhere the same; and only ignorance of the recent history of Communion in South-East Asia allows its apologists in the West, nearly two decades after the B.C.P.'s operations in the Prome area, to persuade citizens that the whole cause of the trouble in South Vietnam is that it had a 'reactionary' government in power. The mind boggles at the ease with which this confidence trick has been perpetrated. And yet it should not boggle: it is now *sixty-two years* since Lenin laid down the principle that has guided the activities of Communist parties ever since: '*The only serious principle for the active workers of our movement should be the strictest secrecy, the strictest selection of members and training of professional revolutionaries.* Given these qualities, something even more than 'democracy' would be guaranteed to us, namely, complete, comradely, mutual confidence among revolutionaries.'

Here is the pattern of events to be found in all revolutionary guerrilla warfare campaigns: ('They the Communists) instituted People's Courts; they called meetings of all villagers, hauled up the accused and asked the meeting to answer "yes" or "no" to the question whether the accused should be killed. The villagers were naturally horrified and shrank away from them. In the Delta (that is, Prome and thereabouts) they prohibited the export of paddy (rice) to Government controlled areas; in other words they blockaded Government areas from their (the peasants') puny pockets. The price of paddy slumped in their areas; the cultivators whose only cash was paddy, starved. Then the Communists granted monopoly of purchase and export to a rice mill owner or a well-known rice merchant. The monopolist bought at starvation prices and sold the paddy in Government controlled areas at Government rates, splitting the margin with the Communists under guise of contribution for purchase of arms.

'In some areas agricultural land was distributed. One or two acres were distributed per head. But the economic unit is an acreage that can be worked by one yoke of cattle. A cultivator family therefore either had an area less than one yoke acreage in which case there was surplus land left uncultivated or sold. The result was such confusion and disorganization that even the landless cultivators began to question the desirability of land distribution.'[1]

[1] *Burma and the Insurrections* op cit.

But of course confusion and disorganization is exactly what the Communists wanted, and they still want it today. Through confusion and disorganization of traditional societies comes the Communists' long sought-after power to manipulate men's minds: manipulation through violence, actual or potential, physical or moral, as was pointed out earlier but always, in the last analysis, resting upon the power of the gun. It was Mao Tse-tung who said: 'Power grows out of the barrel of a gun.' Around Prome it was a British Sten gun; around Pleikku in the Central Highlands of South Vietnam it may be a U.S. or French (or today more likely, Chinese) sub-machine gun. But a gun. Recently much has been made of the fact that European weapons have often been used by the Vietnamese Communists in South Vietnam, as though this proved something about the government; as to that the B.C.P. in 1948, fighting a universally acknowledged left-wing government of whole-hearted neutralism, used British weapons. What did *that* prove except that guerrillas, by concentrating overwhelming force against police posts or by infiltrating government units, can fairly easily obtain some but—as will be argued—never sufficient, arms to launch a truly decisive counter-offensive against the government, whether the government be the left-wing government of Burma or the 'reactionary' government of South Vietnam. And yet the capture of Western arms in South Vietnam has been adduced by the Vietcong's apologists in the West as *proof* that South Vietnam's Government was a 'corrupt' dictatorship opposed only by a 'spontaneous rising' of unorganized peasants smarting under awful disabilities. According to this theory, the peasants of the Prome area in Burma were smarting under similar disabilities months after the Burmese government came to power, and a left-wing government at that.

It is desirable to explore a little more thoroughly yet what the Communist 'response to economic and political conditions' meant to the ordinary people of Burma, because precisely the same conditions have obtained since the North Vietnamese Communist government began slowly (and the reason for the slow beginning will be explained later) to subjugate South Vietnam through what the Burmese left-wing government described in its own, precisely similar case as 'a reign of terror'. U Nu, the gentle Socialist Premier, described it as 'the cult of the gun', a cult which in Burma was adopted by non-Communist groups as well for reasons that will be discussed.

The following is an account of one incident revealed when the Burmese Army recaptured a Communist stronghold area in North

THE BEGINNINGS OF INSURGENCY

Burma after three years of B.C.P. rule which was characterized in this fashion: 'Taxes levied constituted twenty per cent of the entire agricultural produce of a given village. A system of voluntary 'donations' too, was imposed towards the success of the cause of the insurgents. These 'donations' took the form of money, the loan of bullock carts, conscripted human labour and the provision of food.

'The people became impoverished, and no household could manage to store more than twenty pounds of rice against an unnamed day when more provisions might be needed. Disease spread slowly. Lands remained uncultivated for lack of money. People lived under such a spell of fear of the Communist 'masters' that they feared to raise their voices above a whisper.'[1]

Here is the essence of revolutionary guerrilla warfare: control through fear. It was exactly the same in North Vietnam during the Communist-controlled nationalist struggle against the French. A distinguished French journalist described the situation in the Red River Delta of Tonkin (North Vietnam) in 1953: 'The villagers are interrogated (by the French forces) in the normal way: "Who fired on us?" The village chief bows trembling, saying nothing—there are at least two or three members of the Vietminh (the Communist movement) cell amongst the apparently terrified group standing behind him. If the chief talks he will be killed that evening when the French move on to occupy the next village. If he keeps silent, will (the French) shoot him? No, but he will be harassed, bullied, and undoubtedly humiliated and, more often than not, is turned into an implacable enemy'.[2]

This exasperation on the part of forces concerned to put down guerrilla insurgency is by no means new. In 1886, Sir Charles Crosthwaite, a British official engaged in the pacification of Upper Burma wrote: 'As it was impossible to afford adequate protection, villages which aided the enemy were treated with consideration. Flying columns were discouraged. If the people were friendly they were certain to suffer when the column retired. If they were hostile ... they looked upon the retirement as a retreat.'[3]

Dr. Bernard Fall examined the same problem in his *The Two Vietnams* as it affected the revolutionary guerrilla campaign in South Vietnam. How does the Vietcong penetrate areas? Above all through its 'enforcement apparatus' and in particular through the activities

---

[1] *Burma and the Insurrections* op. cit.
[2] Jean Lacouture, *Politique Etrangère*, May–July 1953.
[3] Sir Charles Crosthwaite, *The Pacification of Burma*, Edward Arnold 1912.

of the Dich-Van (the 'Moral Intervention' squads, as they are called). Their job is to prepare the population psychologically in country areas subjugated. 'Ranging from friendly persuasion to murder with deterrent effects', the DV's make themselves felt on what Fall calls a 'specifically Vietnamese level of fighting upon which the foreigner has simply no effect.' 'The violent act (is committed) for psychological rather than military reasons.' Political violence, the indelible mark of the Communist everywhere, is how the Communists rule in South-East Asia, while intensifying their revolutionary guerrilla struggle as time passes and circumstances allow.

This general problem of how to afford protection to the population is certainly not the preserve of colonial or 'right-wing' governments: 'When the Government was able to drive the insurgents out of villages, more often than not, it could not spare the men to garrison the places, with the result that the insurgents came back to wreak reprisals on those suspected or co-operating with the Army.' That refers to the army of the Burmese left-wing government in 1954; an army commanded by General Ne Win, a left-wing soldier, now head of the Burmese nation which pursues a policy of extreme nationalization and neutralism; an army which itself has been an instrument of socialization. The Communist guerrilla is not, in the last analysis, concerned with *popularity* as democratically understood, but with increasing his *control* over a population through 'the violent act for psychological reasons'. He is concerned to induce the defeat of his enemy. And 'defeat', as Miss Coral Bell has nicely expressed it, 'is the name of a process in which the political resolution of a government is broken by military means.'

It is perfectly true that persuasive propaganda is married to violence in Communist revolutionary warfare. That is necessarily so, since the control sought is totalitarian control. To that end a special form of 'correct behaviour' is strictly imposed on Communist guerrillas. It is totalitarian collectivist behaviour: even violence is employed only in collectivized fashion: there is no place for individualistic terrorism (as Lenin discovered more than half a century ago). Otherwise 'pinpoint coercion' is lost. There is no depth unplumbed by Communists in humiliating human beings; no limit to the extent of their atrocities. But every humiliation and every atrocity must always be related to definite political aims.

A juxtaposing of two Communist practices, drawn from very different parts of South-East Asia, may perhaps vividly illuminate the two facets of collectivized behaviour that make Communist revolutionary guerrilla warfare so very formidable. In South Vietnam on 15th January 1962 a young woman named Giau, a propagandist for the Republican Youth Movement (a government organization operating on the village level) was selected for exemplary punishment by the Vietcong. Her 'crime' was to have been trained in the city in modern politics and modern ideas. She returned to her village to proclaim a new dignity for women and to point out—what was literally the truth—that Communist conquest meant that the peasants lost all their landholdings, whether as tenants or owners, and became Communist state serfs on State farms. This was what had actually happened in Communist North Vietnam; and so the revelation of its happening was fundamentally subversive of local Communist propaganda.

The result was that Giau was abducted from her village early in the evening by a group of uniformed Vietcong. People on the outskirts of the village later heard screaming. But no one dared to move. Next morning the villagers found her body. It was mutilated and decapitated. Fastened to her body was a piece of paper which read: 'considering that Giau was a cruel and stubborn person. She was a member of the Republican Youth League, working for the American-Diem regime, helping soldiers to terrorize the people. Giau attended a course for the formation of girl members of the Republican Youth League, specializing in espionage. She took advantage of the magnanimity of the Front of Liberation (that is, the Northern controlled Communist movement in South Vietnam). She came back to live with her parents, she still stubbornly followed the path of sins.

—Many a time she wrote reports to the Security forces regarding the situation of the village.

—she spread anti-propaganda (that is, against the Front).

—she threatened the people.

We appeal to all those who have been wrong and sinful to hurry back to the right path of the people for the people always pardon and welcome those who repent,

People's Front of Liberation
Binh Duong Province.'[1]

That is what is known as 'pinpoint coercion': the brave, the politically effective in each village are killed and mutilated and left for all the village to see and to ponder on. Between 1957, when the campaign to subjugate South Vietnam through revolutionary guerrilla warfare was decided upon, and 1960 the number of assassinations of the kind that

[1] V. L. Borin, *This May Happen to You*, Pamphlet, Sydney, 1963

THE BEGINNINGS OF INSURGENCY

resulted in Giau's death was of the order of 7,000: a pretty effective coverage of much of South Vietnam's villages in which 85 per cent of the population lives.

This incident should be compared with the other facet of Communist revolutionary guerrilla behaviour: exemplary collectivized behaviour in the villages. This example is deliberately chosen from the Philippines in order to show the precise similarity between revolutionary guerrilla warfare throughout the region. Indeed the directive about to be quoted is really only a replica of the directives issued to troops of the Communist Red Army in China. But this one was written by Luiz Taruc, Chairman of the Military Committee of the Hukbalahaps, the Communist-controlled resistance Front in the Philippines.

The directive reads: 'Clean the houses provided by the people . . . Speak in a friendly tone . . . Buy and sell things fairly . . . Return the things we borrow . . . Pay for the things we destroy . . . Do not do, even refuse to do, things which may harm the people . . . Help the people in ploughing, transplanting, harvesting, or in cutting wood whenever it does not hinder the actions of the Army.'[1]

This is the other side of the coin; and its importance must not be underrated. The Communist revolutionary guerrilla in South-East Asia is a puritan fanatic in whose life there is permitted no place for 'private enterprise' corruption—no individualistic killing, no individualistic raping, no individualistic economic exploitation: no place for human love for that matter. He is the servant of a political organization which sees every *human* activity as part of political warfare; and in that warfare propaganda through exemplary collectivized, politically-orientated behaviour is of great significance. He is subtly dehumanized by the apparatus to which he belongs until he reaches the desired point, which was expressed in Red China in this chilling fashion: 'He who does not understand the party line has lost his soul.'

Colonel Jules Roy, in his wonderfully evocative book, *The Battle of Dien Bien Phu*, that battle in 1954 in which part of the flower of the French Expeditionary Corps was defeated by the Communist People's Army in North-West Vietnam, paints a picture of the army of porters bringing the Communist guns and ammunition and supplies to the battlefield: 'If they met or passed a column of women porters, there would be an explosion of gaiety. The two parties would call out to each other, improvise verses and make jokes . . . When two such

[1] *Born of the People*, International Publishers, New York, 1953

THE BEGINNINGS OF INSURGENCY

columns halted together, the river bathing, the bivouacs, and the nocturnal encounters were characterized by an astonishing innocence. It was like an outing of seminarists meeting a party of young nuns. Their church was a total devotion, body and soul, to the fatherland, the sole object of love. In the People's army, the soldiers' language, commonplace by nature, resembled that of children playing at war; the only sentiments expressed in it were a flawless discipline and a boyish fervour. If every group of porters wanted to reserve the role of honour, every soldier's ambition was to sacrifice himself. One begins by smiling, but ends up impressed by the results of this indoctrination.

'Inside each unit, the men were bound together in inseparable cells of three, in accordance with the formula imported from China, in order to facilitate training and make consciences easier to penetrate. What thoughts could remain concealed under these conditions? How could the last barriers of the soul resist this incessant watch? The grip of the political commissars turned every soldier into an instrument in the hands of the Commander-in-Chief and the Party.'[1]

It is necessary to turn back to the area around Monywa in Northern Burma, the liberation of which by the Burmese Army in 1951 was touched upon earlier, in order yet further to penetrate this mode of Communist revolutionary guerrilla behaviour. It is illuminated by the case of a girl called Ma Paw Sein who was desired by one of the Communist guerrillas occupying the area, a young man named Ko Yin Gyi. He wanted to marry the girl but she repulsed his advances and her mother tried all manner of subterfuges to dissuade Ko Yin Gyi from continuing with his proposals.

The story of Ma Paw Sein, as told by villagers afterwards to a member of the government liberating force, ended in this fashion:

'With blazing eyes, Ko Yin Gyi approached the young girl. Paw Sein sprang up to flee behind the oven. But in two quick strides Ko Yin Gyi was on her and enveloping the girl in his arms, began kissing her furiously. "Stop it! Stop it!" Paw Sein called out helplessly. With a loud sob, the mother Daw Paw Lai, sank down into unconsciousness.

'Hearing the screams of the girl and the heart-rending cry of the old woman, anxious neighbours rushed into the house. They found the old woman unconscious. They looked around for Paw Sein. She lay seething in the cauldron. Her body was almost entirely covered by the boiling jaggery juice. In their horror and confusion, some people began dousing the fire, some began ladling off the juices. Finally they

[1] *The Battle of Dienbienphu*, Faber and Faber, 1965.

removed the cauldron from the fire to take out the body of Paw Sein. Mercifully, she died the next day on March 27, 1951.'

Now this was quite obviously a crime of passion, a 'private enterprise' act, and as such not in accordance with Communist revolutionary behaviour. When the villagers approached the Communist commander, he replied to their anger along the following lines: 'Listen to me villagers. I have testimony here that shows that this Ko Yin Gyi was severely wounded in a battle against Government troops. A bullet entered his head, and Ko Yin Gyi had to be operated upon to remove the bullet. But I think the damage was already done. His brain was affected, and that is why such a mentally unbalanced man could commit such a deed that you described. Listen, I am sure that if he were not mentally unhinged, he would not have committed such an act. So, now, if you still intend to take action against mad person, who, after all cannot really be responsible for his actions, then you will only be in the wrong. And, moreover, we cannot just stand by and allow you to take any unfair action against a helpless madman.... This matter of Ma Paw Sein must remain closed. No one must ever mention even the name of Paw Sein again.'

And no one did until the government troops arrived, since the Commander made it perfectly clear that 'power grows out of the barrel of a gun'; and only the Communist revolutionary guerrillas were armed. But this story is interesting for the light it throws on Communist revolutionary guerrilla behaviour: there could be no justification in Communist terms for Ko Yin Gyi's crime, so it had to be represented as the work of a madman.

This chapter has sought to do two things: to show, first, that it is wholly false to argue that Communist revolutionary warfare is a 'spontaneous' peasant rising against 'economic and social conditions'; and secondly to begin to show something of the principles that operate throughout South-East Asia in the carrying out of this kind of politico-military *warfare*.

This Burmese Communist insurrection is not yet over in 1965. That it has not been more successful may be attributed to a number of factors, some of which are specifically Burmese, some of general application to revolutionary guerrilla warfare. First of all, as has been mentioned, Burma has the most acute minority problems of any country in South-East Asia. There have been insurrectionary movements in the Karen State, in the Shan State, in the Kachin State, in the Arakan Division, and amongst the Mons of Lower Burma. Such guerrilla movements have throughout been coloured by regionalist sentiment of a kind deeply unfavourable to the Communists who chiefly represent the majority, Burman group.

Moreover, there were two other left-wing guerrilla movements, the Red Flag (Trotskyites) and the People's Volunteer Organization. Hence lack of unified command, though temporarily achieved on occasion, has prevented the Communists effectively forming a Front organization underground. Secondly the Communists, as is perennial practice everywhere, have more than once tried to achieve power through 'legal' political means; that is, through the infiltrated Burma Workers' and Peasants' party, operating through the official opposition party, the National United Front. This was an impossible task so long as the Socialist-controlled AFPFL government remained united, since the AFPFL (like the Indian National Congress) governed as though it were the only real national party, disposing of an enormous spoils system and making the very apparatus of government, from the high civil servant in Rangoon to the village head, effectively part of the AFPFL party political system. When the AFPFL broke up, the Burmese Army was standing by to fill the vacuum that developed and eventually took over the administration of the state itself.

The Burmese Communists have also suffered from a disability that is of very great importance to an understanding of revolutionary guerrilla warfare throughout South East Asia. It is comparatively easy to acquire sufficient arms to start guerrilla warfare on a limited scale. This can be done by using even the most primitive weapons at first, provided targets are carefully selected and quickly overwhelmed. Sometimes it is not even necessary to overrun isolated police stations in order to capture arms. They can be bought from the proceeds of robberies.

An interesting example of a guerrilla movement growing out of dacoity (armed robbery) can be seen in the Shan State in 1958. The Shan State (in fact a number of States, inhabited by a Thai people who once dominated much of Burma) was until this time ruled in conservative fashion by traditional princelings known as Sawbwas. The pensioning off of the Sawbwas by the central Government in Rangoon was not regarded, as had been expected, as a blow for progress; but rather as a blow against Shan aspirations. Insurgency began to become a problem.

Its development is not to the point here, only its beginnings. The *Rangoon Nation* of 8th October, 1958, reported them thus: 'From being one of the "Safe" zones of Burma, the approaches by road to Lashio (the administrative centre of the North Shan State) have become the most notoriously unsafe of all motorable areas, and the country is agape at the astonishing spectacle of Shan dacoits, sometimes with blunderbusses, defying the law enforcement machinery of the government.

'Yesterday, the Lashio-Tanyang mail van was shot at and a passenger narrowly escaped death when a bullet brazed [sic] his neck. The bus had no intention of running the gauntlet, but it was at speed when called upon by five Shan dacoits to stop and the failure to stop immediately drew the bandits' fire. As soon as the vehicle stopped, the dacoits ripped up the mail bag and scattered the letters. They robbed the passengers of K.5000 (about £380 sterling).

'Again, yesterday, a passenger bus was held up on the Lashio-Kutkai Road, 29 miles from Lashio. . . . The Lashio-Namkham and Lashio-Mongyai Roads being thus accounted, for, the dacoits showing a supreme indifference to the Police said to be scouring the main (North-South) Lashio-Mandalay road, for they pulled off yet another dacoity further down the road. . . . Again there were five dacoits, three of them armed with Japanese rifles, and the rest with locally made matchlock guns.'

On the 11th October, the *Nation* reported further dacoities and remarked: 'The frightening thing in this dacoity was that there were 17 Shan dacoits involved, all of them armed. Observers here are inclined to believe that as dacoity becomes more and more lucrative, and as dacoit bands increase in size, they will become not mere bandits but full-fledged insurgents.'

About sixteen months later the author received in far-away Sussex seven amateurishly typed pages entitled: *The Manifesto of the Revolutionary Council of the Shan State Independence Army*. This document revealed that five months before the above dacoities occurred, a group of Shan leaders met to form this guerrilla movement. The document continued: 'When the Shan State Independence Army intensified its military activities by attacking Burmese Army bases and rendered them ineffective, Burmese propagandists contrived to create the impression that the movement was led by "smugglers and bandits". . . .'[1]

And so from such small beginnings, a guerrilla movement of sorts may grow up—to a certain point. This movement is still in existence and it has done much harassing. This is not difficult, even with very

---

[1] In September 1966 the author received a photograph of Shan insurgents armed with light machine guns and mortars, sent by one of their political leaders.

limited firepower. Provided the initiative is kept and no attempt is ever made to attack except in overwhelming strength, then a very few men can terrorize a whole district. For example, in August 1958 in the Pakkoku district of Northern Burma forty Red Flag (Trotskyites) insurgents were being fairly successful in preventing the extraction of timber by the locals, through threats of violence made during a march through the district. In October of that year the recently retired Burmese Commander of the North Burma Area, Brigadier Kyaw Zaw, made a public analysis of the guerrilla struggle since 1948. He argued that the situation in 1958 was something of a stalemate.

He went on: 'The lesson of China . . . had altered the tactical role of guerrilla warfare. By hanging on and prolonging (the *protracted conflict* concept again) the struggle it was possible to increase one's experience of jungle warfare, to spread out over a large area, and to avoid detection by moving in small groups of ten or fifteen. Without a superior political ideology it was not possible to put an end to such tactics. The army, even if increased in size, could not garrison all areas (the old, old complaint of counter-guerrillas). But if the government were not able to crush the rebels, neither were the rebels able to make any headway.'

'Neither were the rebels able to make any headway. . . .' This fact is a crucial one. Given the Burmese physical terrain, which affords excellent cover and base areas difficult of access, and given its communications systems, which were always pretty indifferent and deteriorated greatly after independence, then guerrillas—whether they be Communists of the White or Red Flag kind, Karens, Kachins, or Shans—could keep themselves in being and make the problems of rural administration exceedingly trying over large areas. *But* they could never get any further with their campaigns for one vital reason: they could not obtain arms and supplies from outside; nor did they have an external 'privileged sanctuary' for training.

The Kachins and Shans, since their states exist alongside Communist China, could easily be supplied with the arms necessary to make them formidable; the modern weapons necessary for their guerrillas to move from harassment and control of localities to actual counter-offensive against the Burmese Army. But though it is more than a decade since Communist China set up 'Autonomous Regions' on its side of the border, containing Chinese-ruled Kachins and Thai (to attract dissidents from Thailand as well as from Burma's Shan-Tai State), neither of these two Burmese minority groups have shown the least interest in accepting aid from that quarter. And for two reasons:

first, their objective is regional autonomy; secondly, they know full well what has been happening across the border in China.

The Burmese Communists of the B.C.P. did attempt to establish a base in the North but this is a very difficult thing to do if, as is the case in Shan and Kachin states, the countryside is both sparsely populated and opposed to any kind of blandishment the Communists could offer: for example, there is abundant land for any tiller anxious to work harder and Burmans, whether Communists or not, are regarded as oppressive aliens. The B.C.P. leaders have for a long time been visiting China, and Chinese influence over the party gradually became paramount; but the task of transporting supplies into Central Burma remains a very difficult one, in fact virtually insuperable without Kachin and Shan acquiescence. As a result, the B.C.P. has for most of the time been wholly confined to Burma proper, and hence has never been able seriously to maul the Burmese Army. This contrasts with what happened in South Vietnam where not only were modern arms imported but, a significant point, cadres able to use them were infiltrated from the north. At present China is content with Burma's *neutralization*.

And so: stalemate, a fact recognized by the B.C.P. Consequently it turned its attentions to older Communist methods: the parliamentary Front organization referred to above; 'Peace Talks' with the government in the hope (not to be fulfilled) that the B.C.P. would be legitimized; the attempted infiltration of both the Trade Union movement and All Burma Peasants' Organization. As has been underlined already, revolutionary guerrilla warfare is but one particular form of Communist conquest through clandestine, conspiratorial violence.

At present, Burma is ruled by a revolutionary council, headed by General Ne Win, an anti-Communist leftist. This government has nationalized practically everything that could be nationalized.[1] A number of significant democratic politicians are imprisoned. The University, its Students' Union building blown up and its curriculum pruned of dangerous political subjects, has ceased to be yet another place of Communist infiltration. The regime becomes evermore state-controlled and inward-looking; and yet guerrilla war continues unabated in the Shan and Kachin States. The Communists have infiltrated some of their members into government posts of importance and the probable successor to General Ne Win, Brigadier Tin Pe, is described as an 'extreme leftist', which in the threatened region

[1] A Swedish match factory appears to be the only Western enterprise remaining.

of South-East Asia might well prove to mean a pro-Communist opportunist, should Communist designs be implemented elsewhere—above all, in South Vietnam.

The 'big drum' no longer throbs under the beat of Moscow hands; but what is to the point here is that even the most left-wing governments have been unable to destroy Communism in Burma; even the most extensive social reforms have not obliterated the activities of that organization. Revolutionary guerrilla warfare has failed of its purpose simply through lack of outside support, which is vital in extending it to the point of serious counter-offensive.

That the B.C.P. really *was* moved by the Calcutta Conference, and most certainly did not rise in arms 'in response to economic and political conditions' was specifically admitted by Yebaw Nyunt Aung, a member of the Central Committee, in August 1958. Extracts from his thesis, couched in that hideous jargon which is so important in world politics, were published in *The Nation*, Rangoon, on 25th August. For present purposes, what is important is his admission that 'the Party has been in error since 1948 in calling the AFPFL and the Socialist party (AFPFL's controlling body) reactionaries and collaborationists of capitalo-expansionists . . . the error in thinking that the armed struggle was the only solution arose in the first instance from the fact that at that time, within the world Communist movement, the fight against Browderism had veered towards left deviationism. The thinking was that so long as there was capitalo-expansionism there was the risk of war, that capitalism had to be ended by war and, as a sequence to this kind of reasoning, that independence could only be won by the armed method.' Which, being interpreted, means that the B.C.P. took to revolutionary guerrilla warfare in 1948, not in response to any kind of 'economic and political conditions' in Burma, but in response to the then requirements of Moscow policy. As was remarked earlier, it is not higher ideas that move Communists but loyalty to an outside source that determines doctrine. And so today, the Chinese source of doctrine for South-East Asian Communists, having decided that Moscow is utterly wrong in striving for coexistence, decrees that revolutionary guerrilla warfare is once again 'correct'. And so today, South-East Asia's Communists prepare to heed the pundits beyond their borders, as the B.C.P. did in 1948.[1]

[1] For example, the Burma Communist party, some of whose leaders live in Peking, were supporting the Ne Win government's neutralist foreign policy as late as 1964. But by 1967 the B.C.P. was advocating the overthrow of the Ne Win government by violence, arguing that 'The ideology and programme of so-called neutrality is, in practice, serving modern revisionism . . .'

Chapter 4

NATIONALISM AT BAY

If further proof were required that Communist risings occur for reasons quite other than mere 'response to political and economic conditions', events in Malaya and Indonesia in 1948 are readily available. In Malaya during the Second World War the overwhelmingly Chinese Communist party of Malaya (M.C.P.) armed and supplied by Great Britain, engaged in guerrilla warfare against the Japanese in co-operation with British special forces.[1] Since Malaya was not only a British colony, in which party politics in the Western sense was scarcely known until after the war, but was also a multiracial society in which Malays, Chinese and Indians lived separate existences often marked by intense mutual suspicion, there was no opportunity for the Communists to build up an effective all-nations Resistance Front movement.

In the years immediately following the war the M.C.P. took advantage of the considerable lawlessness prevailing in rural areas to build up funds through extortion and through what were at the time erroneously believed to be acts of mere 'banditry'. In Singapore they used 'pinpoint' coercion amongst the workers. An incident of industrial violence was reported most vividly at the time by James Taylor, an Australian Reuters' man and former guerrilla fighter with the Independent Companies of the A.I.F. in Timor. It deserves quoting in full.

'The body as we found it was the skinny remains of an engine-room labourer clad in greasy short pants. He lay sprawled under a giant flywheel with his head pulped into the oily sludge by an iron bar and the blooded footprints of the murder mob puddled over his wretched flesh. The flywheel whirled on to the chug of a distant deserted engine and the dull emptiness of the factory and the insensate churning of the wheel made his seem the loneliest corpse in the world. . . .

'Outside, a cordon of police armed with staves and wicker riot shields contained a Chinese mob which confronted them with a wall

[1] F. Spencer Chapman, *The Jungle is Neutral* op. cit. Corgi Books, 1965.

of angry and muttering faces. These were the factory workers, men and women. The men filled a courtyard paved with black asphalt, and the women, arranged in the fashion of a surrealist picture, mounted stairways and galleries running high up the outside of the factory buildings flanking the courtyard. . . .

'Above the mutterings of the mob came the odd shrill vituperative scream of a woman on a gallery, or the yell of a provocateur urging the workers to charge into the police cordon. . . .

'While they wavered, a smooth-faced Cantonese detective moved calmly among them, and one by one he arrested the group suspected of murder.

'Of the five men loaded into a police truck, one never could be forgotten. He was the political organizer who had sparked the fatal dispute. Whirling on the now subdued labourers, he crushed a shabby felt hat on his head and scorned the waverers with an expression of contempt I have not seen equalled in war or peace. Then he roused his cowered comrades from their squatting position on the floor of the truck and bawled out the opening bars of a tune, beating time in the air with a clenched fist.

'As the truck bounced away down the rutted road the arrested quintet hoarsely sang "The Internationale" in the Fukienese dialect. . . .'
By such methods the M.C.P., in the estimate of Alex. Josey in his *Trade Unionism in Malaya*, reached the position where 'nearly the whole of the labour movement in Malaya was under their control.'[1]

In June 1948, obeying the 'big drum' beaten in Calcutta, the M.C.P. threw away all its assets by embarking on a campaign of revolutionary guerrilla warfare in conditions that precluded any chance of success. The decision to rise in open violence was taken in Singapore in March 1948. It was hoped, according to a government report issued soon afterwards, to 'close the port, paralyse transport and all essential services, thereby to confine the army to Singapore and to create chaos in the town. . . .'

This plan utterly failed and the struggle became centred on the countryside. The Communist terrorists (C.T.'s as they came to be called) enjoyed certain advantages. Their guerrilla forces, though normally numbering less than 10,000 were war-experienced fighters with a tremendous amount of jungle cover to shelter them and for a time some 500,000 unprotected Chinese 'squatters' to batten on for supplies, food, and intelligence. Moreover, the C.T.'s were quite specifically engaged in an attack on 'the capitalist' rear—the tin

Trade Unionism in Malaya, Donald Moore, 1955.

mines and rubber plantations—which at first offered up very easy targets for terrorism and 'pinpoint coercion' of the work-force. Their captured directives showed that they aimed to set up base areas from which to launch a revolutionary guerrilla war proper but after an initial period of unpreparedness the British administration quickly moved to deny them any such opportunity.

From the beginning the C.T.'s suffered from enormous disabilities. Because they were chiefly Chinese, the struggle appeared to the Malays to be an attempt at a Chinese take-over of the old Malay homeland. Because rubber and tin prices were high enough to finance most of the counter-insurgency without resorting to additional taxation it was possible to maintain the standard of living in the countryside and the C.T.'s consequently had no basis of agricultural discontent to play on. Because Malaya's only frontier was with anti-Communist Thailand, the terrorists enjoyed no 'active sanctuary', which elsewhere (in Greece as well in Vietnam) was to prove of crucial importance. It took time to make effective border-sealing arrangements and even today the remaining hard-core of the M.C.P. enjoy a 'passive sanctuary'[1] in that border country; but there was never any question of the party establishing a sanctuary that would give them arms and supplies.

The counter-insurgency programme nevertheless took many years fully to implement. By 1956 over 9,000 C.T.'s had been killed, captured, or induced to surrender at a cost of over 4,000 security forces' casualties and nearly 4,000 civilians. More than 2,400 people, mostly Chinese, were murdered. This was chiefly a terrorist campaign and yet it was of course represented at the time by Communists and fellow-travellers as a 'War of National Liberation' arising out of economic conditions.

It would require a separate book to explore fully the means whereby the Communists were defeated, since the British brought to this struggle all the resources of their genius for government. But there are certain points arising out of it that are of general significance in understanding guerrilla warfare and counter-insurgency. First, the British took the decision to win the struggle *before* granting effective self-government, and so counter-insurgency did not take the form of a politically complicated response by a newly independent nation.

The British approached the situation as a problem in police and administrative techniques. Certainly the carrot of future self-government was dangled before the people, but in the meantime everything

[1] This has been reactivated during 1966 as part of a Thai 'liberation struggle'.

was to be subordinated to creating a situation in which the Communists could no longer effectively operate, the central control being placed in the hands of a soldier statesman of extraordinary talents; General Templer.

At the time this approach was fiercely attacked by a senior civil servant and profound scholar of things Chinese, the late Victor Purcell, 'If,' he wrote, '... the present policy is continued [1954], the situation in Malaya will in time not differ materially from that in Indo-China and will be just as hopeless. The official substitute for self-government under the Templer regime is charity and "uplift". On the one hand there is barbed wire, curfews, and abuse; on the other hand a large army of European welfare workers trying to infuse life and hope into the bare shacks of the "new villages". Imagine the aftermath of a moderate earthquake and you have a fair picture of much of rural Malaya today.'[1]

The 'bare shacks' were the areas in which the Chinese 'squatters' had been resettled, removing them from the reach of Communist coercion and their vegetable plots from Communist mouths. This was a move of the utmost importance. But General Templer's countercampaign was a many faceted affair. He himself was not the architect of it. But he infused it with a new life and by his powers of dynamic leadership and a terrifying capacity to blast all forms of complacency out of Malaya's air he brought about a highly practical co-ordination between all those responsible, at whatever level, for maintaining public order and extending its domain. Moreover, far from his appointment as High Commissioner implying the imposition of a military dictatorship, as was sometimes argued at the time, he made public from the very beginning his deep understanding of the fact that the war would not be won by military means alone.

General Templer was in fact a man of profound sensibility and of wide culture. He combined the courage to impose rigorous curfews on recalcitrant villages and publicly to humiliate 'fence sitters' or 'slackers' (whether they were Malayan or British) with a vigorous fashioning of a hitherto non-existent Malayan nation and the sincere encouragement of the various racial groups in bringing their particular cultures to life. He rivalled the great Filipino leader, Raymond Magsaysay, in his personal exertions throughout the troubled areas and in his belief that this was a struggle for 'the hearts and minds of men'. But unlike those liberal thinkers who are prone to reiterate this slogan as though the slogan were sufficient unto itself, he also understood

[1] *Malaya: Communist or Free?* Gollancz, 1955.

that he had to bend the *wills* of 'fence-sitters', if necessary through exceedingly grim administrative measures, so that they became wholly aware of which side was *going* to win. He was as selflessly demanding as were the commissars of the M.C.P. guerrillas; and just as tough without ever losing the respect for the rule of Law that has always marked the best kind of British official overseas.[1]

No praise could be too high for his personal endeavours, but his role must not be exaggerated. He had at his disposal what no South-East Asian political leader has had: a Special Branch, a Civil Service, and armed forces that were not only willing to co-operate with each other (and with the ordinary police force) but which would never for a moment think in terms of personal ambition pushed to the point of thwarting the general effort, let alone to the point of indulging in subversive activities. Just as the Indian Civil Service was the 'iron frame' (in Lloyd George's words) that kept India intact, so the Malayan Civil Service, including the police, and aided by the armed services 'acting in support of the civil power' kept intact the central power-structure of Malayan society and gradually extended it throughout all the important parts of the country. To enable them to achieve this they evolved a committee system and a unified command of great effectiveness.

In these circumstances, the campaign against the Communist terrorists was in general regarded as a *police action*; a total response of the administration in terms of increasing police power over the whole population. This included national registration, extraordinarily rigorous efforts to prevent food and supplies reaching the Communists, the death penalty for carrying arms, closing schools, imposing curfews, detention without trial—all the appurtenances of repression.

At the same time the campaign included most clever amnesty appeals, attention to problems of land tenure, measures making for a multi-racial state in which even the Federation army found itself identified, extra efforts from the dedicated rural development organization (RIDA), and very great devotion to duty on the part of officials at 'District Officer' level responsible for such matters as hygiene and civil engineering. The ambitions of would-be nationalist politicians were at the same time gradually associated with a policy the successful completion of which alone promised the birth of democratic politics in Malaya.

This is not at all to ignore the long, slogging task of the security

---

[1] Sir Robert Thompson's *Defeating Communist Insurgency* op. cit. is the indispensable work on the Malayan insurgency.

forces in killing Communists in the jungle and on its outskirts; nor the new technological devices introduced into the struggle—and new tactics. The use of penetration tactics ('Ferret Force' and special police groups), working on the basis sometimes of such good intelligence that they knew to listen for the cry of babies in the night in order to locate a given Communist camp, not only resulted in kills but in keeping the Communist guerrilla bands off-balance—depriving them of the initiative indispensable for successful guerrilla warfare and, above all, isolating them from the population. This too was *protracted* and its successes were built up from a number of seemingly very minor incidents. 'Notable successes', according to the Federation of Malaya Annual Report of 1956 (eight years after the revolutionary guerrilla warfare campaign had begun) included, for example, a patrol of the 1st Battalion the Fiji Infantry Regiment (one of a number of Commonwealth units, including Australian, who fought there) contacting six terrorists and killing five of them, including 'three ranking terrorists'; a patrol of the South Wales Borderers contacting an unknown number of terrorists and killing four; and a patrol of the 22nd Special Air Service being attacked by five terrorists and killing them all. There are no quick solutions to this kind of war.

In the last analysis, every struggle of this kind depends upon the superior *will* of one side or the other, combined with a superior understanding and deployment of *all* the available resources, political, social, military, psychological, and economic. Conditions are never the same in each country. Drawing parallels between Malaya and South Vietnam, for example, as has often been done is altogether too facile, and is dangerously misleading.

Only one or two points can be made of general validity that have not already emerged from this brief sketch of a situation in which a colonial government did defeat a Communist insurrection which was proclaimed at the time by Western 'progressives' as a nationalist response to economic and political conditions. First, a government which can fundamentally ignore all outside as well as local criticisms because it makes no pretence to be democratic, though it honestly aims to *achieve* a democratic and juster social order, is in the strongest possible position to combat revolutionary guerrilla warfare. Secondly, a government (even a colonial government) which makes service in the villages and the jungle, however great the dangers may be, a point of honour and aspiration for its civil servants, has a tremendous superiority over urban-orientated administrations (even nationalist ones). Thirdly, the sheer political, military and technological *inven-*

tiveness of Westerners remains a weapon of great importance provided it is used in a thoroughgoing fashion.[1] Fourthly, interrogation of surrendered Communist terrorists showed that their motives were often not so much prompted by a concern for social justice as by aspirations towards personal advancement and a sense of security denied to them by a disintegrating traditional society. Once they knew that history was *not* on their side in Malaya, then their ideological commitment frequently collapsed quite quickly, as was also the case with the Chinese Communist prisoners of war in Korea, for example.[2] Since the counter-insurgency campaign in Malaya proved its effectiveness, Malaya has known many problems, but Communist violence has not been one of them.

In 1948 there was an insurrection against the nationalists in Indonesia too, but it was of a different kind. A long-time exiled Communist, Muso, returned with what appears to have been a plan for a 'coup de Prague' or 'palace revolution' of the kind achieved in Czechoslovakia by Klementi Gottwald with the aid of the threat offered by Zapotocky's armed factory militia, the establishment of 'dual power', and the shadow of the Russian Red Army. The upshot was a rising in the city of Maduin in Java which was crushed by the crack Siliwangi division of the Indonesian nationalist army. This may *seem* as though the Indonesian Communists (P.K.I.) acted as they did for reasons of local initiative. But this is most probably not so. In his speech proclaiming the attack on 'the capitalist rear', Zhdanov had specifically mentioned Indonesia (and Indo-China where the fight against the French was well under way) as being countries which were 'joining the anti-imperialist camp'. Obviously, the P.K.I. could not be directed outright to attack a government in which, it had reason to believe, it would soon play a predominant role. What seems to have happened was that the P.K.I. was caught off balance and reluctantly forced prematurely to declare its hand at Maduin.

What is perfectly certain is that the revived Communist party's politbureau declared many years later (on 20th February 1957) that 'The minimum conditions necessary for applying the system of people's

[1] Provided, also, that it is married into a total *political* response, e.g. the remark of a U.S. army officer in Vietnam about 1961, 'What is mobility? Mobility means vehicles and aircraft. . . . The Vietcong have no vehicles and no airplanes. How can they be mobile?', is sheer folly.

[2] Lucian Pye, *Guerrilla Communism in Malaya*, Princeton, 1956. '(Communism's) greatest defect would appear to be the fleeting nature of its charms . . . Its failure to provide advancement and better social status for the Malay (sic) careerist . . . disenchanted many recruits after only a year and a half or two years of service.' Charles W. Thayer, *Guerrilla* op. cit.

democracy do not yet exist.' The men of Maduin had made the same mistake as their forbears had made in 1925, which was castigated in that year by Joseph Stalin in the following terms: 'They were guilty of overrating the revolutionary potentialities of the liberation movement and in understanding the importance of alliance between the working class and the revolutionary bourgeoisie against imperialism. The Communists in Java, who recently put forward the slogan of Soviet government for their country (and advocacy of Soviet uprising) suffer, it seems, from this deviation. This is a deviation to the Left, which threatens to isolate the Communist party from the masses.... A determined struggle against this deviation is an essential condition for the training of really revolutionary cadres for the colonies and dependent countries of the East.' This could hardly be bettered as a condemnation of general application to the events of 1948 in South-East Asia, written twenty-three years earlier by the very man responsible for those 1948 debacles.

However, the P.K.I. had seemingly learned its lesson, until in October 1965 it again embarked upon a 'palace revolution' and decided to avail itself of the opportunities offered by the ego-maniacal President Sukarno. The party doubtless preferred, as every Communist party has always naturally preferred, the chance of entering what was, in effect, so far as influencing policy was concerned, a coalition government, but without the responsibilities of true participation. As a result of 'guided democracy' and its functioning under the ideological umbrella of Nasakom (nationalism-religion-communism) the P.K.I. enjoyed complete organizational freedom, of which they made energetic use, and the chance of identifying their aims with the charismatic appeal of Sukarno. Moreover, the anti-Western offshoots of this ideological standpoint—Konfrontasi ('crush Malaysia') and the diplomatic seizure of West Irian—was not only of immense obvious benefit to P.K.I. propaganda in isolating Indonesia from the West, it also made for a situation in which (desperate coups apart) a *konfrontasi* with the army was much less likely. For a time, though not in the event permanently, it made for an understanding between Djakarta and Peking, both representatives of what Sukarno believed were the New Emerging Forces, and this suited the P.K.I. exceptionally well.

And so the debacle of 1948, so obviously inspired from outside the country, did not prevent the P.K.I. re-establishing itself and building up an impressively large—indeed altogether too large—village-cell (and probably to some extent armed and civil services-cell) organization, which was utterly denied to the Burma Communist party and the Malayan Communist party where the independent governments were determinedly, even ruthlessly anti-Communist. Whether Indonesia will offer up lessons in revolutionary guerrilla warfare will depend upon events which are impossible to predict in rural Central Java and some other areas of Indonesia. But it was clear that the P.K.I. insurgents would enjoy no 'active sanctuary' and so, even if they had acquired quite large quantities of arms, they were ultimately doomed in an armed struggle, unless they had seriously subverted the army in advance.

It is equally clear that the morale of the P.K.I. was seriously affected by events in South Vietnam, for captured documents of the Malayan Communist terrorists show that such insurgents are ever mindful of the general struggle being waged in South-East Asia. Lastly, the pursuit of a 'reformist' image almost certainly hampered the P.K.I. in developing a spirit of revolutionary guerrilla violence amongst its cadres. 'Reformist' activity ineluctably weakens the essentially militaristic spirit of a Communist 'organizational weapon'.

Of course, Indonesia has not been without guerrilla warfare, but it has been of a kind only negatively relevant to the study of revolutionary guerrilla warfare. There have been Darul Islam (Muslim) insurgencies of long duration but so localized and so limited in propaganda value as never to offer the chance of making a nation-wide insurrection. There have been regional (even separatist) guerrilla movements in East Indonesia but though they might have weakened the peripheries, their very aims, together with their isolation from other separatist or potentially separatist areas, deprived them of nation-wide appeal.

The only insurgency that might theoretically have been seen as a generalized threat to the Indonesian government was the 1958 revolt centred (so far as the alternative 'government' was concerned) in Sumatra, and led by a group of regional-minded colonels and liberal politicians driven into revolt by the mess that was being made of the economy. But their cry for a federal, instead of a unitary Indonesian state was hardly an appeal appropriate to a rurally based insurrection. They did not 'think country', being orthodox urban officials or military town administrators by temperament and training, which is fatal for guerrillas. Operating in Sumatra and the Celebes, which produced something like 70 per cent of Indonesia's foreign exchange earnings, they did much economic damage, attacking communications and destroying rubber stocks. But they suffered from a number of disabilities besides 'thinking urban'—even 'thinking Jakarta' in the sense of hoping for negotiations that would, to use Communist terminology, bring them back into the 'legal fold'.[1]

Their leader, Dr. Sumitro, saw the general situation quite clearly, arguing that the Americans who were backing Sukarno were wrong in believing that Sukarno would ever put himself in the position of having to rely solely on the Army. His prediction that the Communists would be used as a balancing force was quite correct. But he never found out what he could do to alter this situation. And the fact that the Americans backed Sukarno and that Malaya (despite insistent rumours to the contrary) would not act as an aggressive 'privileged sanctuary' for his rebel movement put it in the position where the Indonesian army was able easily to administer a military *coup de grâce*. A certain persistent air of unreality about this nobly inspired rebellion was high lighted by the rebels' insouciant protest to Western newspapermen that the airborne troops of the Indonesian army taking over the rebel airfield at Padang were really dummies. Of such stuff guerrilla fighters are not made.

It might be imagined that the infiltration of sabotage and guerrilla bands into Malaya and Malaysian Borneo as part of the Konfrontasi or 'crush Malaysia' policy of Djakarta is of significance for the study of revolutionary guerrilla warfare in South-East Asia, but in fact for a number of reasons, it bore little resemblance to a Communist revolutionary war. First, the whole concept was unsound: the limited and diffused use of guerrillas under the command of Indonesian regular army officers had the effect of achieving the very reverse of the political objective, which was to get the British (and Commonwealth) military forces out of Malaysia. Secondly, attempts to seize control of administrative centres such as Sibu in Sarawak in the face of quickly flown in Gurkhas was simply stupid. The whole of such operations depended upon patient political preparation by the Chinese Clandestine Communist Organization within Sarawak, whereas they were carried out while the C.C.O.'s were still training in the jungle. Thirdly, and much most importantly, Konfrontasi guerrilla operations lacked the political content which makes Communist guerrillas so formidable.

General Haris Nasution has made it plain that he believes that modern guerrillas must be thoroughly indoctrinated politically, 'ideological pioneers' as he calls them, and he sees modern guerrilla

[1] By 1966 this in fact began to happen.

warfare as total political warfare.[1] But of course—and this is very important—it never can be total in this sense unless it is waged by men possessed of a totalitarian ideology (or, for a time, by one *race* against a foreign occupying power). The effectiveness of Communist revolutionary warfare lies in the fact that in *every* field of political activity their 'troops' think as guerrillas, as men self-outlawed and hence unencumbered by doubts and untrammelled by a belief in limits to what is permitted.

Their devotion enables them to merge themselves deeply in the blood, sweat, and tears of war; but their organization with its totalitarian control and limitless objectives also keeps them so to speak, above the struggle as well. The society to which they belong is a society quite literally constructed for warfare on all levels; and it is of its nature offensive in every facet of its activities. There is a world of difference between, on the one hand, the green-clad irregulars calling themselves a 'Liberation Army of Northern Borneo', indifferently indoctrinated in an any way vague ideology, led by regular officers, aiming to cause confusion in Brunei; and men like the Vietcong medical officer, Mai Xuan Phong, writing in his diary, 'One must then live in such a way that one does not have to regret the wasted years and months . . . that one is able to say before passing away: my whole life, my whole strength has been devoted to the most elevated and the most beautiful cause—the struggle for the liberation of mankind.'[2]

And there is a world of difference between the organization acting in Borneo and the organization seeking to impose totalitarian rule in South Vietnam. General Nasution revealingly writes: 'Guerrilla warfare strategically carried out is defensive. A victory in war can only be achieved by an offensive, carried out by an organized army, an army equal or greater in force than that of the enemy.' So says every regular in every non-totalitarian society.

Even an unpleasantly authoritarian society like Indonesia's until recently is unable to claim what the military leader of totalitarian Communist North Vietnam, General Vo Nguyen Giap, claims: 'the army is the people, the people is the army'. There was no comparison between Indonesian officers leading irregulars, even if they harboured pan-Malay ideas and were devotees of Sukarno's Marhaenism (roughly, small-manism), and the politically dedicated army officers of North Vietnam where 'Military training, and political education, are

[1] *Fundamentals of Guerrilla Warfare*, op. cit.
[2] M. Raskin and Bernard Fall, *The Vietnam Reader* op. cit.

the key tasks in building the army in peace time' and where 'We have always given particular attention to the strengthening of the party in the units. From 35–40 per cent of officers and army men have joined it, among the officers, the percentage even exceeds 90 per cent.'[1] Nor was it possible for Indonesians to think in Giap's terms about their country: 'At present North Vietnam is entirely liberated; it is the vast rear of our army. We know that in modern warfare the rear is all the more important.'

It is true that General Nasution, when discussing guerrilla warfare against the Dutch, writes in terms of total war: ' . . . we organized a military form of guerrilla government, consisting of administrative units at village level (desa), under-district (onderdistrik), etc., each headed by a military commander who was also chief of the total guerrilla administration in that area and who operated with full support from the civilian bodies. . . . The government administration was "guerrilla-ized". . . . All government affairs were "guerrilla-ized"— the judicial courts and police, the levying of war taxes, information services, public health, education, manufacturing, communications, etc. In guerrilla-izing in that way the enemy was foiled in his attempt to destroy the organization of our own country so that it was not possible for him to replace it with his government. All the while our side kept the wheels of government going to serve the needs and the struggle of the people.' The Communist 'organizational weapon' with its totalitarian ideology and offensive stance are here altogether lacking. The militarization of politics is wholly different from the political indoctrination of an armed society. The very language of Giap belongs to a quite different mode of thought: 'a people's war is essentially *a peasants' war under the leadership of the working class* (read: Communist Party—italics are Giap's) . . . the Vietnamese people's war of liberation was essentially a people's national democratic revolution carried out under armed form . . . (The) judicious leadership by the party led us to victory . . . the party solved all the problems of the Resistance.' In Indonesia it was the fundamental differences existing between a nationalist regular army and a pseudo-nationalist Communist party which undermined the attempt at imposing Konfrontasi through guerrilla warfare and ultimately led to a confrontation between the army and the party instead.

So far it is clear that, first, no South-East Asian country has opted freely for the Communist 'solution' and, secondly, that no Com-

[1] *People's War, People's Army*, Foreign Languages Publishing House, Hanoi, 1961.

munist revolutionary guerrilla war has arisen simply out of a 'response to economic and political conditions'. In Burma, Indonesia, and Malaya the insurrections arose out of the requirements of Moscow policy and the erroneous belief that violence was the appropriate method to use. In Vietnam, the Communists captured a resistance coalition against the French and owed their success to their politically superior use of guerrilla violence. What about Laos?

Laos has been described geographically as 'a poorly-endowed, thinly-populated, relatively static economy based primarily upon subsistence agriculture and handicrafts.'[1] Until revolutionary guerrilla warfare was introduced into Laos it was a country of gentle Theravada Buddhism. The Lao proper inhabit the lowland valleys and make up rather less than half the total population which is less than two million. The only fighting group are the Meos, probably about 400,000 strong, living high on the crests and ridges of this mountainous country for the most part, and cultivators of a valuable opium crop. There was at the end of the Second World War no poverty by South-East Asian standards, no problems of land tenure (there being land to burn), and no anti-French nationalist feeling of any significance (apart from a very small section indeed of the French educated ruling class). The country is an agglomeration of tribes and languages (eighteen major dialects are spoken in Phong Saly province alone), and there is less a unified society than a multiplicity of feudal societies, in which the family clan is all-important. It has never in any sense been a country in which serious peasant discontents have shown themselves. This is not for a moment to suggest that Laos has been well served in point of medicine, hygiene, or agricultural advancement, only that despite a lack of anything like modernization and an upper class which behave 'feudally', Laos, although a poor, disease-ridden community, can nevertheless easily support a subsistence economy in terms of its present population.

And yet in the years since the defeat of the Japanese, Laos has on a number of occasions become a source of international crisis. It has also become notable for seemingly extraordinarily complex diplomatic manœuvres by the Great Powers; and even more complex moves made internally by groups of men with strange names and vaguely defined objectives: a kind of modernly sinister Ruritania. But from the point of view of understanding revolutionary guerrilla warfare, the pattern of events is not altogether difficult to discern. Laotian political events provide a peculiarly good example of how Communists

[1] Arthur J. Dommen, *Conflict in Laos*, Pall Mall Press 1964.

think strategically and act, both 'legally' and 'illegally' in pursuit of an exceedingly important objective, the true nature of which escaped (one must assume) the otherwise very sophisticated Western diplomats, and probably the Russians as well. The objective was the 'neutralization' of Laos in such a fashion as to preclude future Western intervention, in order to secure the invasion route—the network of roads and tracks southwards which is collectively and most misleadingly known as the 'Ho Chi Minh trail'—to South Vietnam.

Of course, Communist activities after the War began on a quite different basis. As in East Europe and in East Asia, the Communist intention was so to exploit the general 'anti-Fascist' and 'resistance' mentality then widely obtaining, that the would party be accepted into a 'nationalist' coalition, which it hoped to come to dominate. To this end the Communist party of Indo-China chose as titular leader Prince Souphanouvong, a French-educated civil engineer resentful of his treatment by the French and married to a Vietnamese Communist. He was escorted into Laos from Vietnam in 1945 by a group of Vietnamese soldiers, including the young Tran Van Dinh, later to become Chief of Staff of the Lao 'Liberation Army', and later still to become the one diplomat of the Ngo Dinh Diem regime in Washington to remain loyal to his Head of State. Prince Souphanouvong quickly became Minister for National Defence in the Lao Issara 'government', a broad nationalist coalition disposing of very little force or influence, as was shown by the quick collapse of the movement in the face of the very limited French power that was re-established after the war. The Lao Issara leaders were exiled to Thailand; the small guerrilla movement was kept in being chiefly through the activities of Vietminh cadres.

From the very beginning of the post-War revolutionary guerrilla campaign in Laos, the control of what has come to be called the Pathet Lao lay with the Vietminh; and the Laotian leaders of the Pathet Lao have been members of the Communist Party of Indo-China. Since the foundation of that party in 1930, Laos and Cambodia have been included within its ambit of operations. The relationship within the Vietnamese Communist party of Indo-China has sometimes been described as federal. But this is to apply democratic terms to a totalitarian political apparatus; a Laotian Communist like Phoumi Vongvichit operates entirely as a member of a 'party', an organizational weapon, dedicated to the political subjugation of the former French Indo-China. So do the leaders of the 'sleeper' organization known as the Pracheakorn Party in Cambodia. Moreover, as has been the case within Vietnam, the Communist Vietminh has been able to play upon Vietnamese expansionism in this matter: it is not only 'reactionary' Vietnamese who make the joke (privately) that there is only one real Cambodian, Prince Sihanouk. One secret of Vietnamese Communist success has been the marrying of disguised Communist aims with a very genuine *racial* pride. In the trading towns of Laos, such as Vientiane and Paksé, the Vietnamese had proved themselves organizationally superior to the Laotians and Cambodians—and Thai North-Easterners, for that matter, long before Communism became a serious movement.

During the struggle against the French, it seemed as though the Vietminh High Command regarded Laos in purely military terms: as an area for tactically diversionary activities. It was indeed 'invaded' three times by units of the Vietminh army; and one of the many reasons adduced to explain the decision to defend Dien-Bien-Phu was that of protecting Laos. Undoubtedly there was a purely military component in such moves. But the political upshot, which was to be of very much greater significance, was the establishment of Vietminh Communist political power in Phong Saly and Samneua provinces, contiguous with North Vietnam. Once the victory over the French was achieved, which was *political* as much as military, this 'base area' was provided with a 'privileged sanctuary' next door. The Pathet Lao and its political arm the Neo Lao Haksat, the equivalent of the National Liberation Front in South Vietnam, might suffer all sorts of vicissitudes (which it did) but as a result of revolutionary guerrilla warfare an apparently impregnable 'base area' had been set up through what seemed at the time to have been purely military diversionary moves.

It is not to the purpose of this book to examine the attempts of the Neo Lao Haksat to use its 'legal' status in order to carry on the political struggle in an unarmed form, though the fact of this twin-armed approach should be noticed since in some ways Laos was to have been a model, if circumstances proved favourable, for the same kind of twin-armed Vietcong and National Liberation Front approach in South Vietnam. Backed by a seemingly impregnable guerrilla base area, offering a *permanent* threat to the government administration even when it was headed by a coalition including Neo Lao Haksat ministers, attempts were made to prepare for an eventual takeover, including the partial (and impermanent) integration of Pathet Lao guerrilla units into the Royal army.

But the central aim, to which everything else was subordinated, was the creation through revolutionary guerrilla fighting and external political manœuvring of an internationally secured complex of invasion routes to the south. The 1962 Settlement was an astonishing example of how temporary lack of purpose in counter-insurgency was allowed to bring about a conference very gravely disadvantageous to the West and its allies in South-East Asia, for although initially many serious mistakes were made in the conduct of the campaign the turning of the tide in Communist favour in 1961 was combatted for only a short time before the struggle was given up. The Laotian Government's position was undoubtedly bad; perhaps 'the new American administration had to accept the conference proposal, knowing full well that a conference would bring little but embarrassment, but conscious too that it was the only means to avert a collapse.'[1]

This reading of the situation at the time is quite intelligible, though internal events in Laos in the years since 1962 do not wholly support it. What is quite certain is that the internationally imposed isolation of Laos was a marvellous example of the inability of Western diplomats to understand what revolutionary guerrilla warfare is all about. The Declaration on the Neutrality of Laos committed Laos to the 'principles of peaceful co-existence' and 'friendly relations'; forbade it to 'resort to the use or threat of force in any way which might impair the peace of other countries' (including presumably North Vietnam whose forces poured across Laos's countryside as the years went by); required of it the 'withdrawal of all foreign troops and military personnel' (except, in fact, the Vietnamese Communists); and forced it to accept 'direct and unconditional aid from all countries that wish to help the Kingdom of Laos build up an independent and autonomous national economy.'[2] This was being done at the very time General Maxwell Taylor was remarking, wholly truthfully, in Bangkok that 'It is in Laos that the problem of that (South Vietnamese) frontier must be resolved.'[3]

It *was* resolved, wholly in the Communists' favour; the objective had been achieved; and three years later, as a result, the Americans were to find that their every intensification of the South Vietnamese struggle was met by a corresponding North Vietnamese reinforcement of ground troops. What is equally certain is that the guerrilla struggles in Laos have never been in any sense a spontaneous indigen-

[1] George Modelski, *International Conference on the Settlement of the Laotian Question, 1961–2*, Department of International Relations, Research School of Pacific Studies, Australian National University, 1962.
[2] George Modelski op cit.
[3] George Modelski, *Australia's Neighbours*, October–November 1961.

ous rising in response to economic and political conditions; but have always been part of a revolutionary warfare operation directed by Hanoi and carried out by Neo Lao Haksat and Pathet Lao leaders, the most important of whom are members of the Communist party of Indo-China.

The revolutionary insurgency that would seem best to support the left-wing argument that Communist insurgencies are basically spontaneous and indigenous responses to economic and political conditions is that which has been waged in the Philippines. There is no doubt that the Communist-controlled Huk guerrillas drew most of their support from a land-hungry peasantry in part of Luzon Island; there is no doubt that opening up land to the landless played a significant part in what seemed at the time (the late '50s and early '60s) to have been a successful counter-insurgency campaign.

But closer examination shows that the issue has all along been less simple than that. The 'People's Army against Japan', referred to locally as Hukbalahap, and later abbreviated to Huk, was founded by the Communist party of the Philippines in Pampanga province in 1942 under the leadership of Luis Taruc. The movement appears to have had Chinese Communist military advisers and used Chinese Communist guerrilla textbooks.[1] Like the Vietminh, its operations were directed against Filipino political rivals as well as the Japanese; selective terrorism was employed as a politico-military weapon.[2] After the war, the Filipino Communists found their way barred as far as the 'parliamentary form of struggle' was concerned; but as was shown earlier the Communist party used guerrilla warfare as only one arm of its strategy. This pattern is invariable. Its significance is being stressed simply because Communist revolutionary warfare cannot be separated from the political 'guerrilla' approach of Communist parties to every concrete situation. Revolutionary guerrilla warfare is resorted to when it seems to be the most viable form of struggle or the only available form of struggle at a given time.

By 1950 the insurgency situation was serious; and perhaps seemed even more serious than it was because of public concern with ineffectual, corrupt government in Manila. About 10,000 Huks, at least passively supported by large numbers of peasants suffering severe agrarian disabilities in Central Luzon, looked as though they might soon be able to establish areas of 'alternative administration' supported

[1] Maximo V. Soliven, *Vietnam: Seen from East and West* op. cit.
[2] Soliven: 'By war's end, the Huks had eliminated 25,000 persons—and only 5,000 of these were Japanese soldiers'.

by base areas in the Sierra Madre mountains, from which a major Communist revolutionary warfare campaign could gradually be launched.[1]

The counter-insurgency was directed by a former guerrilla hero of the Second World War, Raymond Magsaysay, a man of impeccable public record and great talent for popular leadership. He enjoyed the very great advantage of knowing that though the Philippines are only 600 miles from China, the Huks were cut off by the sea from a 'privileged sanctuary' which could train, arm, and supply their formations. Moreover, the Americans had lightly ruled the Philippines and had long encouraged parliamentary democracy so that there could be no real pretence that the Huks were fighting a quasi-colonial government. The Huks had to take their stand on the basis of agrarian discontents.

Magsaysay, like Templer in Malaya, understood that the whole of society was involved in this kind of insurrection and so his response was as much social and political as military. It was by no means only socio-political, however, as has often been represented. 'Magsaysay acted effectively against the two obvious targets. He made the armed forces an instrument for securing the support of the people for their government; he made them also an effective instrument for pursuing, capturing, or permanently discouraging the guerrilla. He announced his intentions; he announced his dramatic policy of a 'All-Out Friendship' or 'All-Out Force', and then he acted to make good his words.'[2]

Magsaysay was concerned both to remove the sources of grievance and to destroy the political organization responsible for canalizing these grievances into a campaign designed to bring the Communist party to power. The American counter-insurgent expert General Lansdale nicely described the propaganda aspect of the struggle, arguing that 'purely military tactics had failed completely to stop the Huks' because they had 'analysed the people's grievances and made the righting of these wrongs into their slogans'. In other words, the Communists were 'exploiting contradictions' in Filipino rural society in order to move towards their real objective, Communist dictatorship.

---

[1] According to one authority, the Huks were by this time acting according to the 'Calcutta line'. Brian Crozier, *Turmoil in South-East Asia*, Penguin Special, 1965. In another important study, *The Rebels*, Chatto & Windus, 1960, Crozier states that Taruc (like Sjarifuddin in Indonesia) did not announce his Communist commitment until 1948.

[2] N. D. Valeriano and Charles T. R. Bohannan, *Counterguerrilla Operations*, The Philippine Experience, Praegar, 1962.

They campaigned under cover of a bogus Cause; land redistribution, which of course would immediately be disowned by the party when in power; then the indoctrinated revolutionary army would become the instrument of agricultural collectivization, as it did in North Vietnam after the French withdrew.

Magsaysay's answer was not, as it is sometimes supposed, a large-scale land reform programme but rather the offer of land and rehabilitation to surrendered Huks on the same terms as were enjoyed by returned soldiers (retired veterans) of the Filipino Army. In addition he did what was never done during the Diem regime in South Vietnam, because of the orthodox military ideas of American advisers; he transformed the army into a body capable of what has come to be called 'civic action' work, 'helping the villagers build roads, repair irrigation ditches, rehabilitate hamlets destroyed during the fighting or ravaged by (Huk) punitive measures.'[1] Like General Ne Win in Burma, he integrated the constabulary with the Army, hence ending a most unhappy relationship between police and people. A stroke of genius was to introduce army lawyers to represent the cases of peasants in the courts.

The approach was indeed highly effective in terms of desertions from the Huk formations and in terms of winning popular acquiescence in government activities. But they could not possibly have been so efficacious if it had not been for the military corollary; 9,695 Huks killed in action, 1,635 wounded, and 4,269 captured.[2] Magsaysay placed great importance on his battalion combat teams and his 'Large-Unit Infiltration' methods. Everything that could ensure greater mobility was brought into play, including a system of bribery and exemplary punishment. Not the least of his successes was the betrayal and arrest of a major portion of the Politbureau of the Communist party of the Philippines.

An analysis of the reasons why men joined the Huks and why they surrendered, also makes it clear that there was a very great deal more to the putting down of the Huks than the offer of 'land to the tillers' or civic action work in general. Thirty-eight per cent of the Huks questioned (the largest proportion) attributed their involvement to personal friendships; about 20 per cent were 'invited' to join; about 18 per cent were kidnapped or captured; and about 11 per cent voluntarily sought out the organization.[3] Some 61 per cent of those

---

[1] Bernard Fall, *The Two Viet-Nams* op. cit.
[2] Soliven op. cit.
[3] Alvin A. Scarf, *The Philippine Answer to Communism*, Starford University

who surrendered cited hardships in the mountains as the chief reason for their surrender; the next most important reason, cited by 45 per cent of the surrendered Huks, was *failures* of the Huk revolutionary guerrilla movement.

In general, it seems clear that, apart from the special case of Vietnam which remains to be examined later, none of the disturbances that have taken place in South-East Asia since Second World War have had a purely agrarian origin. They have rather consisted of a series of attempts by Communist parties denied access to the 'parliamentary form of struggle' to win through to power by way of revolutionary warfare. There is, of course, on occasion an important stress laid upon land reform by Communist parties engaged in insurgency, but even Burma's sweeping land reforms did not have a clearly definable effect on Communist tactics. In short, revolutionary warfare is a purposeful political activity undertaken according to certain principles of violence and propaganda by the 'organizational weapons' known as Communist parties. As such, revolutionary insurgency can be mounted even where political and economic conditions are by no means peculiarly bad, though of course the undeveloped world—Peking's 'interzone'—is by definition an area where there are all manner of economic 'contradictions' to exploit. It is necessary therefore to examine precisely what is involved in revolutionary insurgency.

Press, His findings may be usefully compared with those of Lucien Pye, *Guerrilla Communism in Malaya*, op. cit. In neither case is 'motivation' simple or obvious or consistent with left-wing ideas of spontaneous insurrection against intolerable economic and political conditions.

Chapter 5

COMMUNIST REVOLUTIONARY DOCTRINES

That revolutionary guerrilla warfare poses one of the greatest political problems in the world today is beginning to become obvious.[1] That this was not for a long time sufficiently recognized in the Western world is not altogether surprising: it is a form of warfare especially *appropriate* to the under-developed world, part of which even now imagines itself to be in revolt against what it sees as a Western world hegemony imposed through superior industrial and economic power and one to which Russia seems, in the eyes of such people, increasingly to belong. Moreover it is especially *inappropriate*, except in conditions of civil breakdown (occasioned today only by armed invasion) to Western industrialized, urbanized societies.

Why is it so vitally important? The answer is quite simple: it is —or at any rate until the American involvement in South Vietnam it seemed to be—the most feasible form of warfare in the present condition of nuclear 'balance of terror'. Total or general war, whether nuclear or non-nuclear, is becoming more and more unthinkable as far as the West and the Soviet Union are concerned and China still lacks a significant nuclear armoury and a delivery system. After Korea, even limited war (that is, limited as to geographical area as well as to weapons employed) did not seem to be decisive enough in relationship to the casualties incurred, at least, such was Chinese reasoning before American involvement in South Vietnam, and it was probably also the consensus of world opinion.

And so, quite obviously the notion of extending revolutionary gurerrilla warfare throughout the under-developed world had a huge appeal to Chinese minds actively bent on altering the balance of world power, but it did not hold the same kind of appeal for Russian minds. Largely as a result of this fundamental difference of opinion, there

---

[1] C. Northcote Parkinson: 'Should they ever turn from science fiction to fact, the politicians would see that their world can be destroyed piecemeal, and has been very largely destroyed already, without anyone resorting to anything much larger than a three-inch mortar.' *East and West*, John Murray, 1963.

occurred the Sino-Soviet split. In order to understand the great dangers to world peace presented by the Chinese doctrine of extending revolutionary guerrilla warfare it is necessary to examine in some detail precisely *what* the differences of doctrine between the U.S.S.R. and China are and *how* they have arisen, for upon understanding this the peace of the world may well depend. Crypto-Communists and their allies are, throughout the U.S.A., desperately working for a Communist victory in South Vietnam, because they know (as General Giap knows and has proclaimed on the basis of deep experience) that if South Vietnam is forfeited, then this revolutionary technique will triumph elsewhere, perhaps everywhere throughout the underdeveloped world. And in order to weaken the will-to-resist, the crypto-Communists and their allies are playing upon every bitter neurosis, every politically uninformed source of generosity, and every historical prejudice existing on the Western 'terrain' on which they are operating.

In order to understand the dimension of the Sino-Soviet split over revolutionary guerrilla warfare it is necessary to go back to Lenin, the man who saw politics as a form of warfare long before Mao Tse-tung; and who saw warfare as part of the human condition and a constant factor in relations between national states until 'capitalism' was blasted off the face of the earth. But Lenin had never seen a thermo-nuclear blast; and this is the crux of the dispute. Lenin being a leader who needed always to underpin the activity of the day with a theoretical explanation justifying it, produced his 'Imperialism: the Highest Stage of Capitalism'.

For present purposes the important argument in 'Imperialism' is that Communism could not be successfully established in the industrialized nations of the West unless the imperialist activities of these nations were also successfully attacked in their colonial possessions. Lenin believed these to be a vital source of the imperialist nations' economic and social well-being: Stalin's 'capitalist rear', in other words. So long as this presumed vital connection existed between European capitalist states and their imperialistically-ruled colonies, then an economic system—a world economic system—existed that would *necessarily* engender wars between 'socialism' and 'capitalism'.

Stalin held to this view firmly; after all, his monstrous behaviour had for most of his life been justified, in his own understanding, by such insights. By 1956 Mr. Khrushchev still appeared to believe that wars of some kind were inevitable; but he also seemed to believe that major wars were not quite inevitably inevitable. As the years passed, such wars became less and less inevitable in Russian eyes, not only because the Soviet Union was beginning to produce a society in which people—particularly, the privileged all-important managerial class—were beginning to enjoy their well-being and did not wish to see it obliterated thermo-nuclearly; but also because, in these new conditions, it was possible for Soviet leaders to understand the objective change which thermo-nuclear weapons had imposed upon Lenin's texts!

Peking was prepared to pay lip-service, for a time, to the doctrine of co-existence; it *had* to while it was exploiting the 'Bandung spirit' of the late 50's. But by 1960 Peking was talking in the ominous fashion that is its stance today: 'We believe in the absolute correctness of Lenin's thinking: War is an inevitable outcome of systems of exploitation and the source of modern wars is the imperialist system. Until the imperialist system and the exploiting classes come to an end, wars of one kind or another will always occur. They may be wars among the imperialists for the redivision of the world, or wars of aggression and anti-aggression between the imperialists and the oppressed peoples, or *civil wars of revolution and counter-revolution between the exploited and exploiting in the imperialist countries*.'[1] As Lenin, following Clausewitz, put it: 'Theoretically, it would be quite wrong to forget that every war is but the continuation of politics by other means.' All these kinds of war represent the continuation of the politics of definite classes or ideologies. Marxist-Leninists must at all costs avoid sinking into the mire of bourgeois pacifism.

Peking in fact was showing itself not only to be unafraid of war even under the thermo-nuclear 'balance of terror' but was beginning to assert its own line firmly, a line necessarily based upon the presumedly abiding truth of everything that Lenin had said, in order to assert its own desire for leadership within the Communist world. The Soviet Union's task, to assert that conditions had changed the validity of Lenin's 'Imperialist' thesis, was not, in theory, at all easy: it may sound simple enough, so far as democratic thinking is concerned, but the Soviet Union was not built on commonsense lines but according to dogmatic beliefs, in which every important work of Lenin's had assumed the role of a quasi-religious text. If one text were to be discarded, what was the value of the others?

Mr. Khrushchev's answer was this: 'Lenin's formulations on imperialism hold their former strength and will serve as the guiding star

[1] Author's italics.

of our theory and practice. But it is impossible to forget that Lenin's views on imperialism were formulated and developed decades ago, when many factors which have now become decisive in the development of the historical process were non-existent.

'Several of Lenin's formulations on imperialism date from the period when there was no Soviet Union nor other socialist states. Today, the Soviet Union with its tremendous economic and military potential is growing and strengthening, and the great socialist camp which today consists of more than 1,000 million people is growing and strengthening, while the understanding of the working class, which is carrying on an active struggle for peace in the capitalist countries, has also developed. Today there exist several factors such as the broad movement of the partisans for peace, and the increasing number of states coming forward for peace. It is also necessary to note that imperialism does not now have such a reserve in the shape of the colonial system which it formerly had.

'Because of this, comrades, it is impossible to mechanically repeat now on this matter of imperialism what was said by Vladimir Ilyich Lenin many decades ago. . . .' On the other hand, Mr. Khrushchev went on record as saying a year later (June 1961), by which time he must have been conscious of his dilemma *vis-à-vis* the hard Chinese line, 'There will be liberation wars as long as imperialism exists, as long as colonialism exists. They are revolutionary wars. Such wars are not only permissible but inevitable, for the colonists do not of their own free will grant independence to peoples.'[1]

It will immediately be noticed that he had contradicted himself: in the first speech the 'imperialists' are said to have lost their 'reserve' of colonies; in the second speech, they still have them. Such are contradictions of Communist dogma in changing circumstances; and as such, they represent fundamental contradictions between the development of the Soviet Union on the one hand and the development of China on the other. This point is not being made facetiously; it is of very great importance. Had Soviet energies not been forced back upon Russian development by the wills of men in Western Europe, then Russia would not today be in the economic and social position to revise the teaching of Lenin in the interests of its own worthwhile survival. Had Stalin's expansionism been allowed to continue, then the energies of the Soviet Russian people would have had to be dispersed, to the detriment of Russian development, across an impossibly wide

---

[1] L. G. Churchward, Soviet Revision of Lenin's Imperialism, *The Australian Journal of Politics and History*, May 1962.

area of imperialist control. So it is with China today: unless the wills of free men impel Communist China to exert its energies internally towards the betterment of its own people, then it will indeed become an 'unmanageable giant', insatiable in its appetites for further political expansion, inhumanly militaristic and subordinating its own people to bitter aggressive misery, not only to their detriment but to the imminence of world war. This is what 'the partisans of peace' do not understand, but it is what the Soviet Union certainly does understand, and is brought out by a further examination of the Sino-Soviet split.

The split was fully admitted early in 1963. As the *Peking Review* of 21st June put it: 'A number of major differences of principle now exist within the international Communist movement.' And the nature of those differences was underlined in the historic Letter of the Central Committee of the Communist party of China of 30th March 1963 in reply to the Letter of the Central Committee of the Communist party of the Soviet Union. The turgid language, the repetitions, the leaden logic of this letter makes dreary reading for the democratic citizens of free countries who are accustomed to speaking to men as men. This is a machine speaking to a machine *but*, unless Communist Chinese ambitions are stopped in South-East Asia and a viable South-East Asian economic and political confederation is established in the wake of that stopping, then this Chinese Letter may prove to be one of the truly significant documents in the history of mankind.

In pristine Marx-Leninist terms—in terms of regarding Marx-Leninism as an eternal truth—this document reads exceedingly impressively. 'The central issue here is whether or not to accept the revolutionary principles of the Declaration and the Statement. (That is, attempts in 1957 and 1960 to forge a political programme acceptable to all the world's Communist parties.) *In the last analysis, it is a question whether or not to accept the universal truth of Marx-Leninism, whether or not to recognize the universal significance of the road of the October Revolution, whether or not to accept the fact that the people still living under the imperialist and capitalist system, who comprises two-thirds of the world's population, need to make revolution, and whether or not to accept the fact that the people already on the socialist road, who comprise two-thirds of the world's population, need to carry their revolution forward to the end.*'

Now it is perfectly obvious what the Chinese were trying to do; they were not merely asserting that they, and not the Russians, were presenting the correct Leninist line; they were also—by repetition of the phrase, 'two-thirds of mankind' in that context, suggesting that they, and they alone, were speaking for the aspirations of the underdeveloped world. And so it is not surprising that this Chinese thesis (similar to Zhdanov's thesis of 1947, though with an added plausibility derived from the fact that an 'Asian', under-developed nation was propounding it) quickly found supporters as far away as Latin America. For example, in the *Peking Review* of 30th August 1963, there appeared a Brazilian article arguing as follows: 'The Chinese Communists have always said that the revolution in their country basically follows the line of the Russian October Revolution. To achieve complete victory, the Brazilian revolution must also follow the common laws of the two great revolutions in history.

'The Chinese Communist party, in accordance with its traditions, demonstrates unbounded loyalty to revolutionary principles; together with Marx-Leninists of the world, it is waging an uncompromising struggle against modern revisionism (that is, the Moscow line on war). At the present moment it is difficult to estimate the depth of the influence of this struggle. . . . On the pretext of developing Marx-Leninism and taking account of realities (see Mr. Khrushchev's argument above) adverse currents tried to induce the working class and its allies to deviate from the correct road of the struggle for socialism, distort proletarian theories and wipe out their essentials.'

In its Letter of 30th March 1963, Peking makes quite explicit just how vitally important it regards its revolutionary warfare thesis. It contains a clear declaration of revolutionary warfare against the West, to be waged throughout the under-developed nations of the world. Without understanding the full implications of China's analysis of the world situation it is quite impossible to understand the true nature of the struggle for South Vietnam; nor the world-wide consequences for the West if it and its allies fail to meet the challenge.

At the risk of leaden repetition it is necessary to spell out the significance of the Sino-Russian split even further. Peking sees the situation thus: 'The strategic objectives of U.S. imperialism have been to grab and dominate (read: support through alliances) the intermediate zone lying between the United States and the socialist camp, put down the revolutions of the oppressed peoples and nations, proceed to destroy the socialist countries, and subject all the peoples and countries of the world, including its allies, to domination and enslavement by U.S. monopoly capital.'

The horrifying unreality of this world-view is not a subject for analysis here. It speaks for itself and for the consequences Peking draws from it: the vital struggle must inevitably be fought in the under-developed world; and in Peking's view this fact enormously assists its objectives. 'The various types of contradictions in the contemporary world are concentrated in the vast (intermediate zone) areas of Asia, Africa and Latin America; these are the most vulnerable areas under imperialist rule and the storm centres of world revolution dealing direct blows at imperialism.' It is on this struggle that the whole *world* struggle 'hinges'.

Attention should be drawn to two points in particular here. First, Peking uses the Communist term 'contradictions', to which reference has briefly been made earlier. Secondly, it refers to what it calls 'world revolution', as though there were only one. In Communist terminology 'contradictions' appear to mean enduring and fundamentally opposed interests between classes, which it is the task of Communist agitators to interpret and illuminate for the benefit of the understanding of the lower class. Clearly there are on occasion real contradictions in some societies, and especially in under-developed societies where the old canons of authority have crumbled and a new, monied but not necessarily productive class battens on the peasantry. All independent South Asian states have felt it necessary to take action, often severe, against the usually foreign money-lending classes (Chinese and Indian for the most part); and most South-East Asian states have to some degree, sometimes (as in Burma) to a very large degree, moved against landlords in the interests of landless peasants or peasants with too little land.

These are real contradictions in two ways: first, they represent a form of easily understood injustice and secondly, they must be removed if the country in question is to develop its resources fairly quickly. In order to remove them, as was suggested earlier, a far greater degree of central direction of the economy is required than might seem desirable to liberal capitalists of the West.

But, as has already been pointed out, the term 'contradictions' can be—and is—applied much more widely than this by the Communists when they wish to wage political warfare. Real contradictions shade off into the kind of tensions that can be found in any society, but particularly (as is obvious enough) in rapidly changing countries, and these tensions are exploited and manipulated by Communists in order to increase social *hatred* where they do not actually create it; and to channel discontents and hatreds along lines favourable to Communist policies. Given the abiding and narrow concern of Communists with seizing power at all costs—'The fundamental question of every revolution is power,' as Lenin roundly declared—then it is not difficult unscrupulously to turn social tensions into sources of political violence; or in the West into sources of national weakness.

What the Peking line is concerned to do all over Asia, Africa and Latin America is to exacerbate every tension and turn it to Peking's advantage. This vast process of political agitation embraces activities as small in themselves as playing off family factions within a Vietnamese village right up to the international level; for example trying to humiliate India at a moment of military crisis in order to embolden Pakistan to intensify the war, or trying to persuade African leaders that a great racial struggle is commencing under Chinese leadership.

This leads to a consideration of what the vital Chinese letter of 30th March 1963 means when it refers to the 'world revolution' as though there were only one. It is the intention of Peking that there shall be only one and that it shall be under Chinese leadership. As Mr. Denis Warner points out,[1] this intention was *implicit* in Peking Communist thinking as long ago as 1949 when the regime had just come to power. Mr. Warner quotes extensively from the speech of Liu Shao-chi, the party theoretician and at one time a likely successor to Mao Tse-tung, a speech which he rightly calls 'of transcendent importance in the Asian scene'.

Liu declared that 'This conference (attended by delegates from all Asian countries *and Australia*) will undoubtedly give an impetus to the development of the progressive labour movement and the widely developed national liberation movements in Asia and Australasia. . . . The labour movements and the national liberation movements in Siam and the Near East as well as in Australasia are also growing. . . . The great victory of the Chinese people has set them the best example. . . . The path taken by the Chinese people in defeating imperialism and its lackeys . . . is the path that should be traced by the peoples of various colonial and semi-colonial countries in their fight for national independence and people's democracy.'

From the beginning then, Communist China has seen itself as having a role to play of peculiar appropriateness to the under-developed world, a role that if played correctly could give it leadership of the Communists in it and indeed of many of the nationalist movements as well. Here Liu laid down what Mr. Warner calls 'four simple rules':

(i) 'The working class (Communist party) must unite with all other classes, political parties, or groups, organizations and individuals willing to fight imperialism.

[1] *Out of the Gun*, Hutchinson, 1956 op. cit.

(ii) 'The nation-wide united front must be led by and built around the working class and its party, the Communist party. It must not be led by the wavering and compromising national bourgeoisie, or the petty bourgeoisie.

(iii) 'In order to enable the working class and its party, the Communist party, to become the centre for uniting all forces working against imperialism and competently to lead the national united front to victory, it is necessary to build up through long struggles the Communist party which is armed with the theory of Marxism and Leninism, which understand strategy and tactics, practices self-criticism and strict discipline and is closely linked with the masses.

(iv) 'It is necessary to set up wherever and whenever possible a national liberation army which is led by the Communist party and is powerful and skilful in fighting its enemies. It is necessary to set up the bases on which the liberation army relies for its activities and to make the mass struggles in the enemy-controlled area and the armed struggles co-ordinate with each other. Armed struggle is the main form of struggle for the national liberation struggles of many colonies and semi-colonies.'

In other words, long before U.S. policies in South-East Asia could conceivably have affected Peking attitudes towards the outside world, the chief theoretician of Chinese Communism, at a conference which saw the formation of a subversive bureau on which even distant Australia was represented, was laying down the lines of the revolutionary guerrilla warfare campaign that rages in 1967. It was a time when it might have been expected that the Chinese Communists would have been concerned entirely with problems of internal reconstruction. But not at all: Peking was concerned immediately to carry on the struggle elsewhere.

Now at that time the effects of the *Moscow* decision to wage revolutionary guerrilla warfare throughout South-East Asia were still being very seriously felt; the results of the Calcutta Conference decision were not at the time clear. But even so China was claiming its special role in the area. Of course, since the Sino-Soviet split was still many years ahead and obvious to no one, the complete revelation of Chinese Communist ambitions had to wait until March 1963. But that declaration of aims was no mere series of debating points with Moscow; it was prefigured as early as 1949. It is extremely important to grasp the enduring intensity of Peking policy towards the outside world, especially for Western democrats accustomed to regarding feebleness of purpose, occasionally interrupted by ill-prepared gestures of dramatic intent as forming a 'normal' foreign policy of general acceptance elsewhere.

In September 1965 the Chinese Defence Minister, Marshall Lin Piao spelled out most aggressively of all what was adumbrated by Liu Shao-chi in 1949. His long speech printed in the *Peking Review* of 3rd September is a battle cry for the times, directed as much against the Khrushchev revisionists, who 'have staked the whole of their future on nuclear weapons and are engaged in a nuclear gamble with U.S. imperialism, with which they are trying to strike a political deal', as against 'U.S. imperialism (which) is preparing a world war.'

This speech is a deliberately apocalyptic essay in praise of revolutionary guerrilla warfare. Quoting Mao to the effect that 'Without a people's army the people have nothing', and Lenin to the effect that wars marvellously hasten 'social development', Lin Piao makes the claim that 'Comrade Mao Tse-tung's theory of people's war is not only a product of the Chinese revolution, but has also the characteristics of our epoch. The new experience gained in the people's revolutionary struggles in various countries since World War II has provided continuous evidence that Mao Tse-tung's thought is a common asset of the revolutionary people of the whole world.'

Lin Piao clearly lays down a challenge before the Western world: '... You fight in your way and we fight in ours; we fight when we can win and move away when we can't win ... you rely on modern weapons and we rely on highly conscious revolutionary people; you give full play to your superiority and we give full play to ours; you have your way of fighting and we have ours.' For Lin Piao, the issue is not in doubt since, as Mao has laid it down, 'All reactionaries are paper tigers'; and so, 'to despise the enemy strategically is an elementary requirement for a revolutionary.'

The intermediate zone is to become a vast battle-ground and 'in the final analysis the outcome of the war will be decided by the sustained fighting of the (Communist) ground forces, by the fighting at close quarters on battlefields, by the political consciousness of the men, by their courage and spirit of sacrifice.' The Russian fears that revolutionary guerrilla warfare campaigns—'liberation wars'—are a danger to world peace are contemptuously dismissed. But should this in fact happen? 'If the U.S. imperialists should insist on launching a third world war, it can be stated categorically that many more hundreds of people will turn to socialism; the imperialists will then have little room left on the globe; and it is possible that the whole structure of imperialism will collapse.'

According to Lin Piao's analysis of the world situation, revolutionary guerrilla wars must proliferate. 'It is certain that such wars will develop vigorously. This is an *objective law*[1] independent of the will of either the U.S. imperialists or the Khrushchev revisionists. The revolutionary people of the world will sweep away everything that stands in the way of their advance.'

Lin Piao extends to the whole world a dictum of Mao's, to the effect that victory in guerrilla warfare depends upon controlling the countryside while the cities will drop like rotten fruit of themselves. 'Taking the entire globe, if North America and Western Europe can be called the "cities of the world", then Asia, Africa, and Latin America constitute the "rural areas of the world". Since World War II, the proletarian revolutionary movement has for various reasons been temporarily held back in the North American and West European capitalist countries, while the people's revolutionary movement in Asia, Africa and Latin America has been growing vigorously. In a sense, the contemporary world revolution also presents a picture of the encirclement of cities by the rural areas. In the final analysis, the whole cause of world revolution hinges on the revolutionary struggles of the Asian, African, and Latin American peoples who make up the overwhelming majority of the world's population.'

The vital significance of the struggle in Vietnam is clearly underlined. 'The U.S. aggressors are in danger of being swamped in the people's war in Vietnam. They are deeply worried that their defeat in Vietnam will lead to a chain reaction. They are expanding the war in an attempt to save themselves from defeat. But the more they expand the war, the greater will be the chain reaction. The more they escalate the war, the heavier will be their fall and the more disastrous their defeat. The people in other parts of the world will see still more clearly that what the Vietnamese people can do, they can do too.'

In the second half of 1966, during the profound upheavals in China leading to General Lin Piao being named Mao's heir, this document again assumed great theoretical prominence. Quite naturally, it was suggested by some Western observers that this argument can hardly be taken at its face value as a profession of practical politics; that it is not a plan which China can implement but rather a morale-boosting statement of aspirations. On the other hand, *The Economist* pointed out editorially on 20th August 1966 that 'Until and unless there is solid evidence that China does not intend to do what Lin Piao says it wants to do, or cannot do it, the only safe assumption for the

[1] Author's italics.

Americans or anybody else to make is that the Chinese mean every word they say. That is where any sober Asia policy starts from.'

It would perhaps be better to regard the South Vietnamese struggle as a 'test case' for a *certain kind of warfare*; revolutionary warfare; and for its response, counter-insurgency. What is at issue is not so much what China itself can or cannot do, but the proof or rebuttal of the Chinese Communists' belief that they have devised a kind of revolutionary warfare that is based on a *scientific* understanding of the laws of warfare and of the social laws of development that obtain in the under-developed countries of the world. The Peking-line Communist insurgents are concerned to demonstrate, particularly in South Vietnam, that what Mao's theory declares to be an ineluctable historical process is in fact what it claims to be. Ideologically, 'China is engaged in a holy crusade to establish credibility before the rest of the world. In that respect, we're both hung on the same hook,' as an American diplomat phrased it.[1] The contest in South Vietnam therefore is enormously important for the Peking-line version of the future of Communism in the under-developed world. General Giap's belief that 'if we win here, we shall win everywhere' will seem to have been made valid in a test case which American public opinion is highly unlikely to permit being repeated elsewhere. More than 500,000 American servicemen and all the genius of American technology that can be used in tropical conditions have been brought to bear in South Vietnam. The Americans too believe this to be a test case.

It is as well to underline the very great dangers involved in the present struggle. Even if Communism is defeated in South Vietnam —really, politically defeated—even if South Vietnam is successfully pacified; even if the pacification also permits the stabilization of South-East Asia, the struggle can be begun all over again by the Communists. There is reason to suppose that all manner of exploitable 'contradictions' will subsist in South-East Asian societies for decades to come; reason to suppose that serious administrative and political defects will continue to exist in the political societies of that region. The U.S.A. has insistently maintained that it will not seek to destroy the Communist regime in North Vietnam, the revolutionary base for the subversion of the South; the rebuilding of the Southern society into one proof against Communist insurgency will be a huge task. Short of some presently unforeseeable diplomatic agreement between Washington and Moscow, which itself would depend upon a hitherto unforeseeable Moscow dominance in Hanoi, it is likely that half a

[1] *Time*, 9th September 1966.

million Americans will be engaged in South Vietnam for five years more in the task of pacification alone.

It is not intended at this point to explore such matters further, except to remark that whereas an American 'victory' in South Vietnam will not necessarily stabilize the region in a long-term fashion, a Communist victory would undoubtedly destroy the will of the other non-Communist nations of South-East Asia steadfastly to combat the stepped-up campaigns of Communist insurgency that would quite soon be directed against them; and it would equally undoubtedly persuade their governments to disavow their alignments with the West. The kind of suffering and destruction occurring in South Vietnam is countenanced only because of the significance of the struggle being waged there. If the struggle proves to have been in vain, then degrees of suffering and destruction will certainly not be accepted by its neighbours. Nor—even more importantly—will it be countenanced again by the public of the United States of America.

And here perhaps lies the greatest danger of all. The U.S.A. can scarcely afford now to appear to have been induced to withdraw from South Vietnam through exhaustion of spirit; but it is still possible that it will be induced to agree to a political settlement that appears to be honourable and satisfactory but proves a little later not to have been satisfactory at all. In which case it is to be expected that the cry will go up in the U.S.A. of 'No more Vietnams!' Apparently thwarted in South Vietnam, Hanoi can then escalate insurgency in Laos to the point where the non-Communist Laotian government cannot cope with it. Laos can be used even during the build-up of insurgency there as a revolutionary base for the prosecution of revolutionary warfare in North-East Thailand and in the Thai–Malayan border area.

What is basically at issue is the new form of warfare, a fusion of Communist political guerrilla behaviour and organization with the traditional skills of guerrilla fighting, and this is what is meant by revolutionary guerrilla warfare.

Chapter 6

THE NATURE OF REVOLUTIONARY GUERRILLA WARFARE

In order to understand Communist revolutionary warfare, it is necessary first to distinguish it from the more traditional type of guerrilla warfare.[1] Though the former must use the *military* techniques of the latter, they are by no means the same kind of warfare politically. As its name denotes, guerrilla warfare is concerned with small wars; often enough in the past there have been wars within wars. This is not to say that very large numbers of people may not be involved, in one way or another, in guerrilla warfare; only that *operations* are normally small-scale. When they have not been, they have usually been disastrous. It may be described as a kind of warfare in which 'the strategically weaker side assumes the tactical offensive in selected forms, times, and places.'[2] The necessity for the guerrilla to seize and retain the initiative is a condition not only of his success but of his continuing existence.

This is because guerrilla warfare is a form of warfare carried out by irregular forces which dispose of inferior fire-power and logistic support in general. They must, as a consequence, keep the initiative through superior mobility, which in turn depends upon a superior knowledge of the geographical terrain and a superior control over (or support from) the 'human terrain'; the society amongst which the war is being fought. Traditional guerrilla warfare also normally includes the substitution of local skills and native ingenuity for the technological and organizational strength of the regular forces opposing them: the substitution of hit-and-run raids or sabotage for fire-power and mechanized transport, ambushes for orthodox manœuvres, the countryside for strong garrisons, mantraps for strongpoints, road destruction for motorized transport, and so on; above all perhaps in modern times, the substitution of men for machines. As T. E. Law-

---

[1] As a result of experiences in Indo-China, the Algerian National Liberation Front appreciated this difference and adopted a Communist-style approach to organization, agitprop, etc.

[2] Franklin M. Osanka (Editor), *Modern Guerrilla Warfare*, op. cit.

rence put it, 'In the Turkish Army materials were scarce and precious, men more plentiful than equipment . . . the aim should be to destroy not the army but the materials,'[1] and a Communist writer confirms that he was as good as his words, '(Lawrence) struck at the weak points of the bourgeois fighting machine, at its clumsy technical apparatus, its inefficiency, its dependence upon supplies.'[2] This has been expressed by General Giap as the 'superiority of the man against the gun.'

Mao Tse-tung developed a theory of substitutions, believing that 'space in China could be made to yield to time, and time, revolutionary organization, and political cohesion, victory . . .'; and he proposed the 'substitution of propaganda for guns, subversion for airpower, men for machines, space for mechanization, political for industrial mobilization.' Some of the things Mao is saying belong to traditional guerrilla thinking; some to revolutionary guerrilla thinking. The differences will be examined below. What the author is attempting to establish here is this: there are certain features of guerrilla warfare, revolutionary as well as traditional, which involve the pitting of material weakness and local ingenuity against apparently overwhelmingly superior forces; and these features have come to confer upon guerrilla warfare of any kind a certain attractiveness of spirit—Davids against Goliaths, Caractacuses against legions, 'peasants' against 'mercenaries', individuals against machines. The Communists have quite improperly become identified with this spirit in places like South Vietnam.

To the urbanized Western intellectual, weary of liberal capitalism, yet disenchanted with the Soviet Union, the revolutionary guerrilla often takes on the characteristics of a new type of Rousseau's 'noble savage', fighting to retain the primitive simplicity of his tropical paradise against the onslaught of a gigantic, Western military machine—the monstrous enfleshment in steel of everything such an intellectual has come to hate in his own civilization. That it is not really quite like that for marine ambush patrols in the scrub around Danang's Marble Mountain is beside the point for such a Western opinion-maker.

Of course, this fantasy is deliberately fed by Communists and fellow-travellers in the West. An Australian Communist pamphlet published in 1965 argued that in so far as it is a war at all in South Vietnam, as opposed to a spontaneous and indigenous rising of peasants, it is in the tradition of Wolfe Tone or Nehru or Kenneth

[1] *The Seven Pillars of Wisdom*, Jonathan Cape, 1946.
[2] Christopher Caudwell, *Studies in a Dying Culture*, The Bodley Head, 1951.

Kaunda or Nasser . . . or George Washington: 'They (Australian Liberals) try to pin it all on Mao Tse-tung when it is really the spirit of Washington as well, of Andreas Hofer, Garibaldi, Jose Marti, Ben Bella, Australia's Peter Lalor and of every other patriot who has ever led his people against apparently hopeless odds. . . . All that is really new about it is the unparalleled ferocity with which it is being waged by the foreign forces of suppression, and the correspondingly unsurpassed courage shown in it by the popular forces.' Such romantically erroneous notions are held by many people in the West who are in no wise Communist sympathizers.

Another reason for the often gross misunderstanding in the West of what revolutionary war is all about stems from the growth of a double-standard of judgement which is very prevalent in self-styled liberal progressive quarters. This malaise was nicely analysed by an Indian observer of the American scene: 'Marxism in America is made up of many strands. Some of the more salient ones are:

'(1) It specializes in double-think. It has two standards. One by which to judge its own country and other free countries, another by which to judge Russia and China and Communism in general. . . . It judges America ethically, Russia dialectically; America in terms of performances, Russia in terms of promises and plans; America realistically, Russia doctrinally. Whatever America may or may not do; America is always in the wrong; whatever crimes Russia and China may perpetrate there is always some reason or justification or provocation for them.

'(2) It is self-alienated and it has a guilt complex. It lacks the discipline and conviction of Communism, but it does flirt with it from the cozy comforts and freedoms of America. It is difficult to say whom it hates more, whether those who see any bad in Russia or those who see any good in America.

'(3) It is anti-Communist in its temper. Narrate before an American audience the worst crimes of Stalin and Mao . . . and the Americans are the very embodiment of patience and understanding, self-recollectedness and cool judgement. But just mention the name of Chiang or Rhee or Diem or McCarthy, and the calm perfection of their cool mien is easily disturbed.

'(4) The tactics of the American liberals is varied. At present they do not say that Stalin or Mao are wonderful. They only propagate that those who may be fighting Stalinism or Maoism are 'corrupt'. Moscow's and Peking's 'reactionaries' very soon become Washington's 'corrupts', thanks to these Marxists. The two accusations from these

THE NATURE OF REVOLUTIONARY GUERRILLA WARFARE

two quarters go together so uniformly and invariably that one can rightly assume a psychological affinity between the two.

'This American liberalism or Marxism has no fixed form, no stereotyped language like the Communists', but it is a great unnamed, almost anonymous force. But it is not unidentifiable. It is soft and sentimental; it sounds reasonable and scholarly; it is roomy, bright and superficial. It feeds on illusion, ignorance and cowardice. With such an amalgam of qualities, it is the best aid and ally of an aggressive force like Communism.'[1]

In the West this double-standard of judgement is greatly exacerbated in the case of Asian problems by a guilty conscience about the past. It is one of the penalties of vicarious living to be burdened with guilt about events in which one has never participated. The guilt-laden double-standard is further exacerbated by the belief that revolutionary warfare is not really warfare at all but rather the expression of an irresistible social revolution in which the Communists just happen to be participating; the corollary of this belief is, quite naturally, the belief that revolutionary warfare cannot be opposed by military force.

Once this viewpoint is taken up, then military opposition to Communist warfare in Asia becomes by definition meaningless and so the evidence of Communist revolutionary warfare campaigns having been put down becomes irrelevant. It is not possible for the proponent of this understanding of events in Asia to see the point of Lucian Pye's argument, for example, to the effect that if an *alternative* kind of social revolution is to be brought about, then 'the matter of first priority must be to ensure that speculations about the outcome of violence cease to play such an important part in determining the behaviour of large numbers of Asians. This means in particular that it must be made clear that any Communist resort to violence will be met and defeated. We should not forget that from India to the Philippines, wherever countries have been given the opportunity to build up other defences against Communism, the opportunity has in each case followed from successful military opposition to the initial Communist challenge. Westerners should be able to appreciate why the political leaders in these countries have been anxious to minimize the roles that their armies played and have stressed instead their welfare programs . . . programs that can win popular support and hence elections . . . the very nature of the Communist appeal in societies

[1] Ram Swarup, *Documents of the Council Against Communist Aggression*, Philadelphia.

THE NATURE OF REVOLUTIONARY GUERRILLA WARFARE

involved in a process of rapid social change suggests that the use of force should be conceived of as an integral part of any counter-policy.'[1]

It is perhaps fair to remark that many Westerners who take up the viewpoint that revolutionary warfare cannot be combatted because it is merely a manifestation of certain vaguely defined revolutionary tendencies within 'emerging' societies are men who have never quite been able to shake off the belief that Communism represents the creed of the future; men who cannot admit to themselves that much of their lives has been spent in a condition of total misunderstanding and so, in the face of an obvious movement away from Communism in Europe, hope for a reprieve in the rice fields and tropical rain forests of South-East Asia, an area which their tired minds transmute from a battlefield into yet another cloudy abode of the Hegelian dialectic, the historical god in whom they still strive to find personal self-justification.

But there are other, more prosaic reasons why the nature of revolutionary warfare is still largely misunderstood in the West. One reason relates to the professional pride of Western military men, reinforced by a pride in technology as such, disturbed by a kind of warfare that is clearly not 'a soldier's war', yet uneasily aware that 'In the last war guerrillas were never decisively beaten by regular armies.'[2] Probably the greatest single mistake made during the Diem regime in South Vietnam was the American decision in 1954 to train a regular, Western-type army. It was not until 1961 that irregular warfare and its countering was taken truly seriously in the U.S.A. despite that country's huge overseas interests. As late as 1966 Sir Robert Thompson felt it necessary to point out that '. . . American military strategy should not be to deploy the maximum possible forces against the regular Viet Cong and PAVN units just to inflict casualties, as it is at present. It should be rather to commit the minimum forces against them sufficient only to keep the Viet Cong dispersed and off-balance. Thus the remainder of the American troops could then be committed to providing the punch and protection without which the pacification programme, still left almost entirely in Vietnamese hands, will not gather momentum.'[3]

[1] Lucian Pye, *Guerrilla Communism in Malaya*, op. cit.
[2] C. M. Woodhouse in Otto Heilbrunn, *Partisan Warfare*, George Allen and Unwin, 1962.
[3] *The Australian*, Canberra, 22nd August, 1966. But in 1967 the North Vietnamese army, by poising 3–5 divisions on the border of North and South Vietnam, began to pose a potential invasion threat on a grand scale, thus tying down large American forces in the north of South Vietnam.

Above all, the Western citizen of an industrialized society just is not, as Fidel Castro put it, 'guerrilla minded'. The modern state has rendered guerrilla warfare impossible except in conditions of acute civic breakdown and then, for the most part, only in geographically remote areas. It is a form of warfare virtually impossible in cities at any time, except in an auxiliary role: for example, the Polish Home army had a far deeper 'popular support' than the French F.F.I. and F.T. but because the Russian army was deliberately stopped outside Warsaw the Home army was destroyed, whereas the French Resistance was able to operate and survive in Paris as an auxiliary of the advancing Allied armies. Even Che Guevara who paid considerable attention to the problem of fighting in built-up areas was constrained to remark that 'the suburban guerrilla is working in exceptionally unfavourable terrain, where risks and consequences of exposure are tremendous. There is only little distance between the guerrilla's point of action and his refuge, so night action must predominate.'[1]

However, the difficulties lying in the way of a Westerner's understanding of guerrilla warfare go much deeper than a mere lack of experience of it. Guerrilla behaviour, though acceptable to a few Westerners for a short time in the extraordinary conditions of war, goes against the whole tradition of civic orderliness and peaceful habit, which has been one of the great achievements of modern nationalism in times of international peace. (It is not without significance that the erstwhile anarchistic 'beatnik', rebelling against the whole social order at home, easily becomes the temporarily disciplined 'Veatnik' demonstrator.) It is something close to a century since that profound student of insurrectionary warfare, Friedrich Engels, remarked sadly, 'It seems that only the barbarians have recognized and made use of the right to fight individually and the civilized nations conform to a certain etiquette that precludes them from fighting on after the official capitulation.'[2] World War II disproved this in certain circumstances, the essential circumstance being the presence of an occupation army.

This goes to the centre of the non-Communist tradition of guerrilla warfare; it is a tradition of warfare directed against occupying armies or foreign administrations. It is not necessarily carried on by the representatives of nations against foreign domination; it may be carried on by a region which sees its cultural integrity threatened by the policies of a modernizing central government. Such was the case with la Vendée during the French Revolution; such is the case today

[1] *Guerrilla Warfare* op cit.
[2] F. O. Miksche, *Secret Forces* op. cit.

with the insurgents in the Shan and Kachin States of Burma. In such cases the government and army of 'the Centre' takes on the appearance of a religious (in la Vendée) or racial (in the Kachin and Shan states) threat. In the Middle East during the First World War the struggle was more complicated in that it was the actual course of the struggle against foreign (Turkish) rule that seemed likely to determine the extent of the Arab kingdom-nations to be established as a result.

But the common feature of these guerrilla campaigns—and the common feature of all traditional guerrilla campaigns—was that they were waged in favour of something that was already *in being*. The struggle was not in itself concerned with altering anything apart from the physical presence of what was regarded as (in some sense or other) foreign over-lordship. In this sense, traditional guerrilla warfare is conservative; it aims to preserve things regarded as precious by the leaders of the revolt, by ridding the country or region of any power that seems to threaten these things, the political independence of the people involved, above all. This does not necessarily mean that the leaders of a guerrilla war are conservative *within* their society; it simply means that the guerrilla struggle is wholly subordinated to the one aim of political independence.

This, as will be shown, is what separates traditional from revolutionary guerrilla warfare. As a corollary to the conservatism of the traditional guerrilla struggle *qua* guerrilla struggle there is its defensive nature: it is concerned to rid a country or region of foreign domination, not to carry the struggle further against the occupying power or centralizing overlord. This is the very heart of the matter. As a result of its conservatism and its defensive character it is not ideological in the modern, totalitarian meaning of the term at all—a meaning which always carries within it connotations of an expansionist dynamic and an aggressiveness directed against neighbouring countries with different political systems.

Again, this is not to say there is no 'ideology' attached to traditional insurgency; some kind of widely acceptable, coherent set of beliefs normally keeps the guerrilla leaders fighting. But this 'ideology' is something *in being*, something that does not have to be imposed as part of the struggle. The guerrilla campaign is designed to liberate this politically. It may be a sense of loyalty to a native leader fighting against the Turk in the Hejaz, it may be Catholicism fighting against the Protestant overlord in Ireland. But it is *there* before the struggle commences. It informs the struggle in all probability; but it does not form it. The Cause in such cases is a real, straightforward one, springing from within, intuitively understood, and accepted by its exponents; not something that arises out of, or is imposed by, the political nature of the guerrilla fighting itself. Traditional guerrilla warfare is designed to open up an area of freedom; Communist revolutionary warfare is specifically designed to contract the area of freedom within the confines of the totalitarian power of the Communist party.

The indigenous advantage of guerrillas against the orthodox forces of Western colonial power—superior mobility—was noticed in Java by the Dutch: 'The most feared of Javanese military tactics was the surprise attack. The Dutch repeatedly fell victim to it, especially when they had ventured over-boldly too far in battle.'[1] It was quickly noticed in the First Indo-China War. Indeed M. Jean Lacouture finds in the Red River delta of North Vietnam in 1953 what Sir Charles Crosthwaite found in the North Shan State in 1886. As the Filipino Communist Luz Taruc put it, 'The plain below changes hands at night: in the daytime it is an oppressed area, ruled by military police and civilian guards, but when night falls it becomes a liberated region, where the people receive our (guerrilla) soldiers with open arms.'

This factor of retaining the initiative, superior mobility and superior intelligence, is not of course confined to Asian conditions. During the Second World War Soviet partisans spectacularly carried out Stalin's instruction of 3rd July 1941: 'In the area occupied by the enemy, partisan units on foot and horseback must be organized to fight hostile detachments . . . blow up bridges and roads, interrupt phone and telegraphic communications and set camps and depots afire. In the occupied areas, insufferable conditions must be created for the enemy; you must follow him everywhere and annihilate his forces. 'Operating as auxiliaries of the Red Army, though under separate command, the Soviet partisans came to dominate 'nearly the entire rear area, and it took every effort of the Germans to keep their one remaining supply route open. . . .'[2] No less than 10,000 partisans' operations were launched before the beginning of the Russian breakthrough in the Bobruisk-Vitebsk area in June 1944. Space, long lines of communications, and a 2,000-mile front allowed the partisans

---

[1] B. Shrieke, *Indonesian Sociological Studies* Part II, J. Brill, 1957. Similar tribute is paid by B. Snodgrass, *The Burmese War*, London, 1827. The works of Sir Hugh Clifford, especially *Bushwhacking*, Harper, New York 1929 is interesting on the problems of 'pacification' in Malaya.

[2] Otto Heilbrunn in F. M. Osanka op. cit. Also Otto Heilbrunn: *Partisan Warfare*, op. cit.

THE NATURE OF REVOLUTIONARY GUERRILLA WARFARE

scope for what was essentially *traditional* guerrilla warfare: a patriotic resistance engendered by the atrocious behaviour of the German Army and designed simply to protect the *status quo* against the Germans.

In the 'thirties in the Middle East a distinguished Englishman saw fit to observe that 'the greatest Power in the world, after near twenty years' experience and experiment, required, in full peace time, an army corps and all the panoply of war to control the 'liberated' population; and the Arabs are able to boast that that in calling off a guerrilla warfare maintained for six months, they yielded neither to British arms nor to the economic necessity of salving their orange crops but to the advice of an Arab (High Command).'[1]

Now though the examples cited all belong to what has been called traditional guerrilla warfare, it became dimly perceptible from the time of the Spanish guerrilla war against the Napoleonic armies, onwards that this kind of military struggle, depending as it did upon popular support, or at least the control of the inhabitants, contained within it political potentialities. Despite the fact that he always considered guerrilla warfare as basically an auxiliary form of struggle, Clausewitz saw not only that 'their (Spanish) universal uprisings interfered with the French armies so much so that the latter were frittered away in small operations without achieving anything decisive' but that 'when, as in Spain . . . the war is for the most part carried on by means of a people's war . . . a truly new power is formed. . . . People's warfare (Volkskrieg) introduces a means of defence peculiar to itself.'

'A truly new power is formed . . .' The development of this potentiality was to be the achievement of Mao Tse-tung, Chu-teh, and the Chinese Communists of Yenan in the 'thirties; and this because Communism as developed as a *technique* of revolution by Lenin *also* contained within itself certain political potentialities which alone could realize the 'truly new power' formed by popular guerrilla warfare. However, between traditional guerrilla warfare, which was always fundamentally a tactical tradition, and revolutionary guerrilla warfare, which has become a strategy for catastrophically altering the balance of world power through the 'Communization' of the underdeveloped 'third world', there stands the thought of that strange man of genius, T. E. Lawrence.

Since Maoist revolutionary warfare is basically a fusing of traditional guerrilla warfare techniques with Leninist political guerrilla doctrine, there is no reason to suppose it would not have developed

[1] Sir Ronald Storrs, *Orientations*, Nicholson and Watson, 1955.

much as it did even if T. E. Lawrence had never lived. Nevertheless, there are three reasons for discussing Lawrence's concept of guerrilla warfare: first, there is good reason to suppose that in fact it has not gone unnoticed in the Communist countries; secondly, he first raised guerrilla warfare on to the plane of strategy; and thirdly, in the light of his thought, revolutionary guerrilla warfare more readily surrenders its meaning, since in some ways it is a half-way house between the two kinds of guerrilla warfare.

Like Mao (and like many of the leaders of European Communism), Lawrence was deeply interested in military history. Deeply impressed by a definition of strategy as 'the study of communications', he found himself operating in a theatre where enemy communications could fairly easily be kept under constant pressure by using 'the silent threat of a vast unknown desert, not disclosing ourselves until the moment of attack'.[1] The Turks had only their narrow gauge railway and Arabia was all about it. To an astonishing degree Lawrence's doctrine and practice anticipate many of the features to be found in the military guerrilla campaigns in China and, on a very much smaller scale, in Indo-China. There was the same retention of the initiative through mobile concentration spreading the 'infection of revolt' and there was the same striving after 'perfect "intelligence" '.[2] Lawrence believed in forcing a long period of passive defence on the enemy, he appreciated the importance of a base (Aqaba), he comprehended the inter-relation between distance and strength and between space and time ('Our cards were speed and time, not hitting power, and these gave us a strategical rather than a tactical strength. Range is more to strategy than force,') and he avoided attacking enemy garrisons. ('The garrison of Medina, reduced to a defensive size, were sitting in their trenches destroying their power of movement ... it was not a base for us ... what on earth did we want it for?') The parallels go down even to the smallest things; to the fabrication of primitive firing devices for mines and a realization that a certain kind of rations (admittedly the Western technological achievement of bully-beef, in the Asian case the shoulder-slung 'sausage' bag of rice) could modify 'land-war more profoundly than the invention of gunpowder'.[3]

[1] All quotations are from *The Seven Pillars of Wisdom* or Capt. B. H. Liddell-Hart's invaluable elucidation, *T. E. Lawrence: In Arabia and After*, Cape, 1934.
[2] Compare: 'For whereas Europe knew nothing of the Mongols, the latter were fully acquainted with European conditions, down to every detail, not excepting the family connections of the rulers.' Michael Prawdin, *The Mongol Empire*, Allen & Unwin, 1941.
[3] But he differed here from the revolutionary guerrilla. Though he was some-

But Lawrence understood something altogether more relevant as well; something that troubles even the finest counter-insurgent experts of the West today: he understood 'motivation', one of those quasi-military terms with which the West hopes—in the field—to disguise its psychological and political lack of understanding of what guerrilla warfare is 'all about'. Lawrence's understanding went beyond the traditional military guerrilla ability of the Vietcong to be everywhere and nowhere, as the French in Indo-China put it, through using the geographical and human environment and superior intelligence. He did indeed understand this problem; and he expressed it better than anyone has ever expressed it, before or since: 'but suppose we were an influence (as we might be), an idea, a thing invulnerable, intangible, without front or back, drifting about like gas? Armies were like plants, immobile as a whole, firm-rooted, nourished through long stems to the head. We might be vapour, blowing where we listed. Our kingdoms lay in each man's mind, and as we wanted nothing material to live on, so perhaps we offered nothing material to the killing. It seemed a regular soldier might be helpless without a target. He would own the ground he sat on, and what he could poke his rifle at.'

And so, nearly four decades later, the troops of the French Expeditionary Force would 'pull back into their blockhouses, drawing their blankets of barbed wire and concrete around them to keep out the chill fear of the night.'[1] The guerrillas were *partout et nulle partout*, like a vapour. There were great differences there, of course, but the psychology of the defenders in the posts like Xuan-Mai, Mo-Thon, Rong-Tam in the Red River delta were manipulated by the enemy in the same way. They learnt what Lawrence knew: '. . . to make war upon rebellion is a messy and slow business, like eating soup with a knife.' They returned deeply dispirited to France, asking themselves like Philippe de Pirey, rhetorical questions such as: 'And what was the main reason for the retreat from Hoa-Binh? The infiltration into this same region of three Viet-minh divisions'; or they died in Vietnam like Guy de Chaumont-Guitry, after noticing that it was nicer to be in Cambodia and Laos where 'one could walk around everywhere unarmed and the inhabitants accept us; or after losing Dien-Bien-Phu,

thing of a 'military romanticist', as Stuart Schram has described Mao Tse-tung, he knew he was not interiorally committed in a totalitarian sense; indeed, he knew, or suspected, that he was taking the Arabs for no more than a camel ride. So, unlike the Vietcong, he could not bring himself to mine trains carrying women and children.

[1] Denis Warner, *Out of the Gun*, op. cit., Hutchinson, 1956.

they railed, like the intelligence specialist General Henri Navarre, against 'la trahison et son allié: défaitisme'; or they simply saw early on, as General Sabatier did, that 'One cannot write or even pronounce the word "Indo-China" . . . without a sentiment made up of regrets, betrayed hopes and powerlessness.'[1]

But other Frenchmen like the parachutist prisoner of the Vietminh, Claude Goëdlhieux, perceived another element in the struggle: self-criticism, which caused a man to lose his individuality and produced, as Jean Lartéguy described it, 'a civilization of insects rooted in their certainty and efficiency.'[2] This seems to be far removed from T. E. Lawrence's 'brotherhood of the desert'. But it is not so. He was only too deeply aware of 'that science (Xenophon called it diathetic) of which our propaganda is a stained and ignoble part. Some of it concerns the crowd, the adjustment of spirit to the point where it becomes fit to exploit in action, the pre-arrangement of a changing opinion to a certain end. Some of it deals with individuals, and then it becomes a rare art of human kindness, transcending by purposeful emotion, the gradual logical sequence of our minds. It considers the capacity for mood of our men, their complexities and mutability, and the cultivation of what in them profits the intention. We had to arrange their minds in order to battle, just as carefully and as formally as other officers arranged their bodies: and not only our own men's minds, though them first: the minds of the enemy, so far as we could reach them: and thirdly, the mind of the nation supporting us behind the firing-line, and the minds of the hostile nation waiting the verdict, and the neutrals looking on.'[3]

This is a simply marvellous statement of the psychology of what Colonel Trinquier calls 'modern warfare'. It is something more and something less than Communist revolutionary warfare. It is something more because it is personal in an exemplary fashion; it is something altogether less because Lawrence was working with nomadic irregulars, adjusting amongst factions, conciliating and directing only subtly, through force of personality not by way of ideology, bribing with gold, appealing to individual ambitions, inflaming appetites within a movement whose only real purpose was to rid the Arab lands

---

[1] Philippe de Pirey, *Operation Waste*, Arco Publications, 1954; Guy de Chaumont-Guitry, *Lettres d'Indochine*, Editions Alsatia, 1951; Henri Navarre, *Agonie de L'Indochine*, Plon, 1956; Général G. Sabatier, *Le Destin de L'Indochine*, Plon, 1952.

[2] Claude Goëldhieux, *Quinze Mois prisonnier chez les Viets*, Julliard, 1953; Jean Lartéguy, *The Centurions*, E. P. Dutton & Company, 1961.

[3] *Seven Pillars*. op. cit.

of the Turkish overlord. It was a loose and fragile unity as soon as the guns ceased firing: an altogether uncertain political purpose so far as ultimate aims were concerned; and plans were always in the long run prisoners of Great Powers whose aircraft could all too easily 'sink' the 'ships of the desert'.[1]

For Communists revolutionary guerrilla warfare is something altogether different. It is simply 'the continuation of the revolution by other means', as Lenin put it. It is not something imposed upon Communist parties; nor is it something chosen in general preference to other forms of political struggle. Communists do not think like that. Lenin again: '.... Marxism does not tie the movement to any particular combat method. It recognizes the possibility that struggle may assume the most variegated forms. For that matter, Marxism does not "invent" those forms of struggle. It merely organizes the tactics of strife and renders them suitable for general use.' Lenin was above all a master of the 'tactics of strife'; and today his most eminent successors in this regard are the Peking-line Communists.[2]

Communist politics are always guerrilla politics, as has already been shown; the 'armed struggle', revolutionary guerrilla warfare, is simply the most appropriate form of political activity in given circumstances and it is at all times subordinated to political aims. 'Legal' status and 'parliamentary struggle' are always preferred. It is a pleasant democratic myth that proscribing a Communist party enhances its power. There is a special reason for this: the Bolshevik 'organizational weapon', being necessarily small, must have access to as many avenues of penetration in the state as possible. It needs freedom of movement in order to advance in power through 'front' organizations. These 'front' organizations are an important component of revolutionary guerrilla warfare as well but in the case of the proscription of the Communist party such fronts are much less easy to control; and there is a grave risk of their being proscribed too.[3]

[1] Compare the personal difference between T. E. Lawrence and Vo Nguyen Giap. The former: 'All our subject provinces to me were not worth one dead Englishman.' The latter: 'Chaque minute, il meurt des centaines de milliers d'hommes sur la toute de la terre. La vie et la mort de cent, de mille, de dizaines de milliers d'humains, fussent-ils nos compatriotes, cela represente peu de chose.' Qu. in Bernard Fall, *Le Vietminh*: 1945–60, Armand Colin, 1960. As Lawrence remarked once, 'All men dream; but not equally.'

[2] Leonard Schapiro, '... Mao is committed much less to a doctrine or to an ideology than to a method or a tactic—which is what Leninism essentially is.' *Problems of Communism* Sept.–Oct. 1966.

[3] Which is precisely what happened in Diem's South Vietnam; and which gave rise to his now much discussed Law 10/59 and the Policy Statement of late 1959, which are to be found on page 268 ff. in Marvin E. Gettleman, *Vietnam:*

THE NATURE OF REVOLUTIONARY GUERRILLA WARFARE

What is chiefly at issue in a revolutionary guerrilla warfare campaign is the expansion (or contraction) or a certain kind of political, armed organization—an alternative administration or 'parallel hierarchies' as Bernard Fall calls them. The administration is simply the extension of Communist party power, although this is often the reverse of obvious. What advances in a revolutionary guerrilla war is not primarily an army of irregulars but a totalitarian, armed political society. In fact, the two are indistinguishable. As *Les Temps Modernes* of August–September 1953 put it, quite correctly: 'Free Vietnam (i.e. the Communist zone) is first of all an army.'

This is where revolutionary guerrilla warfare altogether parts company with traditional guerrilla warfare—though naturally on the military level the rules of guerrilla warfare appear to be the same. The struggle is not directed towards *opening up* the political future, for a society in being oppressed by foreign domination. It is precisely designed to culminate in the *closing* of the future by the Communist party controlling the insurgency. Indeed the actual course of the revolutionary war is, or should be, the creation of the new society and it is here, and not in any of the absurd theoretical arguments as to whether Maoism is, one might almost say (but for the absence of God) 'theologically' different from the Soviet tradition, that the originality of Peking-line Communism lies. It is not that, it is just that having had to choose, in certain circumstances remote from Europe's, the method of military guerrilla warfare, these Communists have come to realize that '. . . a truly new power is formed'. As Mao has put it, 'When the Red Army fights, it fights not merely for the sake of fighting but to agitate the masses, to organize them, to arm them, and to help them establish revolutionary political power; apart from such objectives, fighting loses its meaning and the Red Army its reason for existence.' Or as Giap puts it, 'The Army is the Party, the Party is the Army.' Of course it is put in this stark fashion only *after* victory; before that, the party, like every other Communist party in the world, 'mobilizes' the masses under disguised slogans and under a generally acceptable Cause, which has nothing overtly to do with Communism at all.[1]

History, Documents, and Opinions on a Major World Crisis, Penguin Special. 1966. This will be discussed later in the book.

[1] For example, in Truong Chinh's classic *The Resistance Will Win* op. cit., the party is not mentioned until page 127 in a book of 157 pages. Eventually he writes: 'We must bear in mind that neither the Vietnamese revolution as a whole nor this resistance war can be successful without the leadership of the Communist party.' The English language editor points out that the party was

THE NATURE OF REVOLUTIONARY GUERRILLA WARFARE

Nevertheless the transforming, revolutionary role of the Popular Army (which will be examined further later on) does not mean that this kind of armed struggle is a matter of general preference. It is simply a matter of transforming the political struggle into armed struggle at a given moment for specific reasons. For example, in China the attempt was first made to use 'the machinery of the national-revolutionary (i.e. Kuomintang) government ... to reach the peasantry ... The Communists and their revolutionary allies must penetrate the new governments (in the provinces), so as to give practical expression to their agrarian programme by using the governmental machinery to confiscate land, reduce taxes, invest real power in the peasant committees. . . .'[1]

Admittedly this is a Comintern directive made as part of a policy that in the event proved disastrous; and the disaster had as one consequence the establishment of the Communist agrarian base in Yenan. But as late as 1940 Mao was arguing in favour of a two-step revolution, the immediate stage of which was to be a 'joint dictatorship of all revolutionary classes', a coalition in which the Communist party, because of its far greater organizational efficiency, would quickly be master. Later, moves were made seeking a coalition government with the Kuomintang. The armed struggle is *always* subordinated to the exigencies of political strategy. Precisely the same thing occurred in Vietnam in the 1940's. As will be shown there was no question of an armed insurrection until all possibilities of playing off the interested parties against each other had been exhausted and indeed until the superior world-strategic possibilities of Communism coming to power in France had been proved a chimera. The armed struggle in South Vietnam would be called off tomorrow if it were believed that the National Liberation Front might well win at the conference table what it could clearly not win in the paddy-fields and tropical rain forests. The aim would be to enter a coalition from a position of strength sufficient to enable the N.L.F. to do what the Communists did in Czechoslovakia: make the coalition *irreversible* (a condition that would doubtless be favoured by a tired U.S.A. in the process of withdrawing) and slowly reduce to political impotence the 'partners' in the coalition, as has been done in China and North Vietnam.

This kind of struggle is preferred for a profound reason which is

in fact dissolved at this time, adding 'in truth (the party) continued its activities.'
[1] Robert V. Daniels (Editor), *A Documentary History of Communism*, Volume 2, Vintage Books, 1962.

157

nicely adumbrated by Selznick: 'The nature of Bolshevism cannot be understood unless we grasp the fact that Leninist political doctrine rests upon a broad interpretation of the nature of power. In particular, Bolshevik theory and practice recognize that power is *social*, generated in the course of all types of action (not simply the narrowly 'political') and latent in all institutions. This insight stems in part from basic Marxist theory and in part from the over-all aim of Bolshevism—a transformation of society that will invest every institution with political meaning.' Or as F. O. Miksche has put it, 'The basic element of the People's War is political infiltration through the weak spots of the State's social structure.'[1]

However, for a number of reasons revolutionary guerrilla warfare is now being propagated by Peking and Hanoi as *the* form of struggle for the under-developed parts of the world. The reasons for the development of this doctrine are significant today. Some are obvious enough: the great successes in China and in Vietnam against the French; and the fact that nearly all the governments of Asia have barred Communist parties from participating in the 'parliamentary struggle'. This participation is not open to them in much of Latin America nor, to an increasing extent, in many African countries either. But there is also the positive side to revolutionary warfare doctrine. The struggle being waged in South Vietnam by the Communists is very much an *exemplary* struggle. In the far away Sierra de las Minas in Guatemala, for example, a revolutionary guerrilla leader claims that the *only* road to progress is 'following the road of China, Algeria, Cuba and Vietnam. We cannot make any reform except through a war against the reactionary forces, *and* probably against the North American Marines.'[2] He regards the Vietcong as 'the world's most heroic people'. What Peking doctrine is attempting to achieve is a notion of third world solidarity acquired through the application of an apparently invincible politico-military technique: People's War.

The strategy is to incite by successful example this kind of struggle in as many countries as possible in order to dissipate American military energies through impelling the dispersal of U.S. forces in protracted and seemingly inconclusive 'brush fire' wars to the point where the

[1] Compare Selznick: 'As the Communist technique for penetrating the nerve centres of society is perfected, as the target is extended from key industries and mass movements to government itself, the need for a background of mass upheavals diminishes. The party comes to rely increasingly on its devices of penetration and control, as guided by its own general staff.' *The Organizational Weapon* op. cit.
[2] *Saturday Evening Post*, 18th June 1966.

THE NATURE OF REVOLUTIONARY GUERRILLA WARFARE

cost in lives and material appears altogether disproportionate to the results achieved. It is by no means certain that this strategy will not prove politically successful; it is quite certain that an inconclusive termination of the struggle in South Vietnam will go far towards achieving the strategic objective.

But revolutionary warfare within countries has come to have its special *raison d'être* for Peking-line Communism, and it is to this problem that a return must be made. In revolutionary guerrilla warfare the Popular Army becomes the primary instrument of social change under control of the Communist party. As Giap says, 'The party's leadership of the army is an absolute one. The party is the founder, organizer and educator of the army . . . the system of party committee and political commissar must be firmly maintained . . . a people's war is essentially a peasants' war under the leadership of the working class (read: Communist party). . . . Each person a soldier, each village a fortress, and each party branch a resistance staff.'

Now as was shown earlier there are clear echoes here of the militarized style of politics that is Communist practice everywhere. But as a result of protracted struggle the emphasis shifts: 'Free Vietnam is first of all an army (The civilian intellectuals of *Les Temps Modernes* were after all only quoting Giap); the Popular Army is the expression of the people; the army organizes the people, incarnates the people.' The intensification of revolutionary warfare results in the absorption of the masses by military and political pressures into an all-embracing totalitarian system, into which men are mobilized under false colours or disguised objectives in order to *change* them. The Popular Army is the Communist party's instrument for effecting the social revolution.

It is indeed a class struggle as the Communists see it: 'War is a social phenomenon', as Mao puts it, 'evolved from the system of private ownership and the existence of classes in society. War is the highest and most logical instrument to solve the contradictory interests between classes, nations, races, or any political entities.'[1] And so: 'The main task of revolution is the seizure of political power by force and the solution of all problems is war.' Given this understanding, it is quite natural to believe that, 'Political power comes from rifles. Rifles can found a school, build a civilization and start a popular movement.' But the Communist party must always 'control the rifle, and not the rifle control the party.' Struggle and violence lie at the heart of the

[1] Mao's obsession with the 'theory of contradictions' leads him to find it even as an explanation of aspects of family life.

problem for Mao: 'The postulate must also be clear that only such freedom as is precious is achieved in the process of hard struggle and at the price of human blood, in distinction from those methods which are used by our close enemies.' There is no nonsense about spontaneous peasant risings against injustice in this understanding of the process of history: 'Wherever the Red Army goes, it finds the masses cold and reserved; only after propaganda and agitation do they slowly arouse themselves. . . . The Red Army is like a furnace in which all captured soldiers are melted down and transformed the moment they come over'. . . . 'A truly new power is born,' as Clausewitz dimly perceived.

The art of Communist revolutionary warfare consists in slowly permeating the society under attack with its own armed political infrastructure before subversion has been properly recognized as such and combatted by the government of that society. Once the struggle has been joined, then the art lies in creating such a state of disorder and distress by the disruption of the society under attack that it can only be dealt with by a totalitarian organization such as that which the armed Communist society (the Popular Army of all those under party control) knows how to provide. A tough, disciplined, centrally controlled 'society' advances, first by penetration and then by envelopment, against a society that is of its nature altogether looser in structure, even if the government in question happens to be authoritarian.

A political intensification of the struggle in such a community, wracked by violence and emotionally distorted by the attendant uncertainties of existence, confers a great advantage upon the Communist revolutionary movement since it disposes of a superior organization, superior manipulative techniques, politically superior uses of violence, and a far more politically efficacious ideology. This intensification of revolutionary warfare is something very difficult for Westerners, their minds and attitudes informed at home by notions of conciliation, adjustment, compromise, and a recognition of limits to human behaviour, adequately to understand. It is very easy for a Westerner to interpret as expressions of popular, spontaneous endeavour—popular choice, in brief—situations where in actual fact the ordinary man is being plunged into a morass of fears and doubts, hemmed in by a jungle-like pressure of events, unable economically or unwilling for traditional reasons to flee, continually aware of a pervasive terror and near-chaos, aware also, after a time, that the Communist clandestine apparatus has largely supplanted the real authority of the government; and all too often that government forces, even if they do return, are inadequate in numbers to afford protection for long.

In such conditions there is no question but that Communism can exert a very real attraction. As M. Paul Mus remarked a long time ago, Communism does contain within itself a likeness to the state-religions of East Asia, a clearly explicable coherence and an all-embracing authority, and so can quite easily be seen as inheriting the new 'Mandate of Heaven'. Moreover, as will be shown in the next chapter the majority of men involved in the struggle believe themselves to be fighting for objectives both desirable and noble. This is where serious ambiguities enter the reports of most Western observers so far as the greatly debated question of 'popular support' is concerned.

It is not true that terror is the main motive power of the Popular Army; nor is it chiefly used for controlling the population in Communist-held areas *until* the moment comes, after victory, to pulverize that population through what is euphemistically known as 'land reform' in order to reduce to impotence any potential pluralist elements in the developing Communist totalitarian society. Terror, in the form of 'pinpoint coercion' is indeed used very largely, and always with political discrimination, to prepare the way for the gradual introduction of the Communist infrastructure; and it is used on a very large scale by way of reprisals and example in contested zones of the country. But within their own zones of control, their base areas, the Communists set about creating their own new society and this is done much more through analysis and explanation, and through implementing a local, genuine 'land reform' (which will of course be destroyed after victory), than through the inculcation of fear. It is true that the analysis and explanation are based on disguised objectives, but until the disguise is viciously torn away after victory masses of men are induced to fight for a Cause which they believe to be noble. Two quotations will perhaps illuminate the two poles of the new Communist society, the Popular Army:

'How do you want us to get across the barbed wire and the minefields?' inquired the sergeant (an Algerian serving with the French forces, after the French surrendered at Dien-Bien-Phu). 'Just walk across the bodies of our men,' said the (Vietminh) officer . . . the column came to a halt before a dying Viet-Minh, as the Communist soldiers were then called. He looked up and his lips were moving. 'Get going,' said the officer, 'you can step on him. He has done his duty for the Democratic Republic of Viet-Nam.'[1]

[1] Bernard Fall, *Viet-Nam Witness*, Praeger, 1966.

The second quotation is from the diary of a Vietcong medical officer: 'The most precious thing for a man is his life, because one has only one life. One must, then, live in such a way that one does not have to be ashamed of a pitiful past, that one is able to say before passing away: my whole life, my whole strength has been devoted to the most elevated and the most beautiful cause—the struggle for the liberation of mankind. . . .'[1]

On the one hand there is the pitiless totalitarian society gradually emerging; on the other hand the noble motives of many of these who have been inveigled into the struggle through disguised objectives and fraudulent Causes. And herein lies the tragedy of South Vietnam today: through a protracted form of political struggle, through endless analyses and explanations, through the repeated presentations of noble objectives having no relationship to ultimate Communist party purposes, large masses of Vietnamese fight with extraordinary courage in order to bring about a society in which, all unknown to them, the four corners of earth for which they fight will, in the case of victory, be forever denied to them. Only a Péguy could do justice to this situation.[2]

The point that is not noticed by liberal protestors against the American involvement in Vietnam is that this popular support is but part of a huge confidence trick; and that the essential element in the confidence trick is the engendering of warfare . . . 'the main form of the struggle is war, the main form of organization is the army . . . without armed struggle there will be no place for the proletariat, there will be no place for the people, there will be no place for the Communist party, and there will be no victory in revolution.' (Mao.)

Or again: 'When the Red Army fights, it fights not merely for the sake of fighting, but to agitate the masses, to organize them, to arm them, and to help them establish revolutionary political power; apart from such objectives fighting loses its meaning and the Red Army the reason for its existence.'

In actual fact in China the People's Liberation Army has by no means lost its reason for existence nearly twenty years after the fighting ended: 'All our economic, industrial, agricultural, and commercial departments must study the methods of the P.L.A., must establish and strengthen political work, and then, in this way, we can stimulate

---

[1] Bernard Fall (Editor), *The Viet-Nam Reader*, Random House, 1965.
[2] 'Heureux ceux qui sont morts pour quatre coins de terre . . . Heureux ceux qui sont morts pour la terre charnelle, Mais pourvu que ce fût dans une juste guerre . . .'

the revolutionary spirit of the millions and tens of millions of cadres and masses on the economic front.' (Mao, 1964.) Revolutionary warfare according to Mao has no end while the pulverization of human individuality remains incomplete.

Chapter 7

THE PROBLEMS CONFRONTING COUNTER-INSURGENCY

Communist revolutionary insurgencies in South-East Asia have normally grown outwards from base areas in which the Communists have established local authority through subversion. The major exception to this was the insurgency directed against the French occupying forces, from 1946 until 1954, by the Vietminh coalition government in North Vietnam. It has been an exception of the first importance, since this one successful Communist insurgency was mounted by a High Command which had to a large degree established a popularly recognized 'legitimacy' for itself (not least through the ruthless destruction of nationalist rivals, as well as by incorporating weaker nationalist groupings within the coalition) well before the fighting had begun. The special circumstances attending the Vietminh's assumption of power will be discussed later.

Usually the beginnings of insurgency are very much more difficult to detect and often extremely difficult to define. 'Because of this, a strategic planner of Western counter-insurgency operations is forced to throw away any notions of "quick-fix" plans and unidimensional (for example, economics or military dominated) solutions. He is compelled to scrutinize each insurgency by calling upon virtually all the disciplines of the social sciences. Once a Communist-sponsored insurgency has been identified, the planner is compelled to view this conflict within the microcosm of the specifically affected area and the macrocosm of the international arena.'[1]

It is at this point that the ambiguities and the arguments begin, so far as Western experts are concerned. At one pole of analysis, the emphasis is placed upon Communist conspiratorial methods; at the other upon indigenous notions of 'spontaneous' insurrection, an unplanned violent response to conditions that had come to be regarded as intolerable for one reason or another. This latter argument has even been used by a distinguished observer of South Vietnam in conditions

[1] John S. Pustay, *Counterinsurgency Warfare*, The Free Press, New York, 1965.

where a seasoned, widespread clandestine politico-military apparatus was known to exist.[1]

Of course, as Sir Robert Thompson has remarked, 'The use of the terms 'subversion' and 'insurgency' tends to suggest that the threat is rather ill-defined and abstract. This is not the case. The threat to the internal security of the country arises entirely from the actions and intentions of individual men and women engaged in the subversion or insurgency. It is the individual who plans to subvert others to carry out illegal acts against the state, and it is the individual, acting singly or in a group or in an armed unit, who carries out subversive or insurgent acts. It must therefore be the aim of the intelligence organization to identify such individuals, with a view to eliminating them or at least preventing them carrying out illegal acts against the security of the country.'

But this is to view the insurgency and those involved in it on a level quite different from that of the independent observer; and in the slow development of insurgency out of subversion it is this independent observer—whether he be a journalist or a military representative of a friendly Western power—who is so extremely important, since it is he who affects the decision (or lack of decision) of the potential ally of the government under attack. Very great pains are taken by the masters of a Communist insurgency to represent it as an indigenous and spontaneous rising. And 'it is fairly easy to devise an organizational structure capable of lending verisimilitude to a political fiction, doubly so if one is trying to deceive a foreign audience unversed in local political affairs.'[2]

This much may be said immediately: Communist revolutionary insurgency does not properly belong to the long history of agrarian jacqueries: they were outbreaks of rural violence engendered by the heat of peasant discontents; there was no need for extraneous political leadership to move the 'cold' peasantry to act. It is true that Utopian dreams may be found in this tradition of peasant revolt, but such movements were always dislocated by a lack of 'politically-educated' leadership and a kind of social 'gormlessness' that made it impossible to maintain any sustained campaign. Basically they were of acts of desperation in which the idealistic aspects were socially meaningless.

With the coming of the modern, futuristic revolutions, agrarian revolts were easily translated into a quite different kind of movement, political on the surface, led by men with ultimate aims altogether

[1] Philippe Devillers in Marvin Gettleman (Editor), *Vietnam, etc.*, op cit.
[2] George Carver, *The Faceless Vietcong*, Foreign Affairs April 1966.

dissimilar from that of the peasants. The Communist attitude to the peasants, those 'rural idiots' as Marx called them, was set out as long ago as 1905 by Lenin: 'Let us assume that the peasant uprising has been successful. The revolutionary peasant committees . . . can proceed to the confiscation of any property. We are in favour of confiscation. But to whom shall we recommend that the confiscated land be given? On this question we have not tied our hands nor shall we ever do so. . . . There will always be reactionary admixtures in the peasant movement and we shall declare war on them in advance . . . to whom shall the confiscated lands be given, and how? We do not gloss over that question, nor do we promise equal distribution, "socialization" etc. What we do say is that this is a question that we shall fight out later, fight out on a new field and with other allies. Then we shall certainly be with the rural proletariat, with the entire working class *against* the peasant bourgeoisie. . . .

'At first we support the peasant generally against the landlords . . . but at the same time we support the proletariat against the peasantry in general . . . we can and do say *only one thing:* we shall put every effort into assisting the entire peasantry to make the democratic revolution, in order thereby to make it easier for us, the party of the proletariat, to pass on as quickly as possible, to the new and higher task—the Socialist Revolution. . . .

'The urban and industrial proletariat will inevitably be the basic nucleus of our Social Democratic Labour party (Communist party), but we must attract to it, enlighten and organize all toilers and all the exploited—all without exception: handicraftsmen, paupers, beggars, servants, tramps, prostitutes—of course subject to the necessary and obligatory condition that they join the Social Democratic movement and not that the Social Democratic movement joins them, that they adopt the standpoint of the proletariat and not that the proletariat adopts theirs.'[1]

The essence of revolutionary guerrilla warfare as a political movement is contained in that statement of Lenin's; the history of the revolutionary warfare campaigns in South-East Asia is simply the working out of policy according to this prescription (or the failure to do so). As Philip Selznick puts it, 'The vanguard (the Communist party) is *persuaded*, is won over to Communism as a doctrine, but the masses are *manœuvred* into a position of struggle against the political and economic order.' And so, as Lenin recognized, the party must

[1] Quoted in J. F. C. Fuller, *The Conduct of War, 1789–1961*, Eyre and Spottiswoode, 1961.

always be on guard against finding itself caught up in the mass protest movements which it has to manœuvre in order to achieve its own, disguised ends. That the party has been able to succeed in keeping itself in control is the result of its special organizational principles, which have already been dealt with.[1]

And yet it is often argued that it is 'the land question' that is fundamental to Communist revolutions in South-East Asia, as it was earlier in Russia and China. According to this argument the Communist parties only reflect the great surges of peasant discontent with the prevailing system of land ownership, or at least that it is only by accident that they assume the political leadership of them. For example Professor David Mitrany: 'One might perhaps sum it up this way, that 1917 was a diffused peasant revolution which the Bolsheviks took in hand and organized. . . . Though passive, the Russian armies were still holding the front, but they quickly disintegrated when the peasant soldiers heard that the land was theirs for the taking.'[2] Leon Trotsky expressed the situation thus: 'To realize the Soviet State there was required a drawing together of two factors belonging to a completely different species: a peasant war—that is, a movement characteristic of the dawn of bourgeois development—and a proletarian insurrection, the movement signalizing its decline. That is the essence of 1917.'[3]

The 1917 Revolution is not in this regard a reliable guide to revolutionary warfare in South-East Asia, nor for that matter was the problem of land ownership in reality the cause of Communist revolution in China. The 'Land Question' as a component of revolutionary warfare is altogether more complicated. For example, the 'morcellement' of land in Tongking, the scene of one of the revolutionary warfare successes, was such that no major distribution of 'lands to the tiller' was conceivable.[4] North-East Thailand, the scene of major Communist revolutionary insurgency in 1966, has long suffered from Bangkok's neglect (and a very inadequate rainfall) but land ownership

---

[1] Compare the directive of the Central Committee of the Communist Party of Indo-China in March 1945 preparatory to the anti-French insurrection: 'the movement (the Vietminh coalition) must not be allowed to develop in breadth to the detriment of its development in depth . . .'
[2] *Marx against the Peasant*, Chapel Hill, 1951.
[3] ibid.
[4] David Galula, *Counterinsurgency Warfare*, Pall Mall Press, 1964, cites the relevant statistics from J. L. Buck's monumental *Land Utilization in China*, OUP, 1937, and remarks 'but this fact did not decrease in the slightest the psychological value of the slogan, "Land to the Tiller". An efficient propaganda machine can turn an artificial problem into a real one.'

or tenure is not the issue. Magsaysay's 'land reform' in the Philippines, to which so much of his success has been attributed by believers in the paramountcy of the 'Land Question', was in fact very limited in scope indeed. Other examples could easily be cited.

And yet Mao Tse-tung could write, 'The Kuomintang opposes the agrarian revolution. Hence it finds no peasant support. Despite the great size of its army it cannot arouse the voluntary effort, either of the bulk of the soldiers or of any of the low-ranking officers recruited from small producers to fight desperately on its behalf.' Of course, the Communists in China were greatly assisted by the attitude of the Kuomintang enemy in the later stages of the war: 'The task of the peasant is to provide us with information concerning the enemy, food and comforts for our encampment, and soldiers for our armies.' This attitude has too often characterized the regular armed forces of countries like Thailand and South Vietnam.

It is here that one approaches the kind of 'contradictions' within the under-developed world which the Communist agent versed in the techniques of agitation and propaganda is able so often effectively to exploit. The 'contradictions' between the privileged service-men, representing 'the Centre', and the villager with his strictly local loyalties and hopes is very often equalled by the 'contradiction' between the urban-trained provincial administrator, loathing service in the countryside and showing it all too frequently, and the traditional guardians of village customs and expectations. Sometimes even the police of relatively lowly rank are strangers to the villages in which they are serving; and even should they be of local origin they are usually to some extent estranged from the people by the very nature of their primary loyalty to 'the Centre'.[1] It is not always a matter of Communist attack on so-called 'feudal' privileged at all; just as often it is a question of playing the people off against the recipients of *new* privileges—the army in South Vietnam, for example, which became of local significance in most areas only after 1954. In this sense, Mr. Walt Rostow is right in calling the Communists 'the scavengers of the modernization process.' It is not in the least improbable that the more a government is concerned to modernize an under-developed country

---

[1] The beginning of an insurgency is excellently portrayed in Colin Mason, *Dragon Army*, Horwitz Publications, 1965, and in William J. Lederer and Eugene Burdick, *Sarkhan*, Putnam, 1966, though the latter authors, doubtless in the interest of fictional excitement, speed up events in a misleading fashion. The best answer to the armed exploitation of village-Centre 'contradictions' is the Police Field Force being trained in South Vietnam. This will be referred to again.

quickly, the more 'contradictions' there will be for the Communists to exploit. Moreover, it is the tensions involved in modernization which appear to threaten traditional orders of society such as, for example, the Buddhist monkhood in South Vietnam, who, because they feel vaguely threatened by forces they little understand, find it easy to identify the threat as being represented by the Catholic minority. The regional-minded likewise find it easy to see enemies amongst Saigon's ruling élite, especially when attention is drawn to its Northern component or indeed, under Diem's regime, to those who came from the region bordering the old capital of Hué.

However, while all exploitable 'contradictions' are used as opportunity arises in a revolutionary guerrilla war, the campaign is begun in peripheral areas. Whenever possible, the areas chosen are contiguous with, or at least easily accessible to, a 'privileged sanctuary', a Communist state which provides a refuge, a training area, arms and supplies of the kind necessary for the later, larger-scale phase of this protracted form of politico-military warfare. But some of these starting points, which are expanded into 'base areas' within the country, may be administratively rather than geographically peripheral: for example, Maquis (or Zone D) in South Vietnam, a rugged, densely covered hilly region offering great obstacles to penetration, economically useless, and so well suited to the construction of a 'base area', with all the right geographical features.

What do the Communists set out to achieve during the penetration of the peripheral areas during the subversive phase? Basically, they wish to supplant the existing administration with one of their own; and in time to transform the existing society into a society dominated by—indeed, incorporated in—the Popular Army, which is simply a tool of the Communist machine. The Communists know that the kind of society they are creating, at first only on the hamlet level, is politically *hard* and sociologically *dense* to a degree denied to their enemies. But during the subversive phase it is of the utmost importance *clandestinely* to build up the Communist apparatus within the chosen area. 'Pinpoint coercion', the assassination of those village officials likely to oppose Communist activity with vigour, must follow the build-up of at least a tentative 'alternative administration'; the assassinations simply reinforce its psychological authority. On the other hand, the basic work involved in setting up a network of Communist cells is done through 'armed propaganda' activities. It will be recalled that Giap's second platoon to be formed in the Popular Army was an armed propaganda platoon.

Rifles are necessary from the beginning; out of their barrels power grows. As a result of the Allied policy of supplying resistance movements with arms during World War II, it has nowhere been difficult in South-East Asia for insurgent movements to acquire sufficient arms with which to secure more by carefully planned attacks on country police stations and even on inadequately guarded depots. One of the reasons why the beginnings of insurgency have not been properly recognized is that since it is of the greatest importance to avoid any defeats during the mounting of an insurgency, considerable care is taken only to attack easy targets, a policy that often creates the impression of haphazard activity. This has often been written off for a time by the authorities as 'mere banditry'. Moreover, the essence of the art at this stage lies in a *slow* build-up, which again makes detection difficult. When, added to these two factors, there is the slovenly administration that obtains throughout most of rural South-East Asia, and the disinclination of indigenous governments of recently independent nations to admit (even to themselves) a loss of control, then it is easy to see how the subversive phase of revolutionary warfare is afforded a dangerous lead in point of time.

This is the aspect of the problem that could become critical if revolutionary warfare should spread on a world-wide scale, since the countering of revolutionary insurgency in its later phases is a simply immense task and one in which there is a limit to what even the U.S.A., with all its will and resources, can reasonably be expected to undertake. Unfortunately, however, obviously vital as is the early detection of, and response to, revolutionary subversion, there is an inbuilt unwillingness on the part of recently independent governments (and this is shared even by the Thai government) to accept outside aid and advice at the time when it can be most effective.

In order to illustrate this point it is perhaps useful to cite an article the author wrote in Bangkok in early 1966.

At the end of 1964, Peking announced the advent of a 'Liberation War' and a 'Liberation Front' in Thailand. Scarcely noticed so far in the Western Press, the campaign has in fact begun. As General Prapas, the Minister of the Interior, put it recently: 'The Communists previously only carried out infiltration and propaganda but now they are fighting the police, seizing remote villages, ordering the villagers to work for them, and training them in the use of firearms.'

To someone who has been visiting Thailand fairly regularly since 1951 the situation is eerily exasperating. The same things are being confidently said in Bangkok today as were being said, confidently, in

1953: 'the government is going to assimilate the long-since-Communist-controlled Vietnamese minority along the Thai bank of the Mekong'; 'the Government is going to develop the arid, isolated'; 'the Government has the Communist problem there under control.'

Some members of the Vietnamese community are exiles from the ill-fated Nghe-An Soviet (in North Vietnam, the first in S.E. Asia) of 1930; many took part in the struggle against the French. The community is so well organized that it undercut Thai contractors for government construction work. As long ago as 1958, during the change of regime in Bangkok, it showed its political skills, demonstrating against the authorities, using screens of women to surround police stations. It often conducts its after-hours Vietnamese schools. It is proposed to erect a barbed-wire fence along the Mekong bank of the Nongkai area, 144 miles of frontier, which is the granary for Laos's troubled capital of Vientiane, but the enemy is already within.

Besides, there is the long frontier with Laos running south. Southern Laos is being used as a training ground by the Viet-minh and Pathet-Lao for operations in Thailand. The north-easterners of Thailand are Lao-speakers, resentful of years of neglect, friendly towards the glutinous rice-eating 'cousins' across the Mekong. Guns are coming across the frontier, and Chinese and Russian weapons have already been captured, entering the heartland of the north-east by a number of different routes. Elements of the Vietminh Special Force 44 are believed to have crossed from Thakhek in southern Laos. The assassination of village officials, invariable prelude to the slow escalation of the struggle, is increasingly being reported.

This is no 'spontaneous peasant rising'. The Communists are working through the usual 'front' organizations, the 'Unionists', the 'Pracheachon (People's) Party', 'People's Mobile Development' (this last a clear response to the government's Mobile Development Units), 'Solidarity Movement', 'Mass Development Group', and so on. The propaganda methods are the same as usual: charging the government with oppression, criticizing the government taxes, accusing the government of being 'a slave of the Americans', appealing to a regional, potentially separatist sentiment. As Air Chief Marshal Darwee said, 'Communist guerrilla warfare has begun on a small scale and is at present fragmentary in nature.' (It always seems to be during this phase, though in fact it would never have reached this stage unless the political infrastructure had first been established.) But he admitted that the Communists were acting purposefully, retreating 'strategically' [sic] according to Mao. Moreover, there are ominous signs that the provincial administration is encountering the old problem that faces those responsible for countering insurgency; the presence 'everywhere and nowhere' of guerrillas enjoying superior mobility thanks to a superior intelligence service and widespread local indoctrination. There are already complaints that as the mobile government information teams leave a village 'the agitators return to give their answers to the government's message.'

No, it is not a 'spontaneous peasant rising' but there is no doubt whatsoever that ten years of neglect have allowed the Communists to prepare their ground, as they have been preparing it since as far back as 1955 at least, without let or hindrance. . . . The problems of the north-east have been endlessly talked about; but until the last year disgracefully little has been done about them.

A great deal of blame must also be placed on the 'SEATO mentality': the manœuvrings of warships, the equipment of forces to meet only a phase of the revolutionary guerrilla struggle that is, in essence, comparable with the bloody, all-out war being fought in Vietnam today, the big promises of massive support from 'great and powerful friends'. While the slick hotels mushroomed in Bangkok and television sets proliferated there, it was not until late 1965 that a 100-kilowatt transmitter was set up to match the Peking, Hanoi, and clandestine 'Voice of Thailand' transmitters which up till now have had the thousands and thousands of village transistors to themselves.

During the last year or so the government's Mobile Development Units have done good work in civil engineering, medical pilot projects, hygiene and the like. The army have contributed to the 'civic action' programme. Schools have been erected. Feeder roads to develop the backblock economy have been made—the Australian team has built 150 kilometres—and irrigation dams have been dug. These are good activities, but they should have been under way ten years ago.

It is ominous indeed to hear officials talking about the 'necessity to provide security for the villagers first' before their rural society can be properly developed; it is frightening to encounter this insouciance late in 1965: 'The government has become aware of the Communist danger at this early stage in its development. In South Vietnam the danger was recognized too late.' This is most emphatically *not* an early stage in the development of revolutionary guerrilla warfare. It is the government, not the Communists, who are talking in terms of accelerated rural development and 'crash programmes'.

It is difficult not to have grave reservations about Prime Minister Thanom Kittikachorn's speech of 12th December 1965 in which he, after frankly admitting that 'the subversive aggression against Thailand has been intensified' and after stating that 'we have increased the strength of the administrative officials and police, and the efficiency of the army has been improved . . .', he then said that Thailand has 'tightened relations with trustworthy allies, and we are satisfied that if open aggression is committed against us there will be adequate forces to defend us' and that for indirect aggression 'the unity of the Thai people will be essential in defeating it'.[1]

It is not at all the case that Bangkok's neglect of Thailand's North-East has in itself engendered a peasant revolt; it is simply that this neglect, when opposed to the promises of the Communists, becomes a 'contradiction' to be exploited. In terms of such promises the guerrilla has always an enormous propaganda advantage, since the government's neglect is easily analysed and explained in a demonstrable fashion, whereas the guerrillas' promises are not expected to be made good until after victory.[2]

Again and again the apologists for Communist revolutionary warfare try to argue that guerrilla campaigns are basically *determined* by certain social and economic conditions. But this is at best a half-truth. Lenin put the question more frankly: 'Marxism asks that the various types of struggle be analysed within their historical framework. To discuss conflict outside its historical and concrete setting is to misunderstand elementary dialectical materialism. At various junctures of economic evolution, and depending on changing political, national, cultural, social and other conditions, differing types of struggle may become important and even predominant.'[3] Che Guevara makes the point even clearer: 'It is not necessary to wait for the fulfilment of all conditions for a revolution because the focus of insurrection can create them.'

This is of central importance to understanding what the mounting of a revolutionary guerrilla warfare campaign involves at ground floor level. The intention is not only to manipulate existing 'contradictions' so as to create conditions favourable to the penetration of a totalitarian system, half-political and half-military; not only to erode the administration under attack through 'pinpoint coercion' and hence create a

---

[1] *The Bulletin*, Sydney, 12th February 1966.
[2] Sometimes a start can be made however, particularly in the redistribution of land for example. It was a serious error of Diem's in South Vietnam not to accept the distribution carried out by the Communist-dominated Vietminh before he came to power. But most of the social reforms promised by Communist guerrillas are seen to be incapable of fulfilment before victory.
[3] See F. M. Osanka: op. cit.

vacuum to be filled by the Communist infrastructure; but also to create, through struggle (struggle being seen by Mao as the deepest kind of proper human activity), revolutionary *activity* as a means of radically transforming the 'nature' of the men engaged in it. The Bolshevik 'organizational weapon', while quite deliberately disguising future aims in terms comfortably comprehensible on the traditional plane of understanding, exploits vaguely felt discontents, builds them up in the public imagination and then passes them off as spontaneous reactions; the supposed cause of all the trouble that is being so artfully prepared. By translating discontents and aspirations into terms favouring Communist long-term policy, the 'vanguard' slowly builds a new 'shadow society' that is moved not primarily by terror, which is directed chiefly against those who exert influence of a recalcitrant kind in the areas soon to be subverted, but rather through psychological and (by way of 'front' organizations) social conditioning.[1] Being a 'closed' society *par excellence*, whether on the cell or village or regional level, the Communist area of control can only be loosened by the destruction of its political apparatus. While it continues in being it does violence to the individual or family or group by depriving men even of their solitude, to such an extent that even the *belief* in free choice is temporarily smothered and men come to believe the Peking slogan that 'not to understand the party line is to have lost one's soul'. A counter-insurgency campaign has, therefore, only one proper objective: to relieve the people of the Communist cancer that afflicts them. It is not at all a primary objective of counter-insurgency to kill armed guerrillas; it is to destroy a political organization.

This is why the early detection of the subversion that precedes insurgency is so extraordinarily important: once a major penetration of significant areas of a country has been effected, and insurgency built upon it, the counter-insurgents are likely to find themselves faced not with the prospect of identifying and destroying a comparatively few Communist cadres but with fighting large numbers of psychologically-conditioned (or if it is preferred, 'well-motivated') men deeply imbued with notions (the disguised Causes) that appeal to what is truly noble in them: self-sacrifice for the homeland, the

[1] The argument about psychological and social conditioning is being made strongly in order to counter the all too frequent facile assumption that Communist revolutionary guerrilla forces are terrorized hordes. It is not for a moment being suggested that this conditioning goes truly deep in most men. On the contrary, the efficacy of totalitarian conditioning depends upon the omnipresence of its 'vanguards', its organization, and its credibility as a real representative of the 'wave of the future'. It is easily sloughed off.

fight against corruption, against the selfishness of the privileged, for 'four corners of earth,' for 'the liberation of mankind', and so on.

Early recognition and response permits the blanketing of the revolutionary guerrilla base areas, which are closely integrated complexes of villages prepared for their own defence. They in turn are based upon a politically indoctrinated population in which even children have intelligence jobs, a network of food and weapon dumps, an 'alternative administration' the authority of which is imposed by local guerrilla forces, and the availability of a 'regular' unit operating in the vicinity. All adults, from the age of sixteen to forty-five, are organized to patrol, spy and disrupt the government administration.[1] The aim here is to establish a safe area consisting of a system of militarily organized village communities, some of which will be 'fortified villages', some be responsible for liaison and reporting enemy troop movements. Fundamentally the revolutionary campaign consists of expanding this society at a pace appropriate to political and military circumstances.

Since this phase of insurgency is very seldom recognized and responded to quickly enough, the centre of the struggle becomes the contested zone between the guerrilla's safe areas and those under real government control. Two 'societies' then exist, both of which are concerned to expand towards each other as opportunity offers in order to absorb this zone to their own interests. Having thus acquired an ascendency in terms of territory under control they would possess a springboard for the eventual attack on the other's safe areas, using the approved blend of political and military action.

Here the revolutionary guerrilla is at a huge advantage for a reason that is seldom properly understood: whereas he is concerned to penetrate the existing society with an expanding *infrastructure,* the government under attack is necessarily concerned to preserve its administrative image as the legitimate *superstructure* of society. A collapse in any area of the superstructure is easily observable and can all too easily be construed as a collapse of the whole civilized order. The revolutionary guerrilla is not at all in the same position: he is at first inserting, rather than imposing a *clandestine* politico-military framework the efficacy of which, in the contested zone, does not depend primarily on public performance at all but upon being 'everywhere and nowhere'; an

---

[1] Cp. Lenin: "What other organization except a universal militia with women participating on an equal footing with men can effect these measures? . . . Such a militia would draw the youngsters into political-life, training them not only by word, but by deed and work.'

influence; a vapour drifting where it may, yet deadly against those who compromise themselves by collaboration with visiting government forces which cannot permanently be in evidence throughout the whole territory.

The government is faced with the grave problem of selecting priority areas in which to attempt fully to assert its authority; but there is the even graver problem of the remaining areas, 'where the government must hold out and prevent the insurgents from gaining full control. A very careful assessment is required of the insurgent potential in these areas compared with the reserved available to the government. Depending on this, the government must then decide whether to let a few outlying areas go and to ignore them until such time as the whole programme has advanced sufficiently for further resources to be made available. This is a difficult decision for any government to take, and there is always a risk that such areas, however unimportant, may be declared 'liberated' by the insurgents. This type of operation (the use on occasion of forces in reserve for 'showing the flag') requires very careful handling indeed; under no circumstances must it be carried out as a punitive raid into enemy territory. Its purpose is psychological rather than military, and it is designed to show the population that the government has not forgotten them. The intention of the operation is to encourage the people to welcome the future return of the Government, not, as was so frequently the case in Vietnam, to make them hope that the government forces will never show their faces in the area again.'[1]

But the government's predicament in face of growing insurgent activity in the intermediate territory or 'no man's land' is really much greater than that. In most South-East Asian countries, the central governments are hard put to it, leaving significant insurgent activity altogether aside, to establish a generally accepted 'legitimacy' in country areas, which embrace some 75 per cent upwards of the population. In South-East Asia, the political problem for governments is rather to get themselves accepted as *régimes*—nowhere in the area has there grown up a tradition of oppositions loyal to basic constitutional principles—and no régime so far has managed to assert its 'legitimacy' over as much as a decade.

Therefore, the central government's task in the zone of operations is not really just a question of 'showing the flag'; it is a problem of impressing upon the villages that there *is* a flag. The most extreme example of this problem was to be found in South Vietnam when, in

[1] Sir Robert Thompson, op. cit.

1959, the Communists moved from subversion to insurgency, and where the flag was scarcely known and the régime signified by it meant very little indeed in outlying areas. Apart from Thailand, where the area of attack has certain special features, Communist insurgencies have been directed against new régimes which would anyway have had a struggle to establish their legitimacy for a number of years; in such cases, the battle for the zone at risk is onerous indeed, since however well the government troops might behave, the 'image' of government has not been properly delineated in the minds of the people, and in these areas guerrilla warfare is specifically designed to prevent the people ever forming an accurate assessment of what it is likely to offer. This is not really very difficult, since it only entails employing 'pinpoint coercion' against whatever pilot-projects in the way of social amelioration the government may try to establish; for example, the quick and ruthless destruction of schools and medical clinics and malarial teams and civil engineering projects. Such targets are ferociously attacked by the Communist revolutionary insurgents, as are village headmen who appear likely to help such programmes on the government's behalf, and *this* is where terrorism is so very important a weapon. For example during the Malayan insurgency 3,283 civilians were murdered or abducted against 1,865 security forces killed in action; in South Vietnam in 1960–1, the first phase of insurgency proper, over 6,000 people were murdered and over 6,000 were abducted.[1] From the psychological point of view this is quite sufficient to persuade large sections of people living in the vulnerable zone that the government just cannot protect them.

The writer is of course aware that he has been writing about the activities and aims of an organization, the Communist party, in the abstract as though it were a kind of *deus ex machina*. In a sense it is: the activity of a Communist party in rural South-East Asia is an interposition of something altogether foreign. It is in another sense too, for that matter, because it seeks to impose an artificial solution to the problems of under-developed countries, while the Communists who form the organization which mounts an insurgency are for the most part men who have never left their own country. Most of them, especially the central leadership groups, became Communists because they found in the Communist interpretation of history a psychologically satisfactory explanation of their own disabilities under European colonial rule and of the backward state of their own societies. They also found in this interpretation a great promise for themselves and

[1] ibid.

their countries which seemed to be denied at the ultimate end of things to the presently favoured European capitalists. Moreover, in the colonial era—the period in which the majority of South-East Asian Communist leaders were psychologically and temperamentally formed —it was easy for them to see in the struggle against colonialism a struggle also for the 'liberation of mankind', a struggle in which international human solidarity was raised to great heights of expectation. In South-East Asia these expectations have not yet been soured, let alone eroded, for Communism did not arise here out of the 'mud and rout of defeat' as it did in Russia, but rather out of bright hopes which seemed to be confirmed by the withdrawal of the Western imperial powers after World War II. As a result of this historical accident, the Communists of South-East Asia were at least for a time able to merge their public aspirations with those of the people at large, for both sought national independence. Only the Indo-Chinese Communist party was able to maintain this façade; elsewhere it was destroyed by the unmasking involved in obeying the Calcutta directives of 1947 and 1948.

The prime movers in insurgency are men of the anti-colonialist struggle. But in order to mount an insurgency these small groups of political incorrigibles must recruit the 'resistance movement's' local leadership. And here of course it must be understood that it is the failures of the society under attack that provide the potential recruits. This may or may not be a serious reflection upon that society, since there are disaffected people even in the richest societies. Moreover poor societies, however well-intentioned their governments may be, always contain people who are disaffected simply because there are not enough purposeful and status-bearing jobs to offer the semi-educated or even, sometimes, the properly qualified. This is not seldom the result of the existing family-system, which in South-East Asia tends towards nepotism, as it does in every poor country, whatever its family-system may be.

Anywhere in the world there are in most villages a few people harbouring very localized resentments which can easily be translated by Communist agitators into a generalized Cause. This is particularly so where a traditional structure of authority is in any case being subverted by new modes of behaviour. There are also in most villages a few young men ready for adventure. In many villages in South-East Asia there are in addition a few people who have good reason to feel that they have been maltreated or somehow taken down by the powers-that-be. The Communist technique of deep-level recruitment is to exacerbate such people's sense of not belonging to the existing order by involving them in activities of a purposeful and often dreadful nature directed against the representatives of that order, to make outlaws of them in the special sense that real Communists everywhere feel themselves to be. Such people are the potential recruits for the cadres of the future, their old loyalties wholly analysed and explained away by the propaganda experts, their old status irrevocably destroyed by participation in acts of violence, and their only hopes embedded in the organization which has transformed them; fearful thenceforth only of the loneliness other men call freedom. 'A truly new power is born. . . .'

It cannot be too often emphasized that revolutionary guerrilla warfare is designed to change men through the political and military activities involved in it. Paret and Shy put this very well when they refer to 'the use of guerrilla warfare, not simply as a military means to a political end, but as a political process in itself. Mao implies that the most important aspect of guerrilla warfare may be its effect on the guerrilla and his supporters. The necessarily widespread and protracted experience of guerrilla warfare breaks down passivity (the 'coldness' of the peasantry) and trains political cadres for the postwar tasks of government. An atmosphere of violence creates new emotions and commitments, so that in the end a whole society may become revolutionary. The ancient concept of war revitalizing society is here given new form. . . . Violent experience does change people, whether they are perpetrators, victims, or witnesses.'[1]

It is not terrorism as it is generally understood in the West that from the beginning informs an insurgency, but violence of a number of kinds, military, social, political, and psychological. A guerrilla force is formed in an area in a number of ways: by recruiting cells of three to five men, which in turn recruit other cells ('every party cell is a fortress'); by cadres supplied temporarily from the regular army in order to spread insurgency more speedily, cadres which form armed propaganda units amongst the locals before withdrawing and so intensify the nature of the struggle as well; by permanent cadres from the regular army to stiffen the local movement as a whole; by mixed forces of regulars and guerrillas to accelerate the local fighting potential; by subverting the local militia and turning them into guerrilla bands; even by using local bandits. At the same time the rest of the population is mobilized in 'front' organizations which reinforce

[1] Peter Paret and John W. Shy, Guerrillas in the 1960's, Praeger Paperback, 1964.

the political cohesion of the 'liberated area'.[1] The struggle remains basically political, however fierce the fighting; and simply a continuation of Communist politics by other means; or as Giap put it: 'The Resistance War waged by our people was the continuation of the national democratic revolution by armed struggle. Therefore, to hold firm to the national democratic revolution line in leading the Resistance War was a nodal, decisive question . . . The revolution for national liberation under the leadership of the Communist party never deviated from the democratic revolution. The anti-imperialist task always went side by side with the anti-feudal task, although the former was more urgent; Vietnam was a backward agricultural country and the majority of the population were peasants. While the working class is the class leading the revolution, the peasantry is the main force of the revolution, full of anti-imperialist and anti-feudal spirit. Moreover, in waging the Resistance War, we relied on the countryside to build our bases to launch guerrilla warfare in order to encircle the enemy in the towns. Therefore, it was of particular importance to pay due attention to the peasant question and the anti-feudal question to step up the long Resistance War to victory.' That 'therefore' should be very carefully noticed by those who see in revolutionary guerrilla warfare a spontaneous peasant revolt.

But it is the battle for the areas in dispute that is the more terrible in an obvious way; here the targets are not simply the dispositions of men and women, to be altered by a mixture of psychological suasion and violence, as is the case in the safe areas; here terrorism proper is being used to clear the ground for further expansion while the preparations are being made and the chief targets are not seldom the socially most promising government activities and very often the best representatives of the government: the idealistic volunteers who have left the city to help their countrymen develop a better way of life. In this kind of situation even a foreigner is apt to succumb to gross anger.

Therefore it may be worth while including a personal reminiscence of a new co-operative farm that was being developed in the Central Highlands of South Vietnam, near Ban Methuot, early in 1962. It

---

[1] For example, in 1965, the north-east insurgency in Thailand, based on the 'safe area' of the sparsely populated approaches of the Phupan Range, expanding through Nakhorn Phanom, a Thai-Laotian border province, into Sakol Nakorn, Udorn, and Ubol provinces, established: the Self-Liberated Farmers' and Planters' Association, the Thai Monks' Group, the Federation of Patriotic Workers of Thailand, the Poor People's Group, and the Southern Rubber Plantation Workers' Group. Early in 1966, the Thai Patriotic Youth Organization was founded.

may at least confer an impression of immediacy upon a problem that necessarily remains somewhat cloudy to those unacquainted with the realities of revolutionary warfare as it has been waged in South-East Asia; and so it is quoted as it was written in the dust from the good red soil of the area for an American news digest.

'I went to the countryside, in particular to the countryside around Ban Me Thuot, a garrison town some 200 miles as the Dakota flies from Saigon. It was not my first experience of this war without frontiers—but it may be yours. I hope it is, because this is an ugly kind of war. Oh, there are no big guns firing at you, no crunch of tanks along the road, no screams of bombers overhead. . . . Why so terrible? Because nearly every bullet kills. When you go to an ordinary war, you imagine at first that every shot fired will kill you personally. But gradually you learn to know better. In that kind of war, most bullets kill no one.

'In Vietnam it is different. Most bullets *do* kill. This is not war; it is a Communist murder campaign. Certainly there are skirmishes between Communist guerrillas and Vietnamese government troops— provided the Vietnamese government troops are hopelessly outnumbered. But just as many bullets are fired at civilians—at the head of a district, at a priest who is loved by the locals, a girl who has dared to join the government National Youth Organization, at a young man brave enough to join the militia, or as a village headman. Anyone who opposes the Communists in any way at all is fair game for the Communist murder squads.

'. . . new lands are being opened up by a great task force of bulldozers grinding the softly treacherous jungle into the ground, into the rich red soil of Vietnam's borderlands with Laos and Cambodia. This much maligned government is opening up new territory to whatever peasant pioneers need land. In contrast, the peasant of North Vietnam is being cruelly persecuted, deprived of his lands, forcibly collectivized by a Communist government which, like every other Communist government in the world, has no idea at all of how to solve its agrarian problem. The peasant in the south is far, far better off than his Communist-dominated brother in the north. He has his land as an individual, he is aided by farm credit and fertilizer. One day, he should, and doubtless will, be aided by co-operative methods of marketing his produce. But even now, he knows he is secure.

'So what can the Communists *do* but launch a campaign of terror? They can offer the South Vietnamese peasant absolutely nothing but 'the power of the gun', as Mao Tse-tung calls it; nothing but terror.

Yes, but widespread terror can be a very powerful weapon. I talked with those who are leading, those who are participating in the great land development centres along Vietnam's border with Cambodia and Laos. I saw the remarkable variety of their agricultural produce ranging from rubber to coffee, from turnips to maize. I saw them helping each other to build neat thatch houses. I met the guard of the National Youth Association who, when properly trained, will be armed and constitute the militia to defend the settlement centre. I saw the villagers drawing water from a common well, drawing hope for the future of their children from a common school, drawing health from a common dispensary.

'These are brave and optimistic people. They want to fight for their new lands. They *will* fight for their lands. But terror—the sudden raid from across the border, the assassination at night of the braver spirits of the settlement—this is not an easy thing to stand up to. Soon this terror will come. . . . The Vietcong *must* attempt to obliterate by terror these land development centres of free peasants.

'And given the present policy, the Vietcong *can* do this. Let there be no mistake about it: Terrorism, if properly organized, *can* destroy even the happiest of human communities—unless it is appropriately countered. And here is the crux of the problem: how to counter terrorism? Not in the long run, but in the short run. The answer to this is not a pretty one. It is not an answer that comes easily to those of us fortunate enough to have been brought up in the delightful cloud-cuckoo land of liberal capitalism. Indeed the answer is so tough, so inimicable to our own traditions, that it is not really being faced up to. Instead, a kind of hopeless dilemma exists in South Vietnam, a dilemma that is being allowed to go far towards losing the battle.

'It may best be summed up by the argument of a Vietnamese army officer concerned with civilian problems—though who can separate civilian from military in this situation? He argues thus: 'Yes', he says, 'The Americans have given us, and are giving us, the most wonderful assistance. With their aid, we, a very poor country, are able to have bulldozers to beat down the jungle and settle our overcrowded coastal population on these rich new lands. With their aid we are able to introduce these new settlers to the wonders of modern agricultural science: high-yielding rubber trees, fertilizers, good quality maize, water conservation. Americans have helped teach us to work our agriculture co-operatively. The Americans have in this way done wonders. But therein lies our possible doom.'

'But why?' I asked.

'Ah well,' he said, 'It is really quite simple. We have achieved here something that has removed all grounds for Communist agitation.' He pointed to the young rubber trees, the squat green coffee plants, the fields upon fields of vegetables. 'In the north, the Communist north, the peasant *knows* he is not remotely as well off. This kind of news crosses frontiers.'

'So?' I insisted, watching the great task force of bulldozers tearing down the jungle to increase next year's settlement area—that jungle which is at present such a marvellous lurk and prowling ground for Vietcong marauding bands intent on assassination. . . .

'So,' he said quietly, 'they (the Vietcong) are doing the only thing left open to them. They come in from Cambodia and kill or mutilate or terrorize our headmen, our militiamen, anyone who is brave enough to co-operate with the government. They shoot these people down in front of the villagers and explain to the villagers that anyone else who tries to co-operate with the government will be treated in the same way. They have not really started attacking these land development centres yet in this way—though only the day before you arrived we killed three members of a Vietcong band. But soon they will be attacking us in this manner. They will *have* to.'

'Yes, but why does the government not counter attack?'

'Because if we do counter attack in the only way possible in such a situation,' he said with a wry grin, 'then we shall be accused of adopting Communist methods. Totalitarian methods.'[1]

---

[1] *Documents of the Council Against Communist Aggression*, Philadelphia, February 1962.

Chapter 8

THE GENERAL NATURE OF THE STRUGGLE IN VIETNAM

Three years after the events recorded at the end of the last chapter, the United States, with a few allies, decided to intervene in South Vietnam in order to prevent a complete government collapse in the face of what had become, in the highlands, a mobile warfare campaign. Through a process of phased escalation from passive resistance (or the stage of contention) to active resistance (or the stage of equilibrium), the ground was being prepared by the Communists for a general counter-offensive designed to cut off the northern section of South Vietnam from Saigon control. The phasing of such a campaign varies in different parts of the country; what is important is the proper *pace* of advance in each area, since this determines the appropriate moment for moving from one phase to another, though of course guerrilla fighting in the form of passive resistance goes on till the end, but in an increasingly auxiliary role.

Truong Chinh describes guerrilla warfare as 'the method of fighting in partisan units or with relatively small groups of the regular army disguised as civilians and mingling with the people. Though these forces are armed only with rudimentary weapons, they are extremely active. They attack the enemy from behind, outflank him or launch sudden attacks on his weak points . . . they concentrate for attack and disperse to dodge the enemy's reply. They cut communications, harass the enemy while he is eating or sleeping, wear out his strength, cause him weariness and distress, render his forces lame, lost, hungry, thirsty. . . . The three most generally employed tactics of guerrilla warfare are: surprise attack, ambush and harassment. Fighting must be co-ordinated with sabotage. Sabotage is a wonderful means of resistance by guerrilla forces or by regular troops less well-armed than the enemy.'[1]

During the 'stage of contention', which necessarily follows the

---

[1] *The Resistance Will Win* op. cit. F. Spencer Chapman, *The Jungle is Neutral* op. cit. for an example of the efficacy of sabotage even when carried out by a very small group indeed.

THE GENERAL NATURE OF THE STRUGGLE IN VIETNAM

stage of subversion and penetration, 'our strategy is defensive, but our tactics and campaigning principles are constantly to attack'. The 'stage of equilibrium' comes when 'the enemy no longer has sufficient strength to advance. . . . The two sides seem to be holding each other in the same position. The enemy aims to consolidate, to mop-up, to re-establish order, to set up a puppet government with its armed forces and to divide the people. (This is a reference to the French recognition of Bao Dai's government and is not of general application.) . . . Our military and political aim at this stage is to wear out the enemy forces, annihilate them piecemeal (which was beginning significantly to occur early in 1965 in South Vietnam); sabotage, disturb, give the enemy no peace to exploit the people easily; mobilize the people to wage armed struggle against the puppet administration. . . . Armed propaganda must be carried out on a large scale, particularly in the enemy-held region, to maintain the people's morale. . . .' Guerrillas plus regulars concentrate at 'hinge points', attacking outposts, making sudden strikes at towns, 'where enemy forces are not numerous.' This is a 'hard and complicated stage . . . a relatively long stage . . . the key stage, because it is then that we must pass from an inferior position to a superior position to go forward to the stage of general-counter-offensive.'

At the counter-offensive stage mobile warfare comes into play: 'fighting by the regular army, or by guerrilla forces mustered into relatively big units and co-operating with the regular army, using more or less advanced weapons. . . . The characteristic of mobile warfare is: to manœuvre with flexibility to attack the enemy and destroy him.' It is the stage of general counter-offensive that is vitally dependent upon specialist cadres, modern arms, and supplies which come from the 'privileged sanctuary' next door. 'During the general counter-offensive, the enemy surrenders many positions and withdraws to entrench himself in the big cities. He will possibly hold false negotiations with us with a view to gaining time, carrying out delaying schemes in order to wait for direct and more active assistance from world reaction. . . . As far as tactics are concerned, during this stage mobile warfare at first plays the outstanding role and is fostered and helped by guerrilla warfare. Guerrilla warfare is rapidly and extensively transformed into mobile warfare (many guerrilla groups gathered together form units analagous to those of the regular forces and apply mobile warfare). Mobile warfare is in its turn transformed into positional warfare. Battles for cities and strongpoints take place all the time. . . .'

But it is much more than a phased military struggle: 'As for us, our consistent aim is that the whole country should rise up and go over to the offensive on all fronts. . . . Guerrilla warfare must be the tactic of the people as a whole, not of the army alone. To achieve good results in guerrilla and mobile warfare, we must mobilize the people to support our armed forces enthusiastically and to fight the enemy together with them. The people are the eyes and ears of the army, they feed and keep our soldiers. It is they who help the army in sabotage and in battle. The people are the water and our army the fish.'

The stage of active resistance (or equilibrium) may be described a little differently as the stage when, the guerrilla forces and the political organization being significantly expanded, it is intended to inveigle the government forces into inconclusive engagements—a period of evasion during which it is hoped to disperse, demoralize, and exhaust the government forces, permitting the guerrillas to intensify carefully planned campaigns against areas regarded as of importance for future strategy. It is important not to simplify the ebb and flow of a revolutionary guerrilla war; and not to impose rigid and artificial timetables or procedures upon a very fluid kind of struggle.

As Truong Chinh remarks, a guerrilla war has certain characteristics: a 'war of interlocking' ('. . . the enemy attacks deep behind our lines, and we launch attacks deep behind his. The war has the characteristic of two combs whose teeth are interlocked'); a 'war without fronts . . . without rear lines, without clear front lines'; and a 'war of encirclement'. ('Our guerrilla bases in the enemy-held regions can appear to be mere enclaves surrounded by the enemy. But all these guerrilla bases, together with the bread-free zones, form a huge net encircling the enemy in return.') Moreover, the revolutionary guerrilla high command is always prepared if necessary to return to an earlier phase of the campaign, though from the political point of view, especially in a cultural area like South Vietnam where the peasant in recent decades has been keeping a weather-eye on possible changes in 'the Mandate of Heaven', a changing down of the gears could have very serious consequences so far as the morale of the 'mass base' is concerned.

After all, as Colonel Galula has pointed out, 'The importance of a cause, an absolute essential at the outset of an insurgency, decreases progressively as the insurgent acquires strength. The war itself becomes the principal issue, forcing the population to take sides, preferably the winning one.' Once an insurgency has been defeated, it is easy to forget how potentially formidable it once seemed to be. For

THE GENERAL NATURE OF THE STRUGGLE IN VIETNAM

example, 'The MCP (Malayan Communist party) was well prepared for battle. It had planned its political and military chain of command some years before, in the waning days of the Japanese war. The jungle organization numbered about 10,000. . . . In addition to the force in the jungle a much greater number of sympathizers remained in the towns and villages. . . . The exact number of willing, and unwilling, members of this organization (The Min Yuen network of intelligence agents and suppliers of food and medical supplies) will never be known. In his book *Menace in Malaya*, Harry Miller made a conservative estimate of 500,000. Liaison between the terrorists in the jungle and the Min Yuen was maintained by "Masses Executives", who carried on their everyday business in towns and villages while acting as undercover men for the District Committees. In this way, propaganda could be fed into these communities while, at the same time, the more material means of existence could be smuggled out.'[1]

And compare: 'When he (Magsaysay) assumed command, the Huks were estimated to have about 12,000 armed guerrillas. Furthermore, it was estimated that of the 17,000,000 Filipinos, at least 1,000,000 actively supported the Huks by providing food, supplies, information, and when necessary, recruits. On the other hand, the Philippine army had about 30,000 troops. Neutral observers at the time estimated that the government itself could count on hardly more than 1,000,000 active supporters. The great majority of the population stood aloof muttering curses on both houses.'[2]

It should be remarked also that when a revolutionary guerrilla struggle reaches the dimensions of the one now being waged in South Vietnam the whole system of recruitment and political conditioning is radically altered. So long as the Communists can retain the initiative, not only in military tactics but in politico-military phasing of the struggle as a whole, then it is possible for them to expand their new society according to principles of persuasion and disguised Causes rather than through terror—except of course, discriminate terror as a form of 'pinpoint coercion' in the territory yet to be won over and as traditional guerrilla reprisals against treachery and cowardice.[3] Indeed, provided the phasing lies with the Communists, then their carefully worked-out mode of behaviour towards the population, which

[1] Lieut. Colonel Rowland S. N. Mans, M.B.E. in Lieut. Colonel T. N. Greene (Editor), *The Guerrilla—And How to Fight Him*, Praeger, 1962.
[2] Charles W. Thayer op. cit.
[3] Lenin: 'The firing squad is the legitimate fate of the coward in battle.'

was discussed earlier and the improvement in social conditions, however tactical the motive and temporary the effect, can and do engender quite genuine popular support.[1] This is another vital reason for recognizing and responding to an insurgency in its early subversive phase, since the true face of Communist revolutionary warfare is only revealed to the people at large when very severe pressure comes to be exerted against its organization.

The situation is altogether different when, as is the case in 1967 in Vietnam, no less than two-thirds of the young adult male manpower of the country have been torn away from their occupations by the exigencies of war. Recruiting then becomes a matter of impressment and even abduction; and these recruits and their families are indeed primarily moved by considerations of who is likely to win rather than anything else. The struggle becomes a test of staying-power, with the Communists relying more and more as the months pass upon a weakening of the American will to fight on.

It is interesting in this context to examine once again the thinking of Truong Chinh, even though it relates to past history: 'The guiding principle of the strategy of our whole resistance must be to prolong the war. To protract the war is the key to victory. Why must the war be protracted? ... it is obvious the enemy is still strong, and we are still weak.... The enemy has planes, tanks, warships; as for us, we have only rudimentary weapons. The enemy troops are well-trained, ours are not inured to war ... if while fighting, we maintain our forces, expand them, train our army and people, learn military tactics, to secure in sufficient quantities the things of which we are short, we shall weary and discourage them in such a way that, strong as they are, they will become weak and will meet defeat instead of victory. In short, if we prolong the war, thanks to our efforts, our forces will grow stronger, the enemy forces will be weakened, their already low morale will become still poorer. The more we fight, the more united our people at home will be, and the more the democratic movement will support us from outside. On the other hand, the more the enemy fights, the more the anti-war and democratic movement in France will check his hands; the revolutionary movement in the French

---

[1] Truong Chinh '... verbal propaganda alone is not enough. We should strive to improve the living conditions of the people; restrict usury, take genuine care of the life of the toiling people and the civil servants etc., lighten burdens, reduce land rents ... levy taxes according to democratic principles ... severely punish the thieves of public property, the speculators, smugglers, and saboteurs, confiscate the property of the national traitors and use such property to improve the people's life.'

colonies will oblige the enemy to divide his forces; and he will find himself in a position of isolation in the international arena.'

In 1967 the 'guiding principle' remains the same: protract the war. The expansion of forces has been carried out: the Vietcong 'hard core' (virtually, regular forces) increased from about 30,000 in 1964 to some 90,000 in mid-1966, the North Vietnamese elements of which were built up from two or three battalions in 1965 to a confirmed 25,000; the armament of the irregulars, which increased, despite heavy casualties and higher defections, from 90,000 in 1965 to 105,000 in August 1966, were immeasurably improved. The August 1965 total figure including political cadres, of 190,000–200,000 grew to about 280,000 in late 1966.[1]

It would certainly not be true to imagine that the Americans, Koreans, Australians, and New Zealanders have at any moment suffered from low fighting morale, nor are they ever likely to; and the morale of the South Vietnamese forces could only improve on their situation of early 1965. It is very difficult to judge whether its nearly shattered morale of that time has been wholly restored, since in 1966 the Americans gradually took over more and more of the significant fighting (which did not prevent the South Vietnamese going on taking heavy casualties). It would seem probable that it has been considerably improved but that it remains not nearly high enough for vigorous and consistent pacification work.

Moreover, the 'anti-war and democratic movement' in the U.S.A. has been unsuccessful so far; and with the probable but not yet important exception of Thailand, 'the revolutionary movement in the (American) colonies' has not materialized. Indeed, 'Asian' and African and Latin American public opinion has on the whole been less than enthusiastic about the Vietnamese Communist revolutionary warfare campaign's new, anti-American confrontation, the chief form of the U.S.A.'s 'isolation in the international arena' has been isolation from the understanding of Europe.

Nevertheless, it has become quite clear now to most observers, as it was clear from the beginning to some, that the struggle for South

[1] All such figures can only be estimates; these are taken from *Vietnam: Strategy of 'Measured Response'*, Current Affairs Bulletin Vol. 38, No. 13, 14th November 1966, Sydney. Other estimates suggest that 60,000 men have been infiltrated into the south from the north between 1959–60 and the first quarter of 1965. What is quite certain is that infiltration of men and arms continues on a very large scale, despite all efforts to interdict: by 1966 most Vietcong units were armed with weapons of Soviet or Chinese manufacture. By 1967, the Vietnamese Communists disposed of some 300,000 regulars and guerrillas despite nearly 70,000 defections since 1963.

Vietnam is going to be a long and very terrible one. Assuming that no international initiative brings about a cease-fire, then it is reasonable to suppose that the struggle will take a minimum of five years (as from 1967) to 'pacify' the country; that half a million Americans will be involved in it, not to speak of 700,000 South Vietnamese government troops and security forces; that American casualties will be much greater than in Korea; that civilian destruction will be immense; and that at the end of the struggle it will not be at all easy to demonstrate its international achievement to the public of the United States of America, so far as combatting revolutionary warfare in the future is concerned.

It would require a separate book adequately to describe the dimensions of the struggle, which range from a huge effort to fight inflation to 'search-and destroy' operations in the western Tay Ninh Province, the Vietcong's base area alongside Cambodia where its high command is situated; from providing 500,000 tons of rice and other food grains to waging a bloody battle to cut supply lines emerging across the narrow demilitarized zone between North and South Vietnam; from the flying of 'milk-runs' to supply the beleaguered garrisons of the far south to bombing the Ho Chi Minh network of trails through Laos; from building 7,000 new schoolrooms to training the 15,000-man Police Field Force; from providing 40 varieties of new seeds and distributing thousands of pigs to attacking the Vietcong Yellow Star Division in Binh Dinh in order to prevent it gathering in the harvest; from the First Airborne's dearly won battle of Ia Drang in the Central Highlands to the Marine's slow commencement of pacification of the area around Danang. Pacification during 1966 was confined to four areas, comprising 14 per cent of the population and the real target was only three-quarters of this.[1] The Delta area had scarcely been touched and over six million Vietnamese live there, its pacification will be by far the bloodiest operation of the war, especially in terms of civilians, since over wide areas of this very thickly populated region the Vietcong infrastructure is scarcely indistinguishable from authority as such.

It may be that the experiences of the author in the vicinity of Danang in December 1965 will help in understanding something of the nature of the problem; driving out early in the morning from Danang towards the U.S. Marine battalion headquarters in the shadow of Marble Mountain, it is easy to believe there is a war on—men and vehicles and weapons attest to that—but strangely difficult to get to

[1] John C. Donnell, *Asia*, No. 4, op. cit.

THE GENERAL NATURE OF THE STRUGGLE IN VIETNAM

grips with the reality of sudden violence. An old man in a sun helmet, wispy-bearded like Ho Chi Minh, walks across the sand dunes after a visit to a family grave. Little boys are playing hopscotch; others are walking their beat wherever the traffic is halted to call 'No. One man, give me five piastres.' (It used to be one piastre.) Husband and wife rowing pairs move small boats up-river, bent standing over their oars. Huge fishing-nets hang gracefully above the waterline awaiting the incoming tide.

Across the river we drove past a vast motor vehicle park where on the previous day I had become peripherally involved in a very small incident which was yet significant in certain ways. The U.S. Marine sergeant attached to the corps' public relations department who was looking after me and trying to find me a patrol found me instead a verbal fracas. The participants were a young Marine lieutenant, an Australian warrant officer, a Vietnamese lieutenant, and a Vietnamese civilian. At first everyone became very security-conscious and mumbly at our appearance on the scene but slowly the cause of the row began to emerge as tempers became re-charged. It became clear that a couple of miles down the beach a Vietcong cadre of some distinction had been identified by the Vietnamese civilian, an intelligence agent with bad teeth and a windcheater of which he seemed proud. Apart from that he seemed less than sure of himself, which in the circumstances was altogether understandable.

The Marine lieutenant insisted that nothing could be done about the agent until a truck arrived from somewhere else in the vast motor park. In the truck it seemed there lurked a platoon of Marines. He could not proceed without them. Those were his orders. There was no question whatsoever of the Marine lieutenant being frightened at the prospect of proceeding without his platoon; he was simply obeying orders that had apparently been inadequately conveyed to his platoon sergeant. He was embarrassed but firm in his understanding of how the operation had to be carried out.

The Vietnamese lieutenant, fiery-eyed under his cowboy-style hat fiddled with his bright cravat, and urged on by his increasingly uneasy compatriot, became very angry indeed. He pointed out that this was not the way Vietcong agents were caught. This agent was foreman of a gang of labourers who would by now be assembling outside their place of work—the construction of huts for (of all people) the renowned U.S. Special Forces!—and if he were not nabbed immediately he would probably be tipped off, an event that would gravely imperil the life of the civilian intelligence agent, not to speak of rendering him useless for the future. The Australian W.O., an anyway ruddy-faced veteran of the toughest work of all—leading, while formally 'advising', reactive forces of Nung mercenaries whenever units got into real trouble—began to resemble a shorthorn bull, deeply red of face, pawing his foot in the sand, trembling with irritation in the cool seaborne air. (It transpired later that he badly wanted to go to the lavatory, having been deprived of his normal time for this operation by the unconscionably long argument.)

There was a sudden breakthrough as a result of glances exchanged between the two Vietnamese and the Australian WO: the three of them dashed towards a nearby jeep. Knowing I could not afford to lose face with a fellow countryman, I scrambled into the jeep too, ignoring the despairing, protective cries of the gentle Spanish-American public relations sergeant and the angry remonstrances of the Marine lieutenant. With the WO at the wheel, we drove furiously towards the construction project along a nearby beach, he, taking time off to point out a senior officers' beachside 'shack shack', I, reflecting that it was here in 1858 where at least part of the present struggle had really begun: Danang had once been called Tourane; here the French had landed during the onset of the conquest proper. I also found myself reflecting on our relative lack of arms; all we had, a repeater rifle of small calibre (not the redoubtable Armalite) was held in the delicate hands of the Vietnamese lieutenant.

The jeep struggled, rather than screeched, to a stop in deep fine sand beside a clearing out of which was rising an undistinguished mess hut of local sorts. But nearby the labourers were indeed lined up to receive their day's orders. Since the U.S. Marine lieutenant had insisted that the cadre was likely to be supported by friends with arms cached nearby, I took some time to get my camera adjusted and then picked up a long thick stick, which I affected to use as a shepherd's crook while moving warily towards the labourers. To my astonishment, the civilian intelligence agent was being invited to exchange a few whispered words with a labourer—a bow-legged village wide-boy clad in tattered shorts and dirty hat, disporting only a marvellously ugly steel tooth and a crazily distorted attempt at a smile—in front of the thirty or so labourers most of whose faces were less than amiable yet nearly all of them less than vicious. Then he walked up and down the ranks, peering into faces, trying to look hopeful, but failing. A few minutes later we learnt that the cadre had 'gone to Hué' a few minutes earlier.

This was a perfect example of a lack of liaison between security forces; and as a result, a lack of speedy activity. Moreover, the whole issue should have been one for the police to resolve; they were being welded into a very decent force by a former F.B.I. 'adviser' and could have taken care of the whole show very nicely. The war at this stage was still (and thenceforth always would be) basically a counter-insurgent operation, though it involved large-scale 'spoiling' operations against the Vietcong 'mainforce' units and units of the People's Army from the north (known as PAVNS) in order to cripple their capacity to escalate the war, or even, in some instances, to maintain its intensity. This meant a feet-on-the-ground attempt to erode the Communist political infrastructure—to get the Communist political apparatus, enforced by the 'power of the rifle' as it was, off the backs of the peasants in zones such as that around Danang where control was admittedly imperfect but where anti-Communist power could prevent any really significant return of Communist troops bent upon major reprisals. In such an area it was of the utmost importance to develop the police type of counter-measures to the maximum.

This was an enclave about to be pacified as a safe area from which later to spread out into the hinterland. At night Vietcong companies of perhaps 150-strong (such was the local estimate) could assemble in the dark and make pitch-and-run attacks with their 60-mm. mortars; they had to be sought out relentlessly, their mortar position established by those under fire, and then illuminated by flare planes and blanketed by 81-mm. mortars stationed around the confines of the area. In that way, they could quickly be neutralized. But what was really necessary also was the total destruction of the political infrastructure. In important ways this was being done: the bodies of the Communist 'mayor' of Danang and some of his cronies slung over a fence a few days earlier was evidence of this: they had been cut down while on their way, presumably, to a 'parallel hierarchies' municipal meeting. But the proper destruction of the organization depended upon the quick apprehension of lots of individuals like the foreman at the Special Forces recreation camp; it depended also on good civilian agents who were protected from the kind of comic opera show I had just witnessed. That man was most probably as good as dead and his usefulness anyway at an end in that area—and in a peasant country like Vietnam, an agent is seldom of much use anywhere else in the country on that level of counter-intelligence.

Such were my thoughts as I reported at Marine battalion headquarters, where the soldier's wry, tough humour immediately imposed itself: a photograph of some scrofulous-looking beatniks roughly

THE GENERAL NATURE OF THE STRUGGLE IN VIETNAM

captioned in large inked lettering: THIS MAKES IT ALL WORTH WHILE —KILL A VC AND MAKE A BEATNIK UNHAPPY. Oddly, I remembered a few words (and remembered them almost certainly inaccurately in point of detail) from an article by André Malraux published in *Horizon* (I think) not long after the end of World War II; he wrote about the future being in the hands, he hoped, of those with 'a kind of crazy comradeship': well, here they are, I thought happily—and they've never heard of *Horizon*, nor *Partisan Review* for that matter. Headquarters was waging its war in a large sand-infested tent, duckboards for carpets, gum and soft-drink bottles for ideological replenishment, full of wireless sets tended lovingly by young men who knew they were living in the technological age—and enjoying it.

But what were they like 'out in the bush', as an Australian thought of the feet-on-the-ground war? We set off in the morning, a few of us led by a master-sergeant who seemed to have stepped straight out of the seamier passages of James Jones's *From Here to Eternity*, to join a platoon camped down on the beach, I, armed with a carbine and revolver supplied by Major Ian Teague, an Australian Special Forces officer, disarmed by grave worries about my fitness, re-armed by a feeling that there were a few aspects of this kind of warfare I understood rather better than the Marines.

I began to giggle to myself, as we moved through the small fishing hamlets, every doorway of which was attended by watching children or old folk (one finds oneself using that word in peasant countries for some reason or other), at the recollection of the Marine Corps schools' manual on Small-Unit Operations: 'Deception'. A patrol base is secretly occupied. Secrecy is maintained by practising deception techniques that are carefully planned. Deception plans should include the following considerations: (i) If possible, the march to the base is conducted at night. (ii) The route selected avoids centres of population. . . .'[1] Well, at least we avoided the vegetable plots. We picked our way through the greenery, stepped carefully over the little cactus plant hedges, nodded cheerfully and benignly at the locals, skirted the shrines with their dull lines and peeling white and off-blue paint. The children mostly smiled, since this was the beginning of a pacified area —ju-jubes, medicines, toys and soap—the old people stood in the shadows expressionless, just as I had seen them in other environments oppressed by guerrilla and counter-guerrilla fighting; in Arakan and the Shan State of Burma, in North-East Thailand, in Malaya, in Borneo as long ago as 1945; the old in 'Asia' are curiously imperturb-

[1] *The Guerrilla—and How to Fight Him*, op. cit.

THE GENERAL NATURE OF THE STRUGGLE IN VIETNAM

able, or are rendered gormless by an inadequate diet and the total 'laziness' that goes with it. But they had the strength to gossip and their grandchildren the energy to run. We were a small squad with relatively terrible firepower: scouts with Armalites and the sergeant with M79 grenade launcher. No one was going to jump us by daylight; no one feared our passing.

When we reached the beach a small Vietnamese who had been mooching about tried to make a run for it. He was caught and brought back to where we were resting between long grey fishing-boats. He was not maltreated in any way but he was very frightened. One Marine tried a few phrases from a little book but even though I am tone deaf I knew he was making the wrong sounds. Sign language established that he had lost his ID (Identity Card) while fishing. He probably really had. He was probably a harmless fisherman of about forty years of age who had grown up in one of the nearby villages and played on this beach lapped by the waters of the South China Sea as a child. But no one knew, so his scarf was gently removed from under his shirt and he was blindfolded with it but not before he had begun to cry like a child, loudly. His sobs accompanied us down the beach like a tom-tom.

During the afternoon the platoon positioned on the edge of the beach had to shelter under joined oilskins from heavy downpours which are a feature of this time of year around Danang. In between, it was steaming hot. Corporal Sandbank, a budding journalist from Michigan, my Marine PRO escort who was to show uncommon solicitude for me under fire, exchanged inter-state banter with Scout Boden from California who was looking forward to a long surfing holiday in Australia when he was paid off in a few months' time. It became clear, when conversation turned to the Marine Corps, that they felt themselves to belong to an élite body of men, conditioned by extraordinarily harsh training early on to be far more afraid of letting down the Corps than of fighting the Vietcong.

It also became clear that they still had a good deal to learn about guerrilla warfare when the time came, about 6.30 p.m., to strike camp and get ready to move inland under cover of darkness. We lay down behind light cover but very bunched up. It was obvious that our position must have been given away during the day to any enemy scout who had crawled around on the high ground a mile or so inland.

Suddenly there was the most disagreeably loud explosion very close by. Listening carefully in the silence that followed, it was possible to hear the sounds of the next shell leaving the mortar. We moved rather smartly amongst the sand dunes, I feeling a mixture of embarrassment and relief to find that I had no difficulty at all in keeping up with men twenty years younger in such circumstances.

The Marines took up positions along the ridge of dunes with admirable precision and the platoon commander was quickly in contact with headquarters. Very soon a flare was lightening the dusk above the mortar position which was on the high ground we had intended to occupy. It was only the fact that the mortar's early rounds had dropped behind a sand bank twenty feet behind where we were lying in readiness that had prevented a nasty incident.

Sandbank came back from the platoon's wireless man to explain that it might take some time before the U.S. mortars replied since this was the time when the local population was likely to be exposed on their way home to their villages. I found this solicitude extremely impressive. By the time that Sergeant Chang of Hawaii was explaining to me just how close I should let the Vietcong approach before I threw the hand grenades I had been given after a weak joke about cricket, I began to find this solicitude even a little irritating. The Marines were beautifully calm, perfectly disciplined, and the gentle lapping of the waters of the South China Sea was oddly enchanting. I was seized by a sense of the mysterious greatness of the Americans, a greatness compounded of so many peoples, a variety represented even here; Sandbank, Boden, Chang, Lacqueur. . . . Then came the welcome sound of the American 81-mm. mortars opening up on our enemy who had even the darkness of the night denied to them by the men of the new technological age as the flare plane circled above them. They would find their way home, those who survived, which would be most of them, perhaps by the tiny glow of fireflies in bottles. Though they did not know it, they were fighting with enormous courage for an outworn fantasy first dreamed up in the British Museum and hastily being discarded by the youth of the whole European Communist world. It was Marx who had said, 'Everything happens twice: the first time as tragedy, the second as farce.' Would they ever learn that, the thin men in black out there in the protective shadows thrown by small bushes?

A little while later we set off in the darkness by a devious route through a young plantation area to approach another position inland. The Lieutenant established a tight defence perimeter on a gentle slope and I stretched out on the fine, sandy soil to sleep. But soon I was awakened to be reminded that earlier in the day I had asked to go out on the night's ambush patrol. Since there was estimated to be something of the order of a Vietcong company, about 150-strong, out there in the bush somewhere I had imagined that the idea would have been abandoned. But no: a sergeant lined nine of us up and whispered the kind of instructions I had earlier admired about the Marines but now found profoundly disquieting: 'They'll most likely try to jump us. If they do, there's only one thing for us to do—just move in line towards their fire position until we've walked all over them, giving them everything we've got as we go.'

So we moved off down along the edge of a wide track towards the ambush point. Contrary to stories I had heard, the patrol moved extraordinarily quietly. Even my own smoker's cough altogether left me: perfect fear doubtless stills all maladies. Then the moon began to behave quite atrociously: every time we reached a clearing between lines of plantation, which we always had to cross individually (and most properly so), the moon would peek out from behind dark clouds to illuminate every rut and bush and step-forward across the clearing. I would make my way across the open space aware of the cold pipe clenched between my teeth, the cold grenades strapped to my waist, the revolver's holster knocking against my thighbone, the feel of the repeater rifle in my right hand; aware also—beyond even the croaking of frogs which after a time began to assume the insistence of imagined Vietcong signals—of a sense of horror, probably mostly personal, but (I hope) also a little more generalized about the un-necessity of this war: it did not quite make sense, it did not 'fit' into the pattern of modernization, it was somehow *deeply* unnecessary: for fifteen years I had been meeting Vietnamese exiles in places like Bangkok and Vientiane and Singapore and Rangoon—and in Saigon in 1954 and again in 1962, for that matter—and they had all been 'lovely blokes', as the Australians say, and they all had been quite wildly 'progressive'; and some of the very best of them had seen in the murdered Ngo Dinh Diem the best hope for South Vietnam (and none of these, to the best of my recollection, were Catholics.)

What had gone wrong? I tried to ask myself as I stumbled in ditches, hesitated in patches of moonlight, moved my eyes along the clearing that I was crossing—dry soil, open country, plantations either side of my vision, quite tall trees here, reminiscent in some eerie way of the Western plains of Victoria, which I had known since childhood. What had gone wrong? Why were we nine men, eight of whom were representatives of the least expansionist Great Power that history has ever known, treading warily through the scrub around Danang? What was it all about? In this kind of country at this time of night the odds were not peculiarly unequal: they had their superior knowledge of the geographical terrain, their control still—to some extent at least—of the human terrain, and they most probably had a medium machine-gun. They could 'take' us as they had 'taken' other small U.S. units in the recent past—of that there was no doubt—and in 'taking us' they, the majority of them, would only move one step forward towards state slavery on collective farms, the very theoretical notion of which was being slowly abandoned in the European Communist countries.

But why were *we* here, most of us young and politically uninformed, stumbling around in the scrub seeking out an enemy whom I am sure none of these young men ideologically hated, hated at all for that matter, except as an impediment—and possibly a catastrophic interruption—to what they had been brought to expect from youth: College perhaps, a job certainly, a different kind of struggle for livelihood (meaner possibly, but more nicely circumscribed by far as to likely outcome). Death is not seemingly omnipresent at that age; nor does one consistently address questions to an uncaring eternity, as is the way with cosseted Western intellectuals. Even so, the question hung obstinately in the warm air, between bursts of self-concern, and somehow had to be self-answered there and then. And it was then that I remembered faces near Akyab, the chief town of the Arakan Division of Burma, a country governed by ultra-Progressives, the faces of people who had recently come in from an area bombarded by government gunboats trying to put down a Communist insurgency, as it was believed to be; the faces of plantation workers, Indian, Chinese, and very occasionally Malay, in the Renggam district of Johore State in Malaya in 1951; the faces of Shan villagers on the Namkham-Kutkai-Lashio road in northern Burma; the faces of Borneans as they paddled along the river towards the sea to greet our ungainly convoy of landing-craft which had set off from Mempakaul early in the morning to penetrate the Japanese area of 'pacification'.

In all these cases people had died atrociously—and exact blame could not be attributed—but all these faces, unless one had been all along a fool (which was quite possible) expressed the desire for a restoration of orderliness and kindliness; and that, I felt as I walked full of fear across those bleak moonlit clearings, was most likely, immeasurably most likely, to be achieved through the agency of these gay and gallant young men who were my companions that night. *This* was what it was all about: that young men like these could walk these trails quite without an ideology to sustain them—only a crazy quality of fraternity, carelessness (in the obvious sense of that term), and true democratic graciousness: the graciousness of those who, very young, sought only to bear themselves like soldiers until they could resume their ordinary lives as mechanics and waiters and clerks. . . . There has never been anything quite like this in the world. In their company, it seemed silly to go on asking oneself the question: What had gone wrong?

Which did not prevent the insistent intrusion of quite another question: how long would the pacification, which had only begun in a few areas, take to be completed? Here we were at the ambush point, nine men settled on pine needles in a nook between a well-used wide dirt track and the river which was sometimes used as a night-way for transporting resources, the snipers with their Armalites and the marvellous starlight scope that plucked a mere silhouette out of the darkness, watching the moon-speckled water flowing gently past. It had taken us an hour to move 1,000 yards; probably no one would turn up. How many man-hours were used to kill one Vietcong? In one tight operation in Malaya it had taken 1,500 man-days of patrolling or waiting in ambush for each terrorist killed or captured—plus 60,000 artillery shells, 30,000 rounds of mortar ammunition, and 2,000 aircraft bombs. The tight operations were for the most part far away yet in South Vietnam.

The moonlight on the river was almost unbearably beautiful on this night. The Vietnamese were people of the moon: this dour, combatative sometimes cruel people are also so tender and romantic—in a deeply pessimistic fashion—moved always by a sense of the fleetingness of life, which is symbolized so exquisitely by the pale reflection of the moon in gently running water. . . . 'Thousands of lilies lie between my father and mother and me. My tears flow unceasingly. . . . Little by little the days, and then the months, slip by; each passing spring leaves us a little. Affection and care may be likened to the reflection of the moon in water; Honour and personal advantage pass, like flowers blown in the wind. . . .' So the Vietnamese had sung quietly over the centuries.

No one came down the track; no one used the river. This confirmed my fears that we had been watched all the time. I nerved myself to suggest to the sergeant that we should return by a different route. He said: 'Are you joking? I want to live too.' He led us back by a different route and his sense of direction was unerring: we were inside the platoon perimeter after what seemed to be a much shorter journey. . . .

In the morning darkness the platoon lies in a long line hidden by tall grass at the approach to the beach. We are back in sound of the sea again. There is no smoking, no talking. (There was smoking at the ambush point, to my amazement.) The only things visible besides the silhouettes of tall palms fringing the fishing village we are about to sweep are the lights of fishing boats twinkling close in to the shore. What an immense task it must be to patrol the coast properly when hundreds of thousands of Vietnamese continue to fish regularly, an activity that obviously could not sensibly be interrupted.

Cocks begin to crow in the village; a pink light permeates the dark clouds of the rainy season moving in from the north-east; the village begins to stir in the dawn. But by this time we are moving briskly into positions from which to surround the village, preparing to contract the cordon—the *Kesselring* of major counter-insurgent operations (the chief weakness of which is the ability of a determined enemy to break through at selected points)—and possibly, just possibly, pick up one or two Vietcong resting at home.

At first light the sweep begins. The platoon moves forward (another platoon has been moved up during the night to complete the semi-circle embracing the village up to the seashore), widely spaced out. We are watching for young male faces, fit male bodies: every young man is regarded as a possible Vietcong or a possible deserter. This terrible war has now reached that stage of 'popular mobilization' where all young men are to be involved in it by one side or the other. I remember Saigon a few nights ago, the square outside the oh-so-French Continentale Hotel, and the kindness in the face of Ted Serong (who is one of the greatest counter-insurgent experts operating anywhere today) as he played with the children who make their home in the square, near the sentry box that once guarded 'Parliament House', now just an empty white building with broken windows; remember also his words at that time, 'The manpower shortage may soon become serious.' Such was the price of all the mistakes and misunderstandings of the past.

We skirt the little cactus hedges once more, avoid the pits of sharpened bamboo panji sticks sown like dry, malevolent asparagus in the sandy soil, try to avoid moving across the neat mounds ripe and rich with green vegetables. A Vietnamese soldier attached to the platoon breaks a stake fence to get himself a stick. Nothing changes, I think unfairly (probably): it was that kind of carelessness, hugely magnified and including women, that had helped the anti-Communist government lose the support of a significant part of the peasantry.

We move slowly. I became intrigued by the shards of blue and white pottery littering the paths we tread. It reminds me of Brittany and shellfish; recalls also shards of blue and white pottery found amongst broken glass and rusty implements at the site of a convict work-place on a blustery point in New South Wales. A young Marine begins to help me collect it; it clicks against the hand grenade in the capacious pocket of my jungle-greens. Life begins to seem most pleasantly absurd in the warm morning air; the village fills one with homely aesthetic well-being—the gleaming fishing nets, newly woven, embellished with red and blue and yellow plastic floats, are gay and pure against the thatch and weave of the dust-dulled huts; the great earthenware water pots stand like fecund bellies formed by the swell of the water itself, impeccably formed, an example of natural craftsmanship that seemed to shame the blunt and jagged beastliness of our guns. (No, I did not forget that such earthenware jars often hid subterranean tunnel openings; it just seemed irrelevant—especially as this wasn't soil for tunnelling, I suppose!)

The village is lively with shouted commands but the villagers go on preparing their breakfast—little bowls of rice, green stuff, fish sauce —the older ones studiously avoiding our eyes, the children gazing in puzzlement, quite unafraid. The huts are all entered briefly, men are aroused from bed and some of them rounded up. An old man replaces the movable wall of his hut as the Marines move on. His old, wise, sleepy face betrays no emotion.

The search is brisk and necessarily superficial. I remember Grosthwaite's remarks about Upper Burma in 1886, Jean Lacouture's about North Vietnam in 1953. Someone says, 'It's to keep them on their toes. It reminds them of our presence.' And of course it does indeed do that. Follow-up and continuity, though, are absolutely necessary; and that is not being attempted yet. Two worlds are meeting here— without being able to communicate with each other in any proper manner—in this small fishing village beside the South China Sea. A child comes forward asking for 'five p's' and I know that even here the world is changing rapidly: small change eroding the whole structure of village society, its pottery, its boatmaking techniques, its values, its hopes.

We are now joined by Captain Lloyd who had brought in the other platoon; with him has come a squat motorized child's dream of a 'minitruck' loaded with provisions for the village. We eat our breakfast of tinned rations: sweet wet spam (the guzzling of which provoked the reflection that had the Americans supplied the tinned meat for the Arab campaign in World War I, then all Lawrence's sensitivity to Bedouin Muslim susceptibilities would have been most sorely tested), sweet wet 'sweeties', and sweet dry fizzy powder which I realize too late, was meant to be dropped into one's water bottle in order to re-create the illusion of one's home drug store. Sandbank, solicitous and punctilious as ever, shows me how to grind the empty cans in such a manner as he assumes would prevent their use in the future for nefarious devices. Having arranged to have myself 'marooned' on a peace-time tourist island near Cairns in Queensland over twenty years ago, in order to test certain ideas about survival techniques, I am not altogether impressed by the exercises. But in front of Captain Lloyd and Major King D. Thattenhurst, a much-decorated, quietly spoken Marine hero, I keep my thoughts to myself and grind away at the tins.

Then comes the 'civic action' part of the day's performance and I am completely bewildered: several hundred cans are being handed out with a magnificently generous lack of discretion throughout the village. Fidel Castro's dictum, 'You Americans are not guerrilla-minded', still seems to have some force even amongst these otherwise superbly trained American Marines. The squat Mule (as it is called) trundles its provisions down into the centre of the village, assiduously avoiding the cactus hedge, sometimes helped out of a ditch by embarrassedly eager hands, and begins to disgorge its cargo of rations, medicine, and toys provided by the citizens of the battalion commander's hometown in the U.S.A.

'Doc' Baker, the medic, a Negro with the face of a happy saint, blessed by an incurably humorous—greatly humorous—outlook upon the world, walks alongside the Mule telling me how he and his fellow-Negro soldier have been receiving Vietcong propaganda leaflets about the Los Angeles riots. He is only vastly amused by the whole business: the Marine Corps is infertile ground for such a ploy; indeed so are all the American forces in South Vietnam—maybe the breakthrough in the 'colour question' will come about as a result of companionship in this war. It would indeed be a nice joke if in the greatest of democracies it came to pass that, in one particular, 'the army incarnates the peoples' human equality. Very recently a Negro died very bravely in order to try to save his white buddy; no one in the Marine Corps doubts that the converse would happen whenever the opportunity might offer.

Old women and old men and mothers and children throng around the Mule and 'Doc' Baker, vying for toys and (chiefly) eye treatment and ointment for infected heads. Mothers and grandfathers encourage children to return again and again to the queue formed up by 'Doc'; he begins to recognize faces already encountered, and swishes them away with a laugh. He is not really very effective in this activity because his innate sweetness blinds him to all manner of self-seeking. But he delivers a lecture through the interpreter on the necessity of washing children's heads: 'Tell them to use a bit of soap and they won't need a doctor.' From time to time the mass importunity becomes too much for even the 'Doc' to bear; he signals the Mule to move on. He explains to me that a distribution of soap is to be the follow-up operation; and I have no doubt whatsoever that he will see that it is carried out.

He closes shop and the withdrawal back to base follows. I look at the round-up: thirty men, arranged squatting in ranks of five. They all have Identity Cards, of course. They have all been brought in for questioning before (it transpires later) and one of them could not be more than twelve years of age; but as Captain Lloyd says, 'They're in good condition. There are quite a few young studs amongst them.' This was how it was going, how it had to go at this stage. But how long was this stage going to be? This was what was going to be critical so far as American public opinion was concerned in the years to come.

The senior Marine officers are quite aware of the nature of protracted war, as are other senior officers in Vietnam.[1] And so the job of the professionals is simply to go steadily ahead with their appointed tasks. One of the most interesting of these is the training of the Police Field Force (P.F.F.) at Dalat and Pleikku, Vietnamese personnel being trained at the former place, montagnards at the latter. The task of the P.F.F. is para-military in nature. At this stage it involves little less than the complete rebuilding of rural society; protecting it when the Vietcong main-force units have been cleared out of an area, preventing the movement of guerrilla resources, maintaining the reconstructed government administration. But much more than this: helping re-establish village schools and medical centres (always targets of Vietcong terrorism), injecting confidence into the villagers, even modernizing the village and introducing them to up-to-date ideas of hygiene.

But above all the P.F.F. must be able to maintain security in areas evacuated by regular forces, which have not yet been sufficiently restored to orderliness for the national police to take over. In fact the P.F.F.'s overlap both areas; operating in the rear of the thrusting-out regulars, in the front zone of the spreading-out national police.

[1] Interview with General Wallace M. Greene, Commandant of the U.S. Marine corps, *U.S. News and World Report*, 5th September 1966.

THE GENERAL NATURE OF THE STRUGGLE IN VIETNAM

This has to be a very carefully phased operation, as carefully phased as Giap's—phasing remains at the heart of the problem. The P.F.F. operates as a part of the forces involved in the pacification of selected areas, which includes not only themselves and the regulars but the Regional and Popular (village militia) Forces as well. However, the overall rate of pacification will be significantly determined by the P.F.F.'s ability to play its role alone as the protector of the society that is being rebuilt. If that means a slow rate of advance by the regulars it is just too bad: the great mistake made in this sphere by Diem's regime was to push the pacification programme altogether too quickly forward, allowing Vietcong re-penetration of supposedly pacified areas. This is not for the most part a war of quick armed thrusts; it is a war between two different kinds of society, each trying slowly *totally* to overwhelm the other and permanently to establish its own administrative apparatus and way of life.

The P.F.F. is therefore concerned with policing, but it is of a new kind; above all mobile, self-sufficient, omnipresent and yet disguised as to its exact movements at any time—police who will never offer themselves as a sitting target, as has been the way with police in the past. P.F.F. platoons (the operational unit) will use bivouacs not requisition buildings. They will feed themselves and so never batten on the local population. Being recruited locally, they will visit their families when bivouacing nearby in order to inspire popular confidence. They will also become known for their activities in initiating or taking part in 'civic action' work designed to better the lives of the villagers within their area of operation, which is the village complex of which they are native sons. They will be very like the Vietcong indeed. But they will neither be creating a militarized society nor paving the way for the political and social enslavement of the population through collectivization of agriculture.

This touches upon one of the great problems of counter-insurgency. Given the fact that Communist revolutionary guerrilla warfare basically involves the slow expansion of a perfervidly militaristic totalitarian society, through terrorism as well as exploiting 'contradictions', to what extent can counter-insurgents afford to adopt the enemy's methods? To what extent can it afford *not* to adopt the enemy's methods?

This problem is much more serious than is often realized. At present it is disguised in South Vietnam, because of the methods the Americans have been enabled to adopt during the present phase of the war—'spoiling' and 'bleeding' operations against enemy main-force units, limited pacification in areas which have not been deeply impermeated by the Vietcong politico-military apparatus, penetrative search-and-destroy operations in lightly populated enemy areas, and so on. As General William DePuy, commander of the First Infantry Division, has put it: 'It is a combination of artillery and the Seventh Air Force that kills the Vietcong.'

So far it has been mainly a matter of making technological responses to local military techniques: the starlight scope against night field craft based upon local knowledge of the terrain; the portable landing net against the jungle; the laser illuminator against the penetration of a camp; the heat detector against the smoke-filter oven; photo-reconnaissance against local mobility; the helicopter against the panji stick; the grenade thrower and the Armalite against ambush fire; the heavy bomber against local tunnelling techniques, artillery against booby-trapped hamlets.[1]

The destructiveness of the American method of making war in South Vietnam has quite naturally evoked much criticism in the West but it is worth while considering the alternative approach to the problem of counter-insurgency worked out by the technologically much less richly endowed French. The French experts argued, perfectly correctly, that 'Warfare is now an interlocking system of actions —political, economic, psychological, and military—that aim at the *overthrow of the established authority in a country and its replacement by another regime* . . . traditional armed forces are only of limited importance. . . . This is doubtless why the army, traditionally attracted by the purely military aspects of a conflict, has never seriously approached the study of a problem it regards as an inferior element in the art of war.'[2]

Colonel Trinquier, identifying 'the subtlest aspect of modern warfare' as the 'manipulation of populations', particularly, in his view, through terrorism, argues that the response to this kind of warfare must be total: 'If, like the knights of old, our army refused to employ all the weapons of *modern warfare*, it could no longer fulfil its mission. We would no longer be defended.' Or as one of Jean Larteguy's defeated veterans of Dien-Bien-Phu says, 'He knew it had to come to this, that this was the ghastly law of the new type of war. But he had to get accustomed to it, to harden himself and shed all those deeply

---

[1] The author was intrigued to notice that the U.S. *Popular Mechanics* magazine of August 1966 contained an excellent article on Vietcong booby traps!
[2] Colonel Roger Trinquier, *Modern Warfare: A French View of Counterinsurgency*, op. cit.

ingrained notions which make for the greatness of Western man but at the same time prevent him from protecting himself.' What he had to accustom himself to was the use of 'special methods', called torture by others, as a means of breaking up the political apparatus that was manipulating the population.

Here lies the greatest danger of all to counter-insurgents, the temptation to adopt a synthetic counterpart to Communist totalitarianism. It was not only sections of the French Army that were afflicted by a kind of counter-Maoism; the Diem regime, under the influence of the intellectual ideologue, Ngo Dinh Nhu, went a long way towards attempting the same thing. But it must be understood that the nature of Communist revolutionary warfare is such that the dilemma is a very real one for any counter-insurgent government that does not dispose of the overwhelming power of other kinds that the U.S.A. possesses. As a resolute and outspoken opponent of 'special methods' points out, 'Just as within a country a Communist insurgency can not be dealt with in isolation, so, in a world-wide context, it is not an isolated event but an integral part of the continuing process of Communist aggression by means of subversion and terror. No under-developed or newly independent country can face this threat alone. It will need more than political support from the free world. Economic and material support will be necessary, and military support may be required in addition to military equipment.'[1]

The Americans did not become unnerved, even in the rapidly deteriorating situation of March 1965, as the French did in Algeria, about their traditional effectiveness. They had no need to. Moreover, it is arguable that had international circumstances been different, Algeria could have been retained for France for a much longer time, though at a catastrophic price: the destruction of civil liberty in France. As Peter Paret points out in a remarkable study of French counter-insurgent theory and practice, 'A totalitarian nation within the framework of an aggressively anti-Russian and anti-Chinese alliance might well have won the revolutionary war in Algeria.'[2]

This is a point of very great importance indeed. The nature of revolutionary warfare is such that it almost inevitably evokes a totalitarian response to some extent: a basically civilian society in an under-developed nation simply cannot stand up to the encroachments of a revolutionary warfare campaign without to some extent becoming

[1] Sir Robert Thompson op. cit.
[2] *French Revolutionary Warfare from Indochina to Algeria*, Pall Mall Press, 1964.

THE GENERAL NATURE OF THE STRUGGLE IN VIETNAM

totalitarian too, once the campaign has been got properly off the ground. The country's army may be very good indeed, well-behaved towards the population, adept at fieldcraft, excellent in tactics, great in valour. But killing guerrillas is not the real problem; the problem is to isolate them from the population and hence break their control over a movement that is always more political then military. This is a police, administrative, and intelligence problem too great for the civilian society of an under-developed country to cope with. It is designedly so: it is an application of Communist tactics to a specific kind of social situation. It does indeed 'exploit contradictions', and not just social inequities but the political and administrative weaknesses intrinsic to such developing societies.

The Americans responded to a deteriorating situation by means proper to their own inventive traditions and appropriate to that stage of the struggle in South Vietnam. A typical example of their response was the 1st Cavalry (Airmobile) Division: a whole division of troops, 3,000 of them trained as paratroopers, the remainder being trained in assault by helicopters, which were an integral part of the division. Here are helicopters that can quickly position nearly a hundred men apiece; others firing rockets in their support; here is an air cavalry that can lift its 105-mm. howitzers into battle. Here lies a way of capturing an initiative without the employment of 'special methods'; or so it seems.

But the problem will not really be so simple as that as the pacification phase is entered on a large scale; it will not be nearly as simple as that in the Delta. A hundred helicopters laden with troops cannot remove the stranglehold of the Vietcong over the peasants even in one small hamlet. Again, this is recognized by perceptive U.S. commanders. General DePuy has rightly said: 'As big battles become less productive for them they will end up doing what they can do effectively. And that is where the job begins.' And that is where it suddenly becomes very difficult indeed for the Western counter-insurgent, whose superiority in weapons and technology has so far allowed him to stand back and take an objective view of his battles with the enemy, to identify himself with the task to be done at village level, understanding the problems there to be encountered by sharing the people's thoughts and fears.

The American response to this will perhaps be the continuing build-up of very large forces; and, perhaps, the resolution to fight a very long war. In so far as the problem of revolutionary warfare is mainly confined to South Vietnam, then it is quite possible for young

THE GENERAL NATURE OF THE STRUGGLE IN VIETNAM

Americans to serve there without severe damage to their traditions of behaviour in any permanent sense. There is no danger whatsoever of American officers in South Vietnam developing the kind of quasi-fascist 'counter-Maoism' that afflicted the much more sorely tried French. The effects of reliance upon technological superiority may on many occasions be dreadful for villagers caught under fire (despite prior American warnings) but the alternative to this would be an Algerian style 'crusade' and this is precisely what liberal democracies cannot afford. Today that is simply a sign of loss of nerve.

It is probably true to say that the great issue of the struggle in South Vietnam will be about the manner of pacification, especially in the densely populated Delta region. It is very difficult indeed to see how this can be completed in a civilized fashion without an enormous effort of devoted service by tens of thousands, hundreds of thousands of Americans. There is some reason to believe that this will be forthcoming, because of the importance attributed to South Vietnam. But there is equally reason to believe that it is very necessary that in the future some other approach must be adopted internationally towards the general problem of revolutionary warfare. However, it is extraordinarily difficult to establish what the approach should be.

Though it is quite possible for experts to identify the early stages of a Communist revolutionary guerrilla war, public recognition of such an identification, both in the target society and abroad, is an altogether different matter. Ideally, the United Nations should recognize this form of warfare as a threat to the peace and act accordingly. Ideally, the United Nations should be empowered to send inspection teams to areas of disaffection at the request of the governments concerned, provided such governments could present a *prima facie* case for such inspection. If the UN inspection team were convinced that an armed rising was being mounted, then, ideally, a UN observation team would be stationed in the disaffected area and the economic and social 'contradictions' being exploited by the armed Communist organization would be tackled by the appropriate UN agencies. The threatened society would, as a condition of applying to the UN, have to agree to carry out what the UN deemed necessary economic and social reforms in the countryside, working alongside and under the notice of the UN agencies.

But for a number of reasons such an ideal solution is clearly not in sight. First of all, as the International Control Commission's activities in Vietnam have shown, the kind of inspection team at present established by the UN is of its nature unable to agree upon what constitutes 'aggression' against an established government. The composition of such teams (in Vietnam it was Indian-Polish-Canadian) results in the facts of insurgency being interpreted by the Communist component simply in terms of political philosophy: for Communists, Communist revolutionary insurgencies are still by definition spontaneous popular risings against colonial, neo-colonial, or 'feudal' oppression.

It should be added that even if this at present insuperable barrier to international recognition of the mounting of a revolutionary insurgency did not exist, there would still remain a great reluctance on the part of most governments in the under-developed world to admit that things were getting out of hand in the countryside; and part of this reluctance would be well founded, since an admission of losing control is in itself a fact of very great importance in this kind of struggle. The case of Thailand's North-East which was discussed earlier, serves as a good example of this predicament. Moreover, part of such reluctance would relate to the issue of sovereignty which again is of great significance in this kind of struggle: an important difficulty can be placed in the way of Communist insurgency through an appropriately stated nationalist interest.

Therefore, so far as can be seen into the future, revolutionary insurgencies, if started with due circumspection, may be expected to 'get off the ground' before international public opinion has taken much interest in them, by which time the nature of their origins will have become so beclouded by sedulously infiltrated fellow-travelling propaganda and wish-dreams propagated by guilt-laden 'progressives' that purposeful counter-action on behalf of the target society will become increasingly less likely.

Success against the Communists in Vietnam will not necessarily, as has been argued elsewhere, stiffen the will of the U.S.A. for future struggles of a like kind. It may well have the effect of a general U.S. determination that 'No more Vietnams' shall be the slogan for the future. It is conceivable that the involvement in Vietnam will, in time to come, be regarded as having been based upon a grave strategic misconception. But if that day should come revolutionary guerrilla warfare will take on an invincible aspect throughout South-East Asia and probably much further afield in the under-developed world.

And of course, this is precisely what Mr. Cabot Lodge must have had in mind when he argued that the U.S.A. was fighting in South Vietnam in order to prevent a general 'holocaust'. Such a holocaust will occur, if it occurs, not simply because a Communist victory in the 'test case' of Vietnam will have nerved Communists throughout the third world to embark on an apparently invincible course of action, not simply because insurgencies have begun to proliferate in increasing numbers but also because a failure in Vietnam on the part of the Americans will have deeply subverted *their* confidence in being able to cope with the general Communist threat in *limited* ways. It is not in the least necessary for a supporter of U.S. action in South Vietnam, from the moment the struggle was joined *en masse*, to be an admirer of all the qualities of American character in order to perceive the catastrophic consequences of an American failure in that struggle. Indeed it is to be hoped that such consequences will be foreseen before it is too late by precisely those in Europe who most distrust what they like to call the 'emotional instability' of Americans.

Chapter 9

VIETNAM: THE VIETMINH REVOLUTION

Vietnam is basically composed of two delta regions joined by a narrow coastal strip, less than 50 miles wide at its narrowest. Some 60 per cent of the country's area is mountainous, including high plateaux, inhabited by tribes known collectively as montagnards (or as Mois, savages) having nothing in common except a long enmity with the Vietnamese. As much as 80 per cent of South Vietnam provides tree or bush cover for guerrilla warfare; nearly half of it provides high stand tree cover or real jungle. The coastline of Vietnam is about 1,200 miles long.

The population of North Vietnam was stated in 1964 to be 15,000,000 and South Vietnam 12,800,000.[1] North Vietnam is 60,000 square miles, South Vietnam 66,000 square miles in area. Population density in the Vietnamese areas of settlement are very much greater in the north than in the south; in the north the 'morcellement' of land reached 'pocket-handkerchief' proportions by World War II but centuries-long prodigies of hydraulic engineering developed a control system never yet attempted in the south and more than half of this region is double cropped with rice. In the north ownership of fragments of land by individual peasants was the overwhelming rule; in the south, as a result of French policy, tenant farming was very widespread.[2]

North Vietnam became the centre of the country's mining and manufacturing industry, South Vietnam an important rice-exporter, the two halves of today being clearly complementary to each other economically. On the other hand, as will be shown, there is a long

[1] C. A. Fisher, *A Social, Economic and Political Geography of South-East Asia*, Methuen, 1964. Ellen Hammer, *Vietnam: Yesterday and Today*, Holt, Rhinehart and Winston, 1966, gives the figures of 18 millions and 16 millions respectively; and states that the rate of population increase is 3·4 per cent which, if true, is exceedingly fast in present circumstances.

[2] By 1940, more than 98 per cent of Tonkinese and 89 per cent of Annamese (central region) peasants still owned pieces of land. G. McT Kahin, *Governments and Politics of Southeast Asia*, Cornell University Press, 1959. In the 1930's about two-thirds of the population of the southern delta were tenant farmers paying up to 40 per cent of their crop in rent.

historical precedent for the present political division; and the French policy of ruling through three regions, Cochin-China, Annam, and Tonkin—and ruling Cochin-China in a different fashion, exacerbated historical regionalism.

To confine description as far as possible to South Vietnam; the general employment situation in 1961, according to a Colombo Plan survey was:

Agriculture, forests and fisheries	5,642,000
Mining	1,020
Manufacturing	123,600
Building and Public Works	150,500
Electricity, Gas and Water	2,600
Commerce, Banking, Insurance	206,000
Transport	145,300
Services	34,800
Plantations	61,000
Domestic Services	100,000

Though Saigon, with a population of perhaps 2,000,000, is an important city, and though there are a number of significant provincial centres and (recently) ports, South Vietnam is basically composed of thousands of hamlets, each containing a few hundred people, and villages, the population of each of which may number several thousands. Population density varies considerably; even within the Mekong delta, some 14,000 square miles in area it varies between 500 to 75 per square mile (and even much less in the southernmost swamp country).[1] Even so, an average of 250 people per square mile, when the enclustered peasant village style of collective living is taken into account, will make the pacification of this region a very difficult task indeed from the point of view of preserving human lives; and since it is uncontrolled inundation country, operating there is extremely disagreeable. Moreover, this kind of country is not designed, to put it mildly, for heli-pads, let alone airstrips.

In order to understand the nature of the present struggle it is necessary to consider the Vietnamese people as well as the nature of revolutionary guerrilla warfare. The Vietnamese are not only the most numerous of the peoples of continental South-East Asia; they are by far the most formidable. A recent historian of Vietnam has remarked, 'The very existence of Vietnam as a separate country, and the survival

---

[1] Fisher, op. cit. Fisher makes the interesting point that at the beginning of French colonial rule the average density was 50–60 per square mile.

of the Vietnamese as a distinct people, must be regarded as a miracle, for which scores of historians have so far tried vainly to find a satisfactory explanation.'[1] This is undoubtedly written out of an excess of enthusiasm: a glance at the extent of past Chinese imperial domains and a thought about communications systems in the pre-industrial age, together with a little consideration of the ease with which the Vietnamese could expand southwards, will suggest that there was nothing particularly miraculous about their survival as a people.

Nevertheless, in striving to survive against Chinese colonial encroachment and the even more insistent, and much more turbulent encroachment of the Song-koi (Red River) floodwaters, the Vietnamese have developed formidable qualities.

They were under Chinese subjection for more than a thousand years (III B.C. to A.D. 939) to whom they were known as the 'people beyond the river' or, more significantly, the people of the 'Pacified South'— a benighted area of imperial 'inspection'. Their upper, literate orders of society were thoroughly sinicized, alike as to religions and the ethical system; institutions and ideographs; and military organization and agricultural techniques. Indeed the modern term 'Little China' seemed appropriate enough to some observers.[2]

Certainly political unity of the country has not been usual in modern times: since 1600 Vietnam has only once been a unified state, under the Emperor Gia-Long between 1802 and 1858; during the preceding two centuries it was divided roughly where it is divided today. The noted British authority, P. J. Honey makes much of this: 'Every Vietnamese knows his history and knows that throughout Vietnamese history there have been Chinese invasions. Only when China overruns the whole country is it hopeless. . . . The Vietnamese people believe that if they can keep a part of the country free from Chinese occupation, there is a chance of driving them out. They look upon North Vietnam as being under Chinese influence and South Vietnam as the part that is holding out.'[3]

This understanding is not accepted by a Northerner like Hoang Van Chi, the distinguished author of *From Colonialism to Communism*, who argues that a serious mistake of the Americans has been to under-

[1] Joseph Buttinger, *The Smaller Dragon*, Praeger, 1958.
[2] The English writer, Alan Houghton Brodrick, wrote an interesting account of Vietnam under that title, Oxford University Press in 1942; in 1951 his fellow countryman Norman Lewis wrote an equally interesting account, *Dragon Apparent*, Cape.
[3] But this viewpoint is not easy publicly to sustain so long as northerners play so large a part in Saigon, hence exacerbating southern regionalism.

take in advance not to try to overthrow the Hanoi regime, thereby surrendering, on behalf of the Saigon Government, the all-important nationalist claim. On the other hand, it is perfectly clear that in recent Saigonese politics mistrust between northerners and southerners has been significant: the argument today is very much one about the appropriate political mythology.

Suffice it to say at this point that despite (or perhaps because of) Chinese imperial domination in the past, the Vietnamese do share a dour, tenacious, combative sense of national identity *vis-à-vis* the rest of the world . . . a terrible national arrogance, their Cambodian and Laotian neighbours call it. But because of historical accidents which have kept on occurring up to the present day, not the least being the French policy of ruling the country through the three regions (or kys), there have been very great difficulties put in the way of institutionalizing true modern nationalism or even of freely hammering out in public debate a common language for it.

It is possible for one nationalist to argue that Vietnamese culture was always only a slavish imitation of China, retaining official Confucian studies longer than China itself; and for another to argue that a very real sense of national identity was always maintained through the state patronage of Vietnamese letters. The standpoint of the debaters is usually determined to a large extent by their attitudes (or the attitude of their families) to political nationalism during the recent past. There arose a decisive division between members of a very generalized 'resistance' on the one hand and 'collaborators' with the French on the other, and within both groups there was often a division between those who looked to the old culture to sustain them and those who looked to the modern culture of Europe. It is probably true to say, and some Vietnamese nationalists say it, that French education was brought in too late to effect a thorough Westernization; producing only one generation, for the most part, of Westernized intellectuals, the impact of French culture was subversive rather than restorative of such national morale as existed.

And yet, bearing in mind the argument that continues, it would be difficult to deny that the Vietnamese discovered themselves, in a subtle and profound sense, during the period of Chinese tutelage in the Red River delta. The systems of dams and dykes and canals was a very great human achievement and this effort of at least partly taming a huge natural challenge has left its mark on the national character in a fashion that is relevant today: a toughness not to be found in the easier lands of South-East Asia (and not to the same extent in South

Vietnam, for that matter, since the Mekong is gentler than the Songkoi); a quality of dourness allied with pessimism imprinted by the insistent rising and raging of waters, a king of seasonal fatalism, one might call it. Fatalism is, of course, politically neutral—until it is clear which side is definitely winning.[1]

Equally relevant is the fact that from the tenth century onwards there grew up within Vietnamese society an implacably expansionist mentality; they were not Spartans engaged in a permanent Thermopylae, as Hoang Van Chi has described them, for nothing. Far from confining themselves to the Red River delta, they became a colonizing people, moving south to wipe out (to all intents and purposes) the once powerful Chams who stood in the way, and moving out westwards against the territories of the Khmer (Cambodian) empire. This process of conquest was brought to a halt by the neat mapping pencils and administrative plans of the French imperialists who conquered Vietnam between 1862 and 1884 (though pacification lasted considerably longer) and also brought Laos and Cambodia into union with what the French liked to call their *Balcony on the Pacific*.

The monsoons, the rivers, and the delta plains made for a culture based on irrigation; a culture wholly dependent upon imposing a reasonable degree of water regulation in an area unafflicted by the anopheles mosquito, the destroyer, in all probability of the similar Khmer culture. Rice production was overwhelmingly dominant until the French introduced rubber into the south. This village culture, with its dependence upon the behaviour of the heavens and collective enterprise imposed from above (though leaving scope for the development of village *mores*), its water buffaloes, its pigs, its supplementary fishing, and its peculiar inlook, constituted a manner of thinking and behaving that remains in many parts even today almost impenetrable by Western minds. This is why Bernard Fall argued very wisely that on 'this specifically Vietnamese level' the foreigner can do nothing; and it is also why the Communists have taken vast pains to represent their disguised objectives in terms comprehensible on the traditional level of understanding.[2]

The super-culture erected on this foundation was primarily Confucian; society's affairs were ordered according to the Confucian understanding of man's place in the cosmos, which gave rise to a

---

[1] There is an interesting study of pessimism in Vietnamese poetry in *Asia* No. II, December 1953 (a quarterly then published in Saigon, later in Tokyo, edited by René de Berval.)
[2] See Paul Mus op. cit.

morality 'not founded upon divine revelation, but upon the elevation of the natural life to the level of the order of the Universe.' Confucianism was not exclusive of other religious attitudes in Vietnam, provided the activities of devotees did not appear subversive of the Confucian manner of ordering affairs, but—on this level—rather a code of ethics easily adaptable to Buddhism and Taoism, both of which were intermingled with it. A Vietnamese pagoda is apt to embody elements of the old agricultural cult of the sky and the earth, a statue (or many) of the Lord Buddha, the bamboo cylinders containing the fortune telling riddle-verses of Taoism, all commingling in the heart of the worshipper with devotion to tutelary spirits and ancestors.

But in the traditional Vietnamese society all these facets of belief and practice were contained within a rigidly ordered, hierarchical state or states. Though the Chinese withdrawal naturally appears in retrospect to Vietnamese today as a kind of national 'Liberation', the evacuation of Chinese power in fact rather left control in the hands of a feudal class of mandarin chieftains whose chief source of aversion of the Chinese was doubtless quite selfish: a desire to corner the taxation and corvée system for themselves. However, in imitation of the Chinese emperors, family dynasties did establish themselves as centralized, Confucian seats of power. The relationship of these rulers with the Chinese emperor sometimes involved the delightful device of recognizing themselves as vassals *vis-à-vis* the Chinese Emperor, emperors *vis-à-vis* their own vassals.

The emperor and his state apparatus came to play an important economic role. In bursts of state energy, agriculture was prompted, dykes were built, and new land opened up under a centrally directed military system. Expansion through *don-diens* (military-garrison-ricefields) was in a sense a precursor of Ngo Dinh Diem's attempt to expand his state through 'strategic hamlets'. What was happening was not simply a smashing of Cham and Khmer power but the slow, systematic settlement of lands southwards.

Three factors of contemporary relevance emerged from these developments. First, the Emperor became something of a true Son of Heaven, the progenitor of well-being, the link between a Heaven-imposed destiny and the actual human condition; in his person lay the Mandate of Heaven. By relegating the Emperor to a position of ritual obscurity and removing his meaningfulness—his Mandate—the French not only psychologically emasculated the educated and traditionally ruling class, in the course of time they found that they had created something like a spiritual vacuum which was filled by a new charismatic figure representing a fresh Mandate: Ho Chi Minh with his presumed tidal wave of the future, Communism.

The Mandate of Heaven was always necessarily a conditional mandate so far as the recipient was concerned and the order which supported him; it could be removed and its removal was made manifest in a breakdown in power. So it was with the French attempt to tame the Viets. The French administered the country always in a superficial way, never wholly unopposed, though for some time impregnable as an alien superstructure based on superior weapons and an altogether more efficient mode of administration not the least efficient arm of which was the deadly knowledgeable political section of the Sûreté. Meanwhile the peasants moved in their fields, their senses for ever alert to discern yet another major change in the tide of Destiny, the Mandate of Heaven. This change was recognized as having come with the display of apparently overwhelming military superiority by the Japanese, other 'yellow men', in the 1940's. The duration and intensity of the struggle in South Vietnam will be much affected by the as yet scarcely tested question of how deeply the Communists have been able to impermeate the minds of Vietnamese with the belief that the National Liberation Front really represents a decisive change of social order. If, as the author believes, the long-standing conditions of uncertainty and ebb-and-flow of power have prevented the mass of the people from being more than superficially affected by Communist propaganda, then it is quite possible, though it is most certainly not a hope on which policy can reasonably be based yet, that pacification might be a quicker business than is at present anticipated.

Secondly, there was developed a specifically Vietnamese mandarinate, however culturally slavish to China it may have been, which contained within it elements of a career open to talent and a system of extinguishing titles over a few generations. It has undoubtedly been romanticized as a system by some Vietnamese of the present day for example by the scholar-soldier who wrote to the author: 'Born from the wandering families of pioneers, the Vietnamese had no system of caste and the doors to fame and social position were wide open to anyone, irrespective of social origins. Vietnamese history is full of farmers who made good, of poor students who read books under the light of a firefly in a bottle and who later became the first dignitary of the country and married the beautiful daughter of the prime minister.' No doubt these were often mere yearnings; but they were aspirations too, and as such indicated possibilities of attaining high leadership that were genuinely felt. As Honey has remarked, the mandarinate 'never became fossilized because it was an élite based upon merit and its composition was constantly changing'. This retained a potentially dynamic element in the higher echelons of Vietnamese society from which so many of the leaders of the Communist Party of Indo-China have sprung. No such unified strata of political leadership sustained itself in colonial Burma or Malaya or Indonesia, for example, where most of the modern leadership came from other groups which were usually divided amongst themselves by racial or political divisions or special interests.

Thirdly, even when allowances are made for exaggeration by modern Vietnamese, there was a conscious attempt made to establish ways of incorporating an essentially Chinese-derived culture into a system of values that could easily be thought of as Vietnamese: 'Temples of Literature', the 'Assembly of the Doctors of Literature', the 'National War College' and the like. However peripheral to the mainstream of Vietnamese life they may prove to have been at the time, they are evidence of a spirit that made for the ready acceptance of romanized Vietnamese writing, which was provided by a great Catholic missionary, Alexander of Rhodes, in 1627.

The spirit also appears to be reflected in the tradition of scholar-soldiers and poet-soldiers as heroes of what was theoretically a civilian culture contemptuous of warriors. One of these heroes, Nguyen-Cong-Tru, expressed something important of the Vietnamese spirit: 'Cruel indeed is nature. Man is mortal, his existence short. Many, alas, are those who die young, barely tasting the cup of life. . . . For honour and glory we lead the life of a lion. Our life is filled with bitterness and joy. Tomorrow the flower fades; tomorrow the moon is gone. . . .' His spirit finds an echo still in the diary of the Vietcong medical officer quoted earlier, the man who believed his life had been 'devoted to the most beautiful and the most elevated cause—the struggle for the liberation of mankind . . .' but who could yet write: 'And one has to live in a hurry. A stupid accident, disease, or any tragic hazard may suddenly put an end to one's life. . . .' It can hardly be doubted that many Vietnamese who see themselves as serving their country against the Americans today draw sustenance from a 'nationalist' dream of honourable heroism that was dreamed many times in gentle wood-lands long before those 'dark, satanic mills' of nineteenth-century England provoked Marx and Engels to create a doctrine of liberation that today enslaves the minds of men belonging to races they had never heard of.

The French carried 'the impact of the West' into a society tradi-

VIETNAM: THE VIETMINH REVOLUTION

tional, hierarchical, consistently combative, potentially heroic—as the emperor Le Loi declared in the fifteenth century: 'We have sometimes been weak and sometimes powerful, but at no time have suffered from a lack of heroes.' Traditional Vietnam was also a deeply patriarchical society based upon duties rather than rights: the Emperor was related to his subjects and to his kingdom as a father to his son, as a husband to his wife. By the same token a son owed absolute obedience to his father, a wife to her husband. In the traditional days the funny stories were about the lover, not the cuckolded husband. The culture of France naturally put paid to that attitude.

The French conquest was to be subversive in many other ways. It was a curious mixture of civil engineering and social dislocation,[1] deep economic penetration and superficial administrative care, civilizing mission and reactionary political nihilism, of the Rights of Man and the privileges of the guillotine or the Son-la and Puolo-Condore political prison camps. A society that worked according to its traditional lights and a culture that formed an intelligible whole was shocked and shaken by alien forces, some of them altogether impersonal and all the more shattering for it the integrated intelligibility of which was onerous indeed for Vietnamese to grasp hold of even should they wish to, as many of them undoubtedly did.

Given the appetites and overseas assumptions dominating much of Western Europe late in the nineteenth and early in the twentieth century, it was scarcely to be supposed that 'La Geste Française' would be interpreted by Frenchmen serving in Indo-China in quite the spirit of a United Nations technical agency and there were Frenchmen working selflessly, no doubt, apart from those who proclaimed proudly that they were 'praedicatores, non-predatores', bearers of the Gospel, not exploiters. But in general Vietnam was governed by men without a feeling of economic responsibility, except of course to the Paris *bourse* and manufacturing interests in France and with an utter carelessness about cultures less dynamic than their own. They had a kind of Darwinian optimism (and the cruelty when even minimally opposed which accompanies such arrogance) that was appallingly destructive of the morale of the Vietnamese educated class. The peas-

---

[1] 'France has built thousands of kilometres of railroads, highways and canals, has built and reinforced dykes and has moved enormous masses of earth. All these projects could doubtless be extended and completed. But then there is the question whether . . . it should not give way to the development of smaller detailed projects carried out in close co-operation with the native communities in the canton and village.' Charles Robequain, *The Economic Development of French Indo-China*, Oxford University Press, 1944.

antry for its part found itself thrust ever deeper into the meshes of an increasingly penetrative money economy by vague, yet seemingly irresistible forces. The mandarins of Annam and Tonking were permitted to keep their finger-nails long under the supervision of French residents; and a few Cochinese cultural assimilés were permitted to have a vote in Saigon along with Indians from Pondicherry.

The Cochinese peasant enjoyed a rice ration twice that of his Tongkingese brother; peasants of Tonking and Annam legally owned their little plots but were scarcely more than tenants *vis-à-vis* the moneylenders. The French tried after a fashion to make tenure more secure and usury less exhorbitant but not very successfully. Besides, while the average size of the holdings decreased with the increase in the population, the French administration favoured the establishment of large estates by a generous concession policy and by patronizing and subsidizing plantation owners. Of course in theory the peasant could move out into the sparsely populated areas but he has always been unwilling to do this, involving as it does emigration from the ambience of his ancestors' tombs and of a past-present-future security of belief sanctified by old and intimate surroundings. It would be unthinkable for a peasant to take such a step on his own and central direction of this kind was lacking: the southern plateau country was a marvellous lair for wild game! In time only one in four of Cochin-China's cultivators were owners. But above all there was the question of usury and chronic peasant indebtedness which was never solved, primarily through lack of a settled general economic policy. Pierre Gourou described the situation in Tongking thus: 'The peasant is led to borrow by poverty; when he has exhausted his resources following a bad harvest, he has to borrow. The interest on cash loans is extremely variable, 3 to 10 per cent per month. The lender covers himself by a mortgage on the harvest or goods of the borrower, for loans in kind the interest paid (also in kind) varies from 30 per cent to 50 per cent for one rice-growing season, that is to say, from 60 per cent to 100 per cent per annum.'[1]

An economic system geared rather to the requirements of France than the needs of the Vietnamese was imposed by an apparatus of colonial repression which in times of crisis was extremely brutal; and it was in moments of crisis that the true nature of a colonial overlord-

[1] Apart from the work of geographers like Robequain and Gourou, there is a good description of economic conditions, including that of landless labourers, in Donald Lancaster's book, *The Emancipation of French Indochina*, Oxford University Press, 1961.

ship was revealed. During a time of troubles, 1930–1931 a Frenchman of genius and liberal outlook happened to be working as a journalist in Saigon. He described the aftermath of the unpremeditated murder of a Sergeant Perrier of the French Foreign Legion:

'It's the little tropical station, always the same, with its projecting roof, its heat, its rain, and its tall palm trees like wolf-heads. However, to the isolated tree planted like a flag-pole across from the installation, a living Annamite is tied, the severed head of a friend in his hands. He had been arrested in the morning, hours before Perrier's murder; he had been leading some taxpayers who had unsuccessfully attacked the local militia on a tax-collecting mission. Communists, obviously. The two Legionnaires question him. Visualize that interrogation of a bound man, a severed head held tightly in his hands, by two Legionnaires, one of whom will admit at the trial that he was completely drunk, in the centre of shuttered native huts, where eyes are glued to every crack. . . . He doesn't reply so he's cut down . . . with one or two bullets in the skull. . . . Although it appears that they were within the law in killing this recalcitrant prisoner, the prudent Legionnaires untie the body, not forgetting the severed head on the ground . . . a taste for neatness—and throw both of them into a nearby river.' The soldiers were acquitted; 'Only the dead are not acquitted.'[1]

By this time the nationalists and the Communists were on the scene. However, resistance to the French had begun a long time before; from the beginning of the conquest indeed, in sporadic form. Guerrilla warfare was still being waged in the 1890's in the North.[2] Within a year or so of the final pacification the Vietnamese saw the great Russian fleet shelter in Camranh Bay (today a huge American base) before going north to its shattering and widely publicized defeat in the Straits of Tsushima by the Japanese, the first Asian power to use Western technology successfully against a white enemy. In no time Vietnamese students were writing home from Japan to 'prepare the population for the future'. Before the First World War, demonstrations and assassinations had begun and what were, probably euphemistically, called 'revolutionary banks' had been founded.[3] There was a monarchist movement, a 'Private Schools Movement', and a 'Pan-Asian Movement'.

[1] André Malraux, in Walter G. Langlois, *The Indochina Adventure*, Praeger, 1966.
[2] Lancaster op. cit. and Ellen J. Hammer, *The Struggle for Indochina*, Stanford University Press, 1954.
[3] T. E. Ennis, *French Policy and Development in Indochina*, Chicago University Press, 1936.

VIETNAM: THE VIETMINH REVOLUTION

By the 1920's the chief political movement attracting those unimpressed by the prospect of constitutional fictions looming over the horizon was the V.N.Q.D.D. or National party of Vietnam, founded by a schoolmaster and containing 'small tradesmen, minor officials, in the public services, employees in private business enterprises, and junior officers of the Indo-Chinese troops. A minority of workers, and women too, played an important role'.[1]

The Communist party of Indo-China (C.P.I.) was founded in 1930, after some false starts and divisions, under Comintern aegis and the leadership of a Comintern agent from Nghe-An province in northern Annam, Nguyen Ai Quoc, later to be known as Ho Chi Minh, 'he who enlightens'. The most significant leaders of the 1960's, Pham Van Dong, Le Duan, Truong Chinh, and Vo Nguyen Giap, were all founding figures. From its inception the C.P.I. behaved in all major matters as an orthodox adherent of the Comintern, which amongst other things permitted its legalization in the south after the formation of the 'Popular Front' in 1936 whereas the V.N.Q.D.D., having made an abortive mutiny at Yen Bay in 1930 was very severely repressed. Even Truong Chinh, always a 'hard-liner' and now famous as a 'Peking-liner', appears to have accepted the 'Dimitrov line' of co-operating with the colonial powers.[2] With the Nazi-Soviet Pact of 1939 the C.P.I. dutifully opposed the now 'capitalist' war in principle but in September of that year it was proscribed along with the French Communist party.

The position of the Communist party of Indo-China in the 'thirties seems to have been something like this: having tried to establish a Soviet in Nghe-An province in 1930, it suffered savage repression in 1930–31, a time when real spontaneous peasants' revolts were under way; later its 'legal status' permitted it to do some groundwork in the way of establishing front organizations; but in general the power of the French administration was so overwhelming that it did not make much headway as a political force, and it passed through a period of difficulties which culminated in 1939–40 with the execution of some leaders and the exile in South China of the others. As was the case elsewhere in colonial South-East Asia, the Communists could not effectively challenge the alien administrative apparatus *because* it was alien and hence did not offer organs of power that could be infiltrated

---

[1] Hoang Van Chi, *From Colonialism to Communism*, Popular Library, 1964.
[2] Bernard Fall in his Introduction to Truong Chinh's *Primer for Revolt*, Praeger, 1963. This facsimile edition includes both Truong Chinh's important works, *The August Revolution* and *The Resistance will Win*.

and manipulated by the Communists, nor permit the significant growth of truly popular movements that could be controlled and manipulated by them. The kind of 'contradictions' which Communists rely upon exploiting were held in a state of abeyance by the sheer administrative and repressive power of French colonialism.[1]

It was a series of events quite outside C.P.I. control towards the end of the Second World War that gave a hitherto chiefly clandestine political apparatus of no obvious importance a number of opportunities for which its leaders could scarcely have hoped in their wildest dreams. Nevertheless it was able to exploit these opportunities so successfully only because of the nature of the 'organizational weapon' and through the adaptation of Communist tactics to meet the requirements of concrete situations.

In May 1941 the Central Committee of the C.P.I. met at Tsingsi in South China (in Caobang Province of Tongking according to later Communist propaganda accounts) to form an anti-Japanese resistance movement, which later became famous under the title of Viet Minh. From the beginning leadership was wholly in the hands of the Central Committee of the C.P.I. but immense pains were taken to represent the Vietminh as a nationalist organization which included but was not controlled by the C.P.I. The Secretary-General of the C.P.I. at this time and throughout the seizure of power in 1945 was Truong Chinh, a man whose works are of central importance and who understood throughout the long struggle that was to come how very important it was to represent the Vietminh *Front*, as he candidly calls it, in such a way as to 'enjoy warm support from people of goodwill, and from progressive nations all over the world.'

The C.P.I.'s or Vietminh's (the terms are interchangeable in reality) first stroke of good fortune came when the Kuomintang authorities reluctantly decided that it would serve best amongst available agencies as an intelligence group in Tongking. The Vietminh cadres re-entered Vietnam armed with Thompson sub-machine guns and other light weapons, the backing of the Kuomintang, and the blessing of the Americans—or at any rate of that country's Office of Strategic Services. It had a slogan appropriate for the time: 'drive out the French and Japanese Fascists and restore the independence of Vietnam; unite with all the forces fighting Fascism and aggression; build a Democratic Republic of Vietnam.' Despite the reference to 'French Fas-

---

[1] There is a fine account of the C.P.I.'s existence during this period by Milton I. Sacks in Frank N. Trager (Editor), *Marxism in South-East Asia* op. cit.

cism', the Vietminh made it clear that it sought only friendly relations with France.

The blue-print for the future Vietnamese Republic of course contained no reference to Communism, let alone mention of agricultural collectivization; rents were to be reduced, individual tenure secured, and only the lands of 'Frenchmen and collaborators' were to be confiscated. Universal suffrage, freedom of the Press, equality of the sexes, decentralization of administration and protection for minorities were loudly proclaimed as the aims of the democratic republic-to-be. 'Union of all social classes, all revolutionary organizations and all ethnical minorities' was the slogan of the day. When the provisional government was formed in exile in 1944 it included representatives of other political groupings just as the provisional unified national government in Hanoi on 29th August 1945 was to include what Truong Chinh nicely called 'some non-party personalities'. The aim from the beginning was to seize power under the disguise of a national united front leading to a C.P.I.-dominated coalition government.

The aim differed from that being pursued from 1944 onwards in Europe only in that the C.P.I. did not enjoy the outside support of a victorious Red Army at the time. And so the essence of its tactics had to be that approach hammered out by Lenin between 1907 and 1909: 'Our principle is to eliminate our enemies by setting them against each other. It is a question of exploiting others without allowing ourselves to be exploited.'

The next stroke of luck for the C.P.I. was the *coup de force* carried out by the Japanese in March 1945 against the French administration, which had until then been kept in being. The sequel to this action on the part of the Japanese was the Vietminh insurrection called by Ho Chi Minh, planned chiefly by Truong Chinh, and known in Communist annals as the August Revolution. On 25th August the 'imperial' regime of the puppet Emperor of French-protected Annam, Bao Dai, disappeared without the least incident, the Vietminh Government was installed in Hanoi.

The period between March and August 1945 requires close examination. It is certainly true that the Vietminh enjoyed some strokes of good fortune—a later stroke of good fortune was to be a famine in the north; and it has been argued that the last word still remained with the Japanese who 'decided to cede their position not to their conquerors but to those who could best continue their historic task of liberating Asia from White Imperialism.'[1] Nevertheless the careful

[1] Philippe Devillers, *Histoire du Viet-Nam de 1940 à 1952*, Editions du Seuil, 1952.

preparation for the insurrection and the manner in which account was taken throughout this period of international factors are of the first importance in providing an object-lesson that is a perfect example of the application of politics to revolutionary warfare.

It is also very important that this period should be properly understood in the West, since there remains in being a myth entitled *The Lost Revolution*, to the effect that the return of the French transformed a genuine, non-Communist nationalist movement into a Communist one. It has often been argued in support of this myth that it was French policy which, so to speak, turned nationalists into Communists, that it was the course of Vietnamese-French war itself which 'caused' the Communists to come to power. The fact is that the Communists were in power in the North before a single French battalion landed in Vietnam.[1] The Vietminh's 'Committee of the South' was under the control of the fanatical Stalinist, Tran Van Giau.

The reasons for this gross and persisting misapprehension about the August Revolution and its bloody sequel are various. In the West this was a period of perfervid anti-colonialism in progressive circles, and throughout the U.S.A.; it was the period when many Westerners, particularly Americans, believed that the Communist party of China was really a group of 'agrarian reformers'. A typical view obtaining in the U.S.A. at this time was supplied by Harold Isaacs, a liberal foreign correspondent of scholarly mind: 'The French were shoe-horned into a fresh foothold in Indo-China with the military assistance of the British and American Lend-Lease equipment. They reacted against the new nationalism of Vietnam with *coup d'états* and military force. They have not hesitated to use surrendered Japanese troops and later hired German Nazi mercenaries for the purpose. They offered the Vietnamese and other Indo-Chinese nationalists membership of the 'French Union' but would not offer any real transfer of power. Agreements were made but never became operative. The result was bitter warfare that began in southern Indo-China in 1945 and in the north in 1946.'[2] It will be observed that the word Communism is not used at all.

The Vietminh took great pains to reinforce the naïveté and optimism of the West. The Comintern agent Ho Chi Minh who for two decades had been trying to organize the C.P.I. chiefly from outside

[1] As late as August 1965 the distinguished American journalist and student of Vietnamese affairs, Robert Shaplen, could argue, 'The chance to guide the Asian revolution along legitimate nationalist lines surely existed before the end of the Second World War.' *The Lost Revolution: 1945–6*, Andre Deutsch, 1966.
[2] *New Cycle in Asia*, The Macmillan Company, New York, 1947.

Vietnam was presented to the Western public as a benign nationalist who loved France and George Washington. The Declaration of the Independence of the Republic of Vietnam, issued at Hanoi, 2nd September 1945, began: 'All men are created equal . . . they are endowed by their Creator with certain inalienable rights. Among these are life, liberty and the pursuit of happiness.' Reference is then made to the Declaration of the Rights of the Man and Citizen of the French Revolution of 1791. There follows an eloquent denunciation of French colonialism but, 'Despite all this, our countrymen have continued to maintain a tolerant and humane attitude toward the French.' All the Declaration asked for was the recognition by the Allies of the independence of a democratic, national state.[1]

But how did the leaders of the Vietminh really see the situation in Vietnam in 1945? The answer to this question can be ascertained in clear detail from documents of the time, and from the works of Truong Chinh which in large part embody directives issued by the Central Committee of the C.P.I., of which he was Secretary-General and master-mind.[2] The general aim had been hammered out during the 1930's and corresponds with the general change adopted in China. That is, after the disasters of 1930–31, the idea of the proletariat, 'though young and few in numbers', establishing a 'socialist' revolution in one fell sweep was abandoned in favour of a two-phase strategy: '. . . The most urgent task of the forthcoming revolution is to form a workers' and peasants' government in order to effect the tasks of the bourgeois democratic revolution and liberate the country from foreign domination.'[3]

In order to achieve this, 'the Indo-Chinese Communist party advocated an extremely clear policy: to lead the masses in insurrection in order to disarm the Japanese before the arrival of the Allied forces in Indo-China; to wrest power from the Japanese and their puppet stooges and finally, as the people's power, to welcome the Allied forces coming to disarm the Japanese troop stationed in Indo-China.'[4]

But insurrection was regarded as out of the question in March 1945: 'The political crisis is a deep one, but conditions are insufficiently ripe for an insurrection because:

(a) the French have offered very weak resistance. . . . The Japanese and French are sworn enemies, but whereas the ranks of the French

---

[1] Rima Rathausky (Editor), *Documents of the August 1945 Revolution*, op. cit.
[2] ibid.
[3] Trager, *Marxism in Southeast Asia*, op. cit.
[4] *Primer for Revolt*, op. cit.

are entirely disorganized, among the ranks of the Japanese there are, as yet, no deep contradictions and confusion has not yet become general;

(b) the 'neutral strata' of the population, before resolutely taking the side of the revolution and giving assistance to progressive elements, must inevitably pass through a transition period in the course of which they will come to realize the pernicious consequences of the 'coup';

(c) except for certain regions with favourable terrain which are already occupied by armed contingents, elsewhere in the entire country the progressive elements are preparing for an insurrection, but as yet they are not ready for fighting and sacrificing themselves.

The three following circumstances create conditions for an early insurrection and the start of a broad revolutionary movement:

(a) political crisis (the hands of the enemy are tied and they cannot prevent the revolution);

(b) severe famine (the population violently hates the aggressors);

(c) decisive phase of the war (the inevitability of an Allied landing in Indo-China).'[1]

What was required of the C.P.I.-led Vietminh Front was to create, through agitation and propaganda, a broad movement that 'can make use of all forms of refusal to co-operate with the enemy, starting from strikes in workshops, refusal to supply products for the market and sabotage, and proceeding to the more developed forms of struggle—demonstrations of the strength of the people and guerrilla warfare'. 'Free zones' [bases had to be established in the interior and a 'Liberation Army' built up]; the 'destruction of traitors' [especially the neo-V.N.Q.D.D. and other genuinely autonomous political groupings] had to be seen to, as also the gathering together of all 'patriotic elements' by guaranteeing the inviolability of property.[2] Even Frenchmen willing to enter the anti-Japanese Front were welcomed. Policy throughout might be summed up by the slogan: 'One enemy at a time', which enabled the full exploitation of 'contradictions'.

Propaganda—'Propaganda carried out with arms in hand' by shock brigades—[were very carefully planned in detail]:

'(a) *Slogans:* The slogan: 'Revolutionary power to the people' must be bound up with the slogans: 'Give us rice and clothes' and 'Put an end to the requisitions of rice and the levying of taxes!'

---

[1] Instructions of the Standing Bureau of the Central Committee of the C.P.I., 12th March 1945. Rathausky op. cit.
[2] ibid. And *Primer for Revolt* op. cit. Words in square brackets inserted by the author.

(b) *Methods of Agitation directed at organizing the struggle.* Utilizing the hatred caused by famine, we must develop agitation among the masses and draw them into the struggle (we must organize demonstrations to demand rice and other foodstuffs or to seize rice granaries belonging to the imperialists.)

(c) *Forms of Struggle.* We must pass over to higher forms of struggle —to mass demonstrations, political strikes, public rallies and students' strikes . . . refuse to deliver rice and pay taxes.

We must mobilize self-defence units in order to disarm defeated detachments, deserters and demoralized soldiers.

We must begin guerrilla warfare where the terrain permits us to do so.'[1]

The building up of the revolutionary guerrilla forces was to be a long process: it was only at the beginning of 1948 that what Giap described as 'the first small campaigns' were launched with the equipment seized from the Japanese in late 1945: '35,000 rifles, 1,350 automatic weapons, 200 mortars, 54 cannon, and even 18 tanks from Japanese sources. French booty stocks, and American airdrops.'[2] The Vietminh were perfectly aware that the last word remained with the Japanese until Allied landings were definitely in plan. And so the founding of bases—deep in the northern interior—was at this time essentially for training for an expected long struggle in the years ahead.

In 1945 everything depended upon international events except the ability of the Vietminh Front to mobilize mass support and have in being an alternative administration ready to assume power the moment the opportunity offered, which was not necessarily expected to happen before the Allies landed: 'When the Allies land in Indo-China in order to attack the Japanese, we shall be unable to begin a general insurrection at once. . . . At the point of landing of Allied forces we must organize demonstrations of welcome and at the same time arm the masses and create people's detachments who will fight shoulder to shoulder with the allies. . . . But in all cases *the initiative in the struggle* must be *held by our forces.*'[3]

In the meantime the infrastructure was being built up out of local combat units and 'transitory organizations', committees which 'had at

---

[1] ibid. Compare: 'The general form of struggle was the armed demonstration. Another special form was the guerrilla wherever the topography of the country was favourable, and yet another, the elimination of traitors in towns and country by *picked detachments.*' *Primer for Revolt.* Truong Chinh's italics.
[2] Bernard Fall in *Primer for Revolt.*
[3] Standing Bureau of Central Committee of C.P.I. Rathausky op. cit.

the same time an administrative, political and military character [that is, a pre-governmental character] working in a determined period, simultaneously with the local administrative organisms founded by the Japanese and being transformed, after the general insurrection, into local administrative organizations. . . .'[1] A highly centralized totalitarian society was already being forged within (and behind) a broad national resistance movement. In August 1945, 'the Vietminh, by means of popular demonstrations and a few revolver shots, captured undefended Hanoi'[2] and the independence of the country was proclaimed. In the event the August 1945 Revolution was simple but it had been immaculately prepared.

Soon Vietnam saw the presence of Kuomintang Chinese occupation forces in the north, British-Indian troops in the south. The enemy in the north therefore then became the Chinese; and in order to get rid of the Chinese, to exploit this 'contradiction', the Vietminh had to permit the landing of French troops there. Since this period has often been treated as one in which French duplicity began to create an implacable resistance movement, it is worthwhile noticing precisely how it was viewed by Giap:

'In its foreign policy, our party tried by every means to realize a cordial policy towards the Chiang Kai-shek army and to avoid all conflicts. Dealing with the main enemy, the French aggressive colonialists, on the one hand, our party led the people and army in Nam Bo (Tongking) resolutely to resist against their aggressive army, mobilized the entire people throughout the country to do their best in supporting the South, sent troops there and at the same time actively prepared for the resistance in case the war spread out. On the other hand, it did not miss any opportunity of taking advantage of the contradictions between the French and Chiang Kai-shek forces and to negotiate with the French Government to secure a *détente* and preserve peace.

'The signing of the Preliminary Convention on 6th March 1946 between the French and our forces was the result of this correct policy and strategy. . . . Thus we succeed in driving 200,000 Chiang Kai-shek troops out of our country. Following this, the counter-revolutionary army of the V.N.Q.D.D. which still occupied five provinces along the frontier and the Midland of north Viet Nam was also annihilated. This democratic republican regime grew stronger.'[3]

[1] *Primer for Revolt.*
[2] Hoang Van Chi op. cit.
[3] *People's War, People's Army* op. cit.

This is hardly the language of a spontaneous rising; nor was the co-operation Giap refers to with the French in destroying the forces of the neo-V.N.Q.D.D. (and of the Dai Viet). The 'eradication of traitors' to which Truong Chinh constantly reverts was interpreted to mean in fact the terrorization of any potential rivals. The leader of the Dai Viet party, Truong Tu Anh was assassinated in 1946; in October 1947 almost on the same day Nguyen van Sam, of the National United Front, and Dr. Truong Dinh Tri, Chairman of the anti-Communist Northern Administration Committee suffered the same fate. Earlier that year the Vietminh arranged the execution of the head of the neo-Buddhist Hoa Hao sect.[1] 'Another tactic . . . was to send nationalists as vanguard troops to be killed by the French. This was the case of the 'Tu Ve Thanh', or auto-defence youth groups, who were left to defend Hanoi (in December 1946) as hostilities broke out, while all Communist troops withdrew from Hanoi. Two thousand young people, aged 15 to 20, managed alone to defend Hanoi for two months. The Communists were ready to fight to the last nationalist in that city!'[2] At the same time of course, pliable 'representatives' of these other political groups were given portfolios in the broad national front government.

It is not to the purpose of this book to explore the manœuvrings of the Vietminh and the French on the diplomatic plane which led the French to bombard the port of Haiphong, killing some 6,000 Vietnamese on 23rd November 1946 and the aggressive action of the Vietminh on 19th December 1946. It is perfectly clear that French policy was shot through with so many 'contradictions' (even within the colonial administration in Indo-China itself) that it must have given the impression of duplicity; and the actions of a man like D'Argenlieu who, seeing the struggle from the beginning as one against international Communism, set out to detach Cochin-China from Vietnam, could not but confer upon French policy an aura of fundamental unreliability. But it is difficult not to agree with what Devillers saw as the judgement on Vietminh policies made by non-Communist Vietnamese in 1946: 'In their haste, in their unwillingness to temporize, the Vietminh leaders, with their fathomless vanity, had driven their country straight into conflict with France—and this after having assented to the re-installation of the French Army in the capital itself and at the most strategic centres. At the same time, with the Commun-

---

[1] Hoang Van Chi op. cit. and Philippe Devillers in William L. Holland (Editor), *Asian Nationalism and the West*, The Macmillan Company, 1953.
[2] Vu Vau Thai, *Asia*, No. 4 op cit.

istic character of its leadership, the Vietminh had isolated Vietnam on the diplomatic level.' Is it really to be supposed that the armed totalitarian society that was coming into being under the guidance of Truong Chinh's Central Committee would have been prepared under any circumstances to have accepted an abiding *modus vivendi* with the French within the French Union?

The long-term culpability of French policy lay elsewhere: it utterly failed to permit, let alone assist, the growth of true Vietnamese nationalism within its zones of control. This was symbolized in terrible but dramatic fashion by D'Argenlieu being 'too busy' to see Dr. Thinh, the nominal President of Cochin-China, on the day of the latter's suicide through political despair; and later by the refusal of the administrator, Ngo Dinh Diem, to serve the French-restored Head of State, Bao Dai.[1]

It is quite certain that men like Truong Chinh and Vo Nguyen Giap were not thinking in terms of spontaneous outraged indignation. Truong Chinh put it this way: 'The Vietnamese people do not hate the French people, nor are we fighting against them; so why should we not be on friendly terms with them. However, the Vietnamese people know that in order to establish relations with the French people, they must resolutely break down the wall that separates the French and Vietnamese peoples—that wall is the French colonialists. We are determined to annihilate the French reactionaries, who daily widen the gulf which separates the two peoples, both of whom love peace, justice and freedom. . . . We must wage a resistance war, we must take military action. . . . Here are the military aims of our resistance war—To annihilate the enemy forces in our country.'[2] Giap put it more briefly: 'The Resistance War waged by our people was the continuation of the national democratic revolution by armed struggle.' And this is the heart of the matter: as was suggested earlier, revolutionary guerrilla war has become something existing in its own right and going far beyond the politico-military destruction of an enemy: revolutionary guerrilla warfare *is* the revolution and once victory has been achieved, it is turned against the population itself in order to transform society.

Moreover, it should be noticed that except for a tactical dissolution in order to make the broadening of the national resistance front simpler, Communist leadership has always been quite clearly the leadership not of a *Vietnamese* Communist party but of the Com-

[1] Ellen Hammer op. cit.
[2] *Primer for Revolt* op. cit.

munist party of Indo-China.[1] This is no mere matter of nomenclature. Communism in Laos and Cambodia (and amongst the Vietnamese migrant group in North East Thailand) has always been controlled by the C.P.I. through Front organizations, the Pathet Lao and its political arm, the Cambodian Pracheachorn party, and since 1944 the Overseas Vietnamese Association in Thailand and Laos. By 1917 this minority group in North-East Thailand, numbering perhaps 100,000 had become something of a Communist-controlled power unto itself; and later its organization, the 'hard-core' elements of which had been survivors of the ill-starred Nghe-An Soviet of 1930, was reinforced by veterans of the Vietminh units it had itself furnished for the anti-French struggle.

And so the Communists who found power so easily in North Vietnam in 1945 were from the very beginning intimately concerned with affairs outside Vietnam. 'Even when the Vietminh was very short of military personnel and armaments, the Communist party directed a group of Vietnamese officers to escort Prince Souphanouvong (titular leader of the armed Pathet-Leo) to organize the army for the liberation and defence of Laos. . . . The same pattern was followed in Cambodia where the C.P.I. member Nguyen van Tay (alias Than Son) organized the Free Khmer or Khmer Issara. . . . In Thailand Nguyen van Long (a veteran of the Nghe-An Soviet) organized the Vietnamese community into "agricultural settlements" which even the Thai police could not penetrate . . .'[2] Nguyen van Long (also known by such aliases as Ly Bac Son) operated as far West as the Shan State of Burma 'with at least liaison functions extending into Malaya and Indonesia'.[3] As early as 1953, 'units of Vietnamese volunteers, cooperating with the Pathet-Lao liberation army began the campaign in Higher Laos. . . .' (Giap).

Had the French withdrawn in 1946, the immediate minimum political consequence would have been the totalitarian collectivization of Vietnam and the domination by Hanoi of Laos and Cambodia, with the subversion of North-East Thailand as an almost certain sequel to the Calcutta conference. In all probability an attempt would have been made by 1950-51 to establish a revolutionary base in southern Thailand designed gravely to hamper the counter-insurgency cam-

---

[1] It was tactically dissolved 'in order to demolish all misunderstanding at home and abroad which might hamper the liberation of our country'.

[2] Private communication from the former Chief of Staff of the Liberation force in Laos.

[3] Contribution by the above to *South-East Asia Review*, Bangkok, January 1952.

paign in Malaya. In addition, the role of the supporters of Pridi Pahnomyang in Thailand would have been altogether more dangerous at the end of the 1940's and in the early 1950's than proved to be the case.[1] This Thai political leader has long since been living in Peking.

It is not proposed to follow the course of the Franco-Vietnamese war here: the methods adopted by the Communist revolutionary guerrillas have been briefly discussed.[2] Nevertheless certain points of general significance should be underlined. The character of the war altered catastrophically for the French with the arrival of Chinese Communist troops at the Sino-Vietnamese frontier in 1949; the fact that the Vietminh was no longer internationally isolated, and that it now enjoyed all that a privileged sanctuary could offer, was deeply appreciated by Giap. It was not until 1950 that the final conquest of the Caobang and Langson frontier provinces was accomplished. Mobile warfare was impossible without Chinese assistance, the later attack on Dien Bien Phu was inconceivable without Chinese artillery. The French made serious strategic mistakes: amongst them were first, a refusal adequately to reinforce in Tongking; later, a refusal quickly to withdraw into the Tongking delta, a refusal that resulted in reverses which were subversive of morale; thirdly, the failure to implement the plan of Marshall de Lattre to use the concrete block-house defensive system as but a corollary to large-scale mobile penetrative warfare; and lastly, the terrible mischoice of Dien Bien Phu as the bait for the set-piece battle the French regulars so desperately longed for, and its sequel in a defeat that was not in itself militarily catastrophic but assumed that character in the light of international politics.

It is by no means true that the French were everywhere unsuccessful or stupid: long before the Americans, the French used the combination of artillery and airpower with often devastating effect. And yet the battle of Dien Bien Phu did to some extent symbolize a French failure of imagination: air power was greatly relied upon in conditions hopeless for its proper use; too much was expected of the few tanks that were available in conditions of limited application; the artillery proved useless against the Vietminh commanding the heights (the French chief gunner committed suicide during the battle); the use of partisans raised from amongst the non-Vietnamese minorities, though effective in some ways, failed altogether to cut the Vietminh supply

[1] 'Whether this was intended or not by the French, the Indochina war for a time bought freedom for about twenty-one million people out of thirty-eight million . . .' Bernard Fall, *Street Without Joy*, Pall Mall Press, 1964.
[2] See Lancaster op. cit. and Edgar O'Ballance, *The Indo–Chinese War*, 1945–54, Faber, 1964.

line to Dien Bien Phu; and the long-planned exercise in entrenched static warfare ultimately depended upon the willingness of the Americans to arrive at the eleventh hour with their heavy bombers, possibly using atomic bombs, a decision evaded in the event by the Americans' request for British support at a time when 'England did not want to spoil the prospects which had been opened up for markets by her recognition, back in 1950, of the Chinese Communist regime.'[1]

This failure of nerve in the West, as it must have seemed to be to Communists everywhere, had a grave consequence: it allowed a theory of the efficacy of 'liberation wars' to become much more widespread and it permitted the Vietnamese Communist High Command in Hanoi to believe that, provided it escalated the struggle carefully in a suitably 'disguised' manner in South Vietnam, then an unwillingness to risk war with either Communist Great Power would inhibit Western military intervention at *any stage*: the new (North Vietnamese) 'privileged sanctuary', according to this understanding of the Communists, would henceforth be immune; Communism could either advance or suffer temporary setbacks in new fields but it could not be destroyed anywhere it had established itself. The partial acceptance of this understanding by the U.S.A. is still underlined by its repeated declarations that it does not seek the destruction of the North Vietnamese regime.

In the final analysis, North Vietnam fell to the Vietminh in Paris and Washington, in the sense that the effort necessary for the destruction of the Vietminh was never made. It could have been made; the Vietminh could have been defeated. But the effort seemed increasingly less worthwhile just as it became increasingly more onerous as Vietminh strength built up. And this is what 'protracted war' is all about: to nibble away at liberal capitalist political will in the seats of metropolitan power while strengthening the will of the expanding Communist society.

On the other hand it would be very wrong not to take full account of the particular strengths of the Vietminh in North and parts of Central Vietnam. The result of the August Revolution in 1945, and the clever exploitation of 'contradictions', was that the Communist-controlled Vietminh was left as the sole important Vietnamese political force in North Vietnam—a situation that never looked like obtaining in the south—and as such, as 'the Resistance' to returning French Colonialism, it undoubtedly attracted into its ranks the noblest Vietnamese in the North and evoked in them a very real belief that

[1] Jules Roy, *The Battle of Dienbienphu*, Faber, 1965 op cit.

they 'were fighting against a colonialism in the process of disappearing from the face of the earth. If they died, it would be with the cry of liberty on their lips.'[1]

Though some efforts were made from 1953 onwards to transform the struggle against colonialism into one against the local 'feudalists' as well, through limited land reform, the emphasis throughout the anti-French was laid upon the broad patriotic front. The Communist party was indeed resurrected officially as the Lao-daong (Workers') party, just as it was to be officially resurrected in the south in 1962 as the People's Revolutionary party, but as a corollary to this the Vietminh Front was given greater breadth by the creation of the Lien-Viet Front. The true meaning of Communist Conquest was not to reveal itself to the great majority of peasants until the terrible aftermath of countrywide 'Land Reform'. It was not until then that most Vietnamese realized just what Giap meant when he said, 'The People's army is the instrument of the (Communist) party and of the revolutionary State for the accomplishment, in armed form, of the tasks of the revolution.'

The only alternative Vietnamese political forces lay in the south and parts of the centre in 1954; and as a result of French policy they remained in an embryonic state. The Catholic minority in the north could never be an alternative to the Vietminh, simply because it *was* a clearly defined *minority*. When the French High Command decided to sign an armistice with the Vietminh High Command, cynically disregarding the Vietnamese Government which France had established, it gave the Vietminh much more than a political victory in the north; it conferred upon this Communist-controlled movement the appearance of having assumed a fresh Mandate of Heaven. The author himself wrote early in 1955, 'It is more than possible that the weather eye of the Vietnamese peasant may come to see a new cosmos in Communism where others see only an historical monstrosity; a natural mutation where others see only a temporary and fortuitous seizure of power. In that case the Vietminh will have succeeded to more than the outward trappings of the Heavenly Mandate.'[2] But that was certainly not true of the south; if it had been, the Americans and their allies would never have been granted the opportunity to intervene.

[1] Jules Roy op. cit.
[2] *Australian Outlook*, March 1955. cp. Paul Mus, *Vietnam: Sociologie d'une Guerre*, '. . . in the perspectives of the Far East, by its double principle of rationality and authority, controlling the truth in everything . . . (Communism) presents itself without difficulty as a Way, Tao . . . not without precedents, though built upon very different foundations, in the history of state religions in Asia, which virtually *is* the history of Asia.'

Chapter 10

VIETNAM: THE ASSAULT ON SOUTH VIETNAM

Though the division of Vietnam in 1954 more or less accorded geographically with past divisions of the country, it was in fact divided as a result of a military truce. The Geneva Conference of 1954, the chief purpose of which was to end the Indo-China war and put forward proposals for the future, referred to only one Vietnam and to the demarcation line on the 17th parallel as 'provisional and not in any to be interpreted as constituting a political or territorial boundary'. The government of South Vietnam (as it became, in effect) refused to associate itself with the final declaration of the Geneva Conference, which provided for the temporary division of the country, and sought instead the demilitarization of the whole country under temporary United Nations' control.[1]

It was envisaged by the Conference, the government of South Vietnam[2] abstaining, that *under certain circumstances*, a nation-wide general election should be held in July 1956 under international supervision. Since this provision of the final declaration of the Geneva Conference has been most widely used abroad to support the Communist-led insurrection in South Vietnam, it is desirable to quote it in full, suitably italicized: 'The Conference declares that, so far as Vietnam is concerned, the settlement of political problems, *effected on the basis of respect for the principles of independence, unity, and territorial integrity, shall permit the Vietnamese people to enjoy the fundamental freedoms, guaranteed by democratic institutions established as a result of free general elections by secret ballot.* In order to ensure that sufficient progress in the restoration of peace has been made, and that *all the necessary conditions obtain for free expression of the national will*, general elections shall be held in July 1956, under the supervision of an international commission composed of representatives of the Member

---

[1] Claude A. Buss (Editor) *Southeast Asia and the World Today*, Van Nostrand, 1958.
[2] The government of South Vietnam will henceforth be called the G.V.N., the government of North Vietnam, the D.R.V.

States of the International Supervisory Commission, referred to in the agreement on the cessation of hostilities. Consultations will be held on this subject between the competent representative authorities of the two zones from 20th July 1955, onward.'[1]

Whatever the complexion of the G.V.N. in the years 1954-56, short of being Communist it could not possibly have agreed to nationwide elections in 1956, since the Government of North Vietnam (D.R.V.) had used the intervening period to pulverize the population of North Vietnam through an extraordinarily vicious 'Land Reform'. It is necessary to examine this first, since it is the crux of the matter; and as such it has been far too little alluded to during the so-called 'Vietnam debate'. Moreover, it is central to the theme of this book in that it supplies a striking example of the way in which revolutionary warfare does not cease at the termination of hostilities against organized political opposition represented by a government in office; that struggle is but part of the process of the revolutionary indoctrination of the masses towards the totalitarian state.

Having used the peasant in the war against the French by promising him alleviation of his *personal* condition as a poor cultivator, the now increasingly overtly Communist Vietnam government set about using state power in order to reduce him to the status of a collectivized serf. He was subjected to a 'series of operations, psychological, social, and quasi-judicial' which ended with him being deprived of his land. This is what is ultimately meant by the term 'mobilization of the masses'.[2] It is designed to create through systematic, state-controlled disorientation of the population, a society in which the Communist party exercises *total power*. As Stalin said, 'Some think that the peasant problem is the fundamental thing in Leninism. . . . This is absolutely wrong. The fundamental problem in Leninism . . . is not the peasant problem, but the problem of the dictatorship of the proletariat.' Since the proletariat cannot logically exert a dictatorship over itself, what is in fact meant is the dictatorship of the Communist party; 'The fundamental question of every revolution is power. . . .' (Lenin.)

But of course the question cannot at first be publicly phrased in that way. Typical of Communist phrasing is the following statement by Liu Shao-chi: 'The Communist party has always been fighting for the interests of the labouring poor, but the viewpoints of Communists have always been different from those of the philanthropists . . . the basic aim of agrarian reform is not purely one of relieving peasants. It

[1] Gettleman, Penguin Documents, op. cit.
[2] Bernard Fall, *Le Vietminh*, op. cit.

is designed to set free the rural productive forces from the shackles of the feudal land ownership system of the landlord class so as to develop agricultural production and thus pave the way for New China's industrialization.'[1]

For many years it has been quite clear that a collectivized agricultural society is for ever under attack by 'the invisible worm of private ownership', as Mr. Khrushchev once described it, and simply does not evoke the productivity claimed for it. This was to be observed in North Vietnam where it was admitted in 1961 that farming private plots of land 'was providing co-operative members with some 30 to 40 per cent of their total income even though private plots comprised only 5 per cent of the total area of the co-operatives. In 1962, he (Le Duan of the Central Committee) forecast, private operations would provide co-operative members with 55 per cent of their income'.[2]

However, a reversal of this agrarian policy would mean the fatal weakening of Communist party control and even to a large extent of its very *raison d'être*, particularly in overwhelmingly peasant societies. And so a new struggle began in North Vietnam, the struggle finally to create a totalitarian society through 'land reform'. 'Agrarian reform is a systematic and fierce struggle,' as Liu Shao-chi admitted; '. . . a revolution is not the same as inviting people to dinner, or writing an essay, or painting a picture or doing fancy needlework. A revolution is an uprising or act of violence whereby one class overthrows another. . . . To put it bluntly, it was necessary to bring about a brief reign of terror in every rural area. . . .' (Mao.) Elsewhere Mao suggests that the reign of terror may not necessarily be brief: 'Confronted with such enemies ("landlords") the Chinese revolution becomes protracted and ruthless in nature.'[3]

This kind of 'land reform' is carried out by the state exploiting 'contradictions' between what it *itself* denotes as 'large landowners', 'rich peasants', and 'poor peasants', the aim being to produce the appearance of spontaneity in order to shatter all will to resist. In theory the task is carried out by peasants' associations but these are in reality merely extensions of state power through 'front' organizations. More serious resistance, as occurred in Ho Chi Minh's home province of Nghe-An, is obliterated by the artillery of the People's Army. That it was indeed a reign of terror was later admitted by the Press of the D.R.V. and by Giap. Estimations of how many people were killed

---

[1] Speech at the People's Consultative Council, 14th June 1950.
[2] P. J. Honey, *Communism in North Vietnam*, Ampersand, 1963.
[3] Mao Tse-tung, *Selected Works*, Lawrence and Wishart, 1954.

vary greatly, between 50,000 and 200,000 people. Since the families of those executed were abandoned in such a fashion as to make starvation likely, the figures of those who died as a result of this policy may well have been very high indeed.[1]

Since this period has been closely examined by Mr. Hoang Van Chi, two quotations from his work will suffice to illuminate it: 'People were arrested, jailed, interrogated and cruelly tortured,' reported the C.P.I. journal, *Nhan Dan* in October 1956, 'people were executed or shot on the spot and their property confiscated. Innocent children of parents wrongly classified as landlords were starved to death.'

One of those arrested, and they included 12,000 Communists, Tan, was told later that it had all been a mistake: 'Tan counted on his fingers . . . eight months in gaol awaiting execution, one month more attending the (thought reform) course: in all he had been absent from home nine months.' He returned home and talked with his friends: 'They recalled how the villagers had been compelled to denounce and torture one another, to sever all family ties and to suppress all human feeling. There was sorrow in every heart.'[2]

This was no gratuitous outburst of state savagery; it was a calculated exercise in pulverizing the nerves of all who might not otherwise easily adapt themselves to the new society, and as such it involved not only state terrorism but thought reform and widespread social upheaval. A whole society was to be transmitted into a totalitarian collectivity through physical and psychological shock treatment. It was during this period that Diem stated: 'We do not object to the principle of free elections as peaceful and democratic means to achieve that unity. However, if elections constitute one of the bases of true democracy, they will be meaningful only on the condition that they are absolutely free.'[3] It is perfectly clear that no international supervisory team could possibly have ensured free elections throughout Vietnam in 1956, since well over half the population, those residing in the north, were under the control of a totalitarian regime in a much more than political sense.

As Truong Chinh put it, 'The aim of the present revolution is that the entire people . . . should thoroughly absorb the socialist ideology, that they should abandon their previous outlook on life and on the world and replace it with the Marxist viewpoint. Thus Marxism-

[1] Hoang Van Chi, op. cit.
[2] ibid.
[3] *Studies on Viet Nam*, Department of External Affairs, Canberra, Australia, August 1965.

Leninism will assume a leading role in guiding the moral life of our country and will become the framework within which the thoughts of the whole nation are formed. It will serve as the foundation upon which the ethics of our people will be built.'[1] The relationship between North and South Vietnam was thenceforth to be between a totalitarian society with a built-in expansionist dynamic and an increasingly authoritarian society, which in moments of ebullience might find its leaders talking in all-Vietnamese terms but which throughout lacked an expansionist dynamic and from 1957 onwards was a target under attack by the methods of revolutionary warfare that this book has been concerned to discuss.

For a number of years the target under attack was not South Vietnam as such but rather the regime which Ngo Diem fashioned from 1954 onwards, it being clearly believed that if this regime could be brought down, then no effective opposition to Communism would remain. Of course the ultimate aim was the political subjugation of all of South Vietnam; but the method adopted was that of creating an alternative society in the hinterland, moved by disguised aims, and directed very pertinaciously, so far as many politically interested Vietnamese could see, against the Diem regime itself. And so there was in South Vietnam a revolutionary guerrilla warfare campaign waged in peculiarly intense circumstances from the beginning, since because of the manner of his coming to power, Diem's regime was also trying to establish its own legitimacy, alter the old society, and expand its own organization, and—after a fashion—advance its own ideology. One result of this situation was that Diem's mistakes could be observed much more clearly by foreign observers than has been the case in South-East Asian countries where the regimes were more easily established or were established over a longer period of time.

Diem was always a man in a hurry; and this fact was to cost him the destruction of what he wanted to stand for and ultimately his life. A devout Catholic from a mandarin family of Hué in Central Vietnam, a former administrator of distinction under the French, a perfervid nationalist, he was in 1954 given little chance of survival in power for more than a few months by most observers in Saigon, principally because he had no obvious basis for support and even his supporters were acutely aware that they lacked any clear mass base. The author well remembers the faces of some young army officers in Saigon in October 1954 when it was suggested to them that if they clashed, as seemed likely at the time, with dissident troops then the French army

[1] Hoang Van Chi, op. cit.

would probably have to intervene to restore order. Their faces lit up with hope and one of them exclaimed, 'Exactly! And you see, if the French fire on us—and only if they fire on us—then the people may understand that we represent their cause!' It was in this kind of atmosphere, redolent of make-shift hopes, obscured by all manner of local feuds, that Ngo Dinh Diem came to power.

In a sense, the Americans were behind him, but in no obvious fashion; and moreover all shrewd Saigonese politicians—and they are exceedingly shrewd in their coteries—were perfectly aware that the Americans had placed themselves in a position of acute ambiguity. Unwilling to intervene at Dien Bien Phu, unwilling to accept the Geneva understandings, they had nevertheless undertaken not to upset the provisions of the Geneva conference. But in 1955 John Foster Dulles made it clear that, 'South Vietnam must be strengthened; and we must not be trapped into a fictitious legalism that would condemn ten million potentially free people into slavery.'[1] And much earlier a U.S. military mission had been established to train a regular army in South Vietnam. The reason for this step was quite intelligible, since on the 8th November 1954 Sir Anthony Eden had announced in the House of Commons that the Vietminh had 'continued to reinforce their army and that by the end of 1954 would have twice as many regular field formations as at the time of the Geneva Agreement.'[2] It was quite sensible to argue that without an army no authority could be seen to exist in the south, especially in the face of the growth of armed power and state terrorism in the north. Diem accepted American advisers with the clear intention of refusing elections in 1956 and of building up an internationally recognized *State* in South Vietnam; he doubtless welcomed the South-East Area Treaty Organization which took it upon itself to designate South Vietnam as a potential area of intervention even in the case of 'indirect aggression'; but it is doubtful whether he ever trusted the American capacity for meeting a crisis.

He was a man who believed that he could save South Vietnam from Communism; and he and his brother Ngo Dinh Nhu between them believed they knew *how* to do this. They were not men disposed to 'play it by ear', except towards the end of their regime when they showed themselves to be singularly tone-deaf. They were prepared only to conciliate a small section of the population; to tolerate within limits most of the population; and to crush whatever political groups

[1] *New York Times*, 21st July 1955.
[2] B. S. N. Murti, *Vietnam Divided*, Asia Publishing House, 1964.

—and sometimes individuals—would not support what the Ngos believed were the sovereign remedies for South Vietnam. In trying to implement this policy they gave their first hostages to what came to be known as the National Liberation Front (N.L.F.): they tackled head-on the private armies of the religious sects, the Cao Dai and Hoa-Hao, which controlled whole rich provinces in South Vietnam and might have been persuaded to continue to play the anti-Communist role they had been playing. Instead, the Cao Dai were to provide probably the largest number of rank-and-file in the early days of the N.L.F.

The approach of the Ngos to this problem is understandable in the light of their intentions *quickly* to create a modern state; and for a long time it looked as though they had plucked out these thorns from their flesh. But this was precisely the kind of miscalculation of the undercurrents of Vietnamese life that was to bring about their downfall; it persuaded them to rush ahead faster, alienating to some degree other sections of the population; and to rely more and more upon Catholics in the army and the administration. Very often these Catholics came from amongst the 800,000 refugees permitted to leave under the Geneva Agreement.[1]

If the army had been a very different kind of army and if the administration had been very different too, it is quite possible that the Ngos might have won out even pursuing the intransigent policy they adopted from the beginning. What was at fault with the army was not its disproportionate number of Catholic officers—Catholics very often had the combative and educational equipment that was required for the job, and advanced for this reason and no other—but in its almost complete lack of openings for talented men of less than bourgeois origin and its totally inappropriate organization. Here both Diem and the Americans showed they had not learnt from the Vietminh victory at all.

In the Vietminh army—and later in the Vietcong—the career open to talent was the normal thing and hence a truly modern professionalism was allied to the political indoctrination; in the army of Diem's regime this kind of psychological professionalism was altogether lacking. It seems clear that Diem had an ambivalent attitude towards modernization: he wanted it but was personally not very interested in the social problems involved in it. He believed that the existing form of military service was 'an expression of the principle of equality for

---

[1] Between 50,000 and 75,000 Vietminh cadres appear to have moved north. But these figures are unreliable.

all citizens'[1] when it manifestly was nothing of the kind. Only the paratroops and special forces built up a true fighting élan. Outside the élite formations, the lack of opportunities for promotion to commissioned rank was a deadly inhibiting factor. (And this inhibiting factor is only slowly being removed in 1967.)

The second grave mistake must be attributed to the Americans who concentrated on building up a professional army trained and equipped for orthodox warfare. The combination of social privilege in the army and orthodoxy in its general approach to war problems resulted in an army that was singularly unfitted to do the kind of things *vis-à-vis* the population which Magsaysay had long since discovered in the Philippines were absolutely necessary components of a counter-insurgent campaign; that is, primarily, to regard itself as much as a reconstruction corps as a fighting force; to see one of the determining factors in its efficacy as correct and friendly relations with the people.

So far as civil administration was concerned, Diem's regime suffered from the same malaise as has afflicted most South-East Asian administrations: the unwillingness of the educated to go out into the countryside or, if they found themselves submitted to this exile, their unwillingness to study local conditions and so identify themselves with the fears and aspirations of the peasants. When this unsympathetic attitude was combined with the decision to abolish the election of village headmen a most unsatisfactory state of affairs existed in the countryside. There were arguments of efficiency in favour of abolishing these elections and they were the kind of arguments that would appeal to a centralizing mandarin in a hurry, but in order to justify such a decision a far, far more efficient administrative service was required than that available to Diem.

This leads to the problem of why and how the insurgency began to develop, since the successful mounting of an insurgency is quite clearly in part proof of a government's administrative weakness. Doubtless all rebellions are born out of a frustration and a capacity for violence,[2] both of which factors are evident in every under-developed country undergoing the stresses of quick change, but the organization and development of a rebellion depends in large part on administrative weaknesses, which are in turn intimately related to weaknesses of communication: the peasant village society is virtually impervious to centrally generated 'public opinion'. It can only be influenced and altered at close-range by the spoken word, disseminated by local

---

[1] *President Ngo Dinh Diem on Democracy:* Speeches, Saigon 1958.
[2] Brian Crozier, *The Rebels*, Chatto and Windus, 1960.

means, and directed towards locally felt needs and perplexities and fears.

Now those observers who believe the insurgency has been a basically *South* Vietnamese matter argue that Diem's policies were so intolerable to certain sections of the population that they caused certain groups more or less spontaneously to rise in arms against oppression. Various forms of oppression are adduced to prove this thesis: the introduction of concentration camps early in 1956 (a clear breach of the Geneva Agreement's provisions forbidding reprisals);[1] the returning of land distributed by the Vietminh to its former owners; the persecution of some political figures; the draconic Law 10 of 1959;[2] the denial of political rights (in fact if not in theory) to opposition groups in the National Assembly or at elections; the disabilities imposed (by a pre-Diem ordinance) on Buddhist organizations; and the callous use of firepower during pacification operations in the countryside.

'It was in such a climate of feeling,' as M. Philippe Devillers argues in the most persuasive exposition of this thesis, 'that, in 1959, responsible elements of the Communist resistance in Indo-China came to the conclusion, that they had to act, whether Hanoi wanted them to or not.'[3] There is no doubt that Diem was determined to destroy the Communist movement in South Vietnam; there is also no doubt that the speed with which he attempted to do this resulted in non-Communists being treated unfairly, sometimes brutally.[4] As a result the Communists were able to recruit to the National Liberation Front a number of dissident groups and what Truong Chinh would call 'non-party figures'. Whether Diem was wrong in acting (as he believed) so as to prevent a recrudescence of Communist revolutionary guerrilla warfare depends upon how such warfare is regarded; that revolutionary guerrilla warfare would not have been reverted to in any case, once the question of re-unification had been put out of court,[5] is exceedingly difficult to believe. Is it really to be imagined that the politico-military methods which had proved so effective against the French would not be used against the Diem regime? If this is to be supposed,

[1] B. S. N. Murti op. cit.
[2] Marvin E. Gettleman, *Vietnam Documents*, op. cit.
[3] *The China Quarterly*, January–March 1962
[4] Robert Scigliano, *South Vietnam: Nation under Stress*, Houghton Mifflin, 1963.
[5] According to P. J. Honey, the D.R.V. Foreign Minister even at the Geneva Conference never expected nation-wide elections: *Communism in North Vietnam*, op. cit.

then it must be based on the assumption that the former Vietminh cadres underwent a strange change of mind. Moreover, the notion that the Vietminh and its political allies (henceforth to be called the Vietcong) were forced into activity implies a pervasiveness of administration which the Diem regime never looked like attaining; and it ignores the problem of bases, arms, and organization.

Diem was indeed ruthlessly attacking the Communist movement; but it was an armed movement already in being. Some of its bases— in the Chaudoc Province which marches with Cambodia, in the Plain of Reeds, in the swamp areas of Vinhbinh Province, in the U Minh forest of An Xuyen Province, for example—were never really subject to Diem's administration at all. Complaints of persecution in the early stages were normally relayed to the International Control Commission through Hanoi with despatch, implying close liaison between these areas and that city.

It is of interest to notice that in Mr. Wilfred Burchett's apologia for the Vietcong, he argues that the important Quang Ngai campaign was begun in order 'to take some heat off the tribespeople' (the montagnards who were indeed badly treated, as they always have been, by the Vietnamese); 'they could do this because Quang Ngai was the only place in Central Vietnam where there was any armed resistance.'[1] Quang Ngai was an old seat of Communist revolutionary guerrilla activity.

Diem's first reference to what he called 'this form of cold war' related to the country along the Cambodian border, which has all along been a major Vietcong base area.[2] Discontents cannot of themselves mount an insurgency, though they are necessary in predisposing recruits in favour of the insurgency. Arms, bases, and organization are essential. The Vietminh had cached sufficient arms with which to begin the insurgency, they had a number of secure base areas, and the organization necessary for gathering together various dissident elements and welding them together under disguised aims in the National Liberation Front. Whether Diem's repressive policies forced the insurgents' hands or not is of only academic interest now; as is the much bruited about question of whether the Southern Communist leaders forced Hanoi's hand or not. This is simply a question of *timing*, it is not a question in itself of the Communist command structure or of Hanoi's political strategy.

[1] Wilfred G. Burchett, *Vietnam: Inside Story of the Guerrilla War*, International Publishers, 1965.
[2] *President Diem on Democracy* op. cit. Speech 7th October 1957.

It can of course be argued that Diem's authoritarianism forced the Communists to take up arms, since they had no peaceful alternative left open to them. But this is to ignore the whole development of Indo-Chinese Communism under the teaching of Truong Chinh and Vo Nguyen Giap, the whole development of 'Peking line' Communist policy, and the whole attitude of Communists to non-Communist societies. Above all, it is to ignore the fact that the Diem regime was faced by an *armed* organization. As was shown earlier very few Asian governments are prepared, for very good reasons, to accept Communist parties into the 'legal fold' and permit them to wage 'the parliamentary struggle', since the overriding aim of the Communists is always to seize total power in perpetuity. To acquiesce in this is to acquiesce in the destruction, not only of one's government, but also of one's society.

By 1959 Ho Chi Minh had made the aims of North Vietnam quite clear: '. . . we (the Communist party) are building socialism in Vietnam. We are building it, however, only in half of the country, while in the other half, we must still bring to a conclusion the democratic-bourgeois and anti-imperialist revolution. Actually, our party must now accomplish, contemporaneously, two different revolutions, in the north and in the south. This is one of the most characteristic traits of our struggle.'[1] But though this was to make Hanoi's aim explicit in a Press interview, as also on various other important occasions in the north, very great pains were taken to disguise the nature of the National Liberation Front.[2]

The disguising of the N.L.F.'s real nature was necessary for two reasons; first, in order to exploit 'contradictions' in the south under the banner of a broad-based organization and secondly, to create the impression abroad of a spontaneous indigenous rising which could never be decently opposed by Western intervention. The men in the north who believed in the principle that 'it is better to kill ten innocent people than to let one enemy escape,'[3] knew perfectly well that such principles could not be revealed to southerners or Europeans until after victory had been achieved.

In the meantime, disguised aims of a generally acceptable nature had to be promulgated. They were essentially those of the Vietminh in 1945: the aims of the first stage of the two-stage takeover referred

---

[1] *Unita*, 1st July, 1959, quoted in George Carver, *The Faceless Vietcong*, Foreign Affairs, April 1966.
[2] *Aggression from the North*, U.S. State Department, February 1965.
[3] Hoang Van Chi op. cit.

to earlier: the establishment of a democratic and liberal regime which after Diem was overthrown and all foreign bases removed from Vietnamese territory,[1] would reduce land rents and implement a scheme of land redistribution, the land to be purchased from existing owners, unless they were 'American imperialists and their servants'. This statement of aims naturally avoided reference to relations with Hanoi, since the struggle had to be represented as one confined to the aspirations of South Vietnamese. And so the N.L.F. has even on occasion talked in terms of a 'neutralization' of South Vietnam. This kind of statement was very important in influencing those in the U.S.A. who wished to believe that the struggle was indigenous to the south and therefore should not be opposed by American troops, or who today believe that negotiations should be undertaken with the N.L.F. as the representatives of an essentially *southern* rising.

It is surely arguable that even had the struggle been entirely an internal war—that is, 'the use or threat of violence to effect a change in the body politic'[2]—the government of Vietnam would have been justified in calling for outside help against a terroristic attempt to impose a Communist dictatorship in perpetuity on the mass of the people. After all '. . . the insurgents' strengths, including active supporters, in both Malaya and Vietnam (until the end of 1964) were at no stage more than 1 per cent of the population, and initially a great deal less than that.' Why should a 'form of warfare designed to enable a very small ruthless minority to gain control over the people'[3] be internationally recognized as a legitimate activity in a period of great world tensions?

The question is particularly valid when the implications of its success are considered. As Malcolm Browne puts it, 'The Vietcong expects to win its war in South Vietnam. But it is also offering the techniques it developed here to all other Communist revolutionary groups in the under-developed nations throughout the world, especially in Latin American and Africa. A growing number of these nations are showing interest in the Vietnamese patent and, before long, many of them may be paying royalties to Hanoi, Peking and Moscow. . . . Accordingly, South Vietnam is a laboratory.'[4]

However, despite the careful disguises, the struggle in South Vietnam gradually revealed its true nature. There can be argument about

[1] Marvin, C. Gettleman, *Vietnam: Documents etc.*, op. cit.
[2] T. P. Thornton in Harry Eckstein (Editor), *Internal War*, Free Press of Glencoe, 1964.
[3] Sir Robert Thompson op. cit.
[4] *The New Face of War*, Cassell, 1965.

precisely how it started; there is no real argument about how it developed. A consensus of informed opinion supports the finding of a severe critic of everything to do with Diem, David Halberstam: 'The new Indo-China war was not a spontaneous uprising from the south. It was part of a calculated and systematic conspiracy on the part of the government in Hanoi to take over the south. But it was the most subtle kind of conspiracy, for though Hanoi directed the war, set its pace, controlled its overall strategy, and on the international front articulated the propaganda aims of the Vietcong, it did not in those days (1959) send North Vietnamese troops to fight in the south. . . .'[1]

Even a protester against the American commitment, Gerald Stone, reported that by early 1965 'it (infiltration from the north) was indisputably taking place on an ever-increasing scale with growing numbers of northerners included. At the same time, North Vietnam, aided by China, was pumping large quantities of arms, munitions, and other supplies southward. This was open aggression—a calculated, illegal invasion of territory aimed at toppling an opposing government that had shown itself capable of suppressing internal opposition. No quibbling over numbers of infiltrators and tonnage of arms could obscure this fact.'[2]

But the great gains had been made long before open escalation of the struggle by the north had given the U.S.A. an excuse for intervening against aggression. It began in 1957 on a small scale and in an apparently haphazard fashion as is the way with the beginning of revolutionary guerrilla wars: the assassination of 43 troops, 23 civil guards, 40 militiamen, 8 social cadres, 68 village headmen, and 228 private persons.[3] By 1965, some 20,000 minor officials in the countryside had been murdered: village chiefs, nurses, school teachers, policemen, and public health officers. By 1960 the Vietcong was attacking in up to battalion strength. The infiltration of specialist cadres through Laos, 'that open sieve' as Philippe Devillers has called it, was got under way. By 1964 the 325th Division of the army of the D.R.V. had entered South Vietnam. Then came the Americans, tardily, unwillingly, but in such a fashion as to put paid to the 'aggression from the north' as the U.S. State Department correctly enough

---

[1] *The Making of a Quagmire*, The Bodley Head, 1965.
[2] *War Without Honour*, Jacaranda Press, 1965. See also Denis Warner, *Reporting South-East Asia*, Angus and Robertson, 1966; Michael Field, *The Prevailing Wind*, Methuen, 1965; Robert Shaplen, *The Lost Revolution: Vietnam 1945–1965*, André Deutsch, 1966; and Brian Crozier, *South-East Asia in Turmoil*, Penguin 1965.
[3] Diem Speech, 7th October 1957 op. cit.

called it at that time in 1965. Bernard Fall estimated that between 1959–63 at least two full divisional staffs of the army of the D.R.V. had been moved south to co-ordinate the operations of the N.L.F. Details of infiltrators and plans of the command structure were supplied in various Vietnamese and U.S. white papers from 1960 onwards.[1]

There is no reason whatsoever to doubt the veracity of P. J. Honey's statement that '. . . the D.R.V. leadership (decided) to change its tactics toward South Vietnam and procure its overthrow while not ostensibly engaging in warfare against that state.'[2] Elsewhere he wrote, 'In an effort to conceal North Vietnam's role, a bogus National Front for the Liberation of South Vietnam was formed.'[3] The relationship between the N.L.F. and the D.R.V. was nicely described by George Carver in *The Faceless Victory* as 'essentially the relationship between a field command and its parent headquarters'.

Nevertheless, the development within South Vietnam of the N.L.F. was a very great organizational achievement; the Hanoi direction, control, officering, and supplying of the movement notwithstanding, this revolutionary warfare campaign was basically self-generating. It had to be, since its expansion of political control depended as much on the exploitation of 'contradictions' as upon terrorism; and the 'contradictions' were most of them local issues that could only be properly exploited through an intimate understanding of them. Of course it is not really possible to isolate the exploitation of 'contradictions' from other activities. As has been shown, the politico-military assault launched against a target society by the *necessarily* expanding (as Giap has pointed out) armed Communist society is always a total one in which the rifle complements the 'gift of the gab'. 'The exploitation of 'contradictions' is not our activity for propaganda by itself, but for agitational-propaganda; and wherever it is truly effective it is the achievement of *armed* propaganda.'

This becomes very clear if an actual local Communist plan of operations is studied. Part of the first page of the Military Plan of the Provincial Party Committee at Baria reads as follows:

'The responsibilities and duties of armed groups:

'In order to carry out the present policies of the party to meet the new situation: increase armed activities to the level of political activi-

---

[1] *Threat to the Peace*, U.S. State Department, December 1961, fins *La Politique Aggressive des Viet Minh Communists*, G.V.N., July 1962.
[2] *Communism in North Vietnam*, op. cit.
[3] *Pacific Affairs*, 1962. Ellen Hammer, *Pacific Affairs*, Spring 1962; Scigliano op. cit.

ties and the policies appropriate for each region—in base areas, armed intervention or activities are the mainstay; in rural areas armed activities should be at the same level as political activities; in towns and cities, political activities are the most important.

'To carry out the policies of the party appropriate to the new situation, the common task of armed units of the military forces is to press forward measures to overcome encircling pressures, propaganda under armed protection, and military attacks on the enemy in a continuous, spreading and well-co-ordinated manner to serve the needs of the revolution. Weaken and annihilate enemy military forces, then regroup for recovery. Build up our forces.

'Concrete activities:

'Overcome encircling pressure; co-ordinate closely with the political branch to carry out plans for this purpose.

'However, we must move forward with determination, planning places for concentration, targets and areas of activities. Forces at the district level should co-ordinate with a number of villages having guerrilla and people's militia security forces. Wipe out the enemy in one area at a time under the guise of liberating the people in that particular area. Concentrated forces of a district should co-ordinate to establish a beachhead in a village or inter-village. . . . Village forces under encircling pressure and having guerrilla groups must progress into inter-village formations.

'Squads in charge of villages and agrovilles must carry out assassination missions right at the centre to immobilize the enemy. Prime targets should be security forces and civil action officials, hooligans and thugs. Besides, propaganda under armed protection must be carried out on a regular basis with a view to establishing bases.'[1]

Other relevant passages in this document are:

'All personnel who meet standards and support the directives can be formed into guerrilla-militia. To be left out: hooligans, spies, police, sons and daughters of landlords and businessmen.

'Deliver villages from pressure. Assassinate hooligans and oppressors. Disperse reactionary organizations carrying out propaganda to soldiers.

'Protect the people, protect production, maintain security and order in villages. Information and labour duties. Fight the enemy in order to take over weapons and establish bases.

'Oppose military service, labour assignments, concentration of people in agrovilles, and fight against corruption.

[1] *Threat to the Peace*, U.S. State Department, 1961.

'Secret Militia:

'Fight against pressure, suppress corrupt officials, carry out military logistics, sabotage, provide and disseminate information.

'Training requirements:

'The cells supervise the execution of all missions, maintain discipline, administer punishment and rewards. In all party committees, military training must be given to members as well as to the party secretary.'

This document relating to plans for the expansion of revolutionary warfare in what is now known as Phuoc Tuy province, the Australian area of pacification today, provides a useful idea of the total approach to the problem adopted by the Communists and also of the expansionist combativeness required of such guerrillas. A summary of another captured document of the same year, 1961, complements it and further fills in the picture of activities:

1. 'Special caution should be used in handling members of the civil guard who defected to the Vietcong: "they might be spies". Such persons should be subjected to thorough investigation for a period of three months. "After this period", the instructions added, "if the case remains suspicious, immediately liquidate the suspect to avoid further trouble for the revolution."

2. 'Step up extermination activities against traitors. All those refusing to have rice collected, to pay taxes or make money contributions to the Front can be considered reactionaries and punished like other traitors.

3. 'Step up activities (aimed at) encircling and paralysing strategic roads, means of communication used for transporting rice, pigs, and charcoal, such as canals. These activities are aimed at ruining the economy of the enemy, of raising the cost of living in the city of Saigon.'[1]

It will be observed that the plans are conceived in terms of encirclement, penetration, and inducing paralysis through terrorist and economic warfare tactics; that the armed Communist society is in this fashion breaking down the G.V.N.'s attempt to retain or restore order so that it may insert its own authority into the disputed zone—and where this cannot presently be done, at least undermine G.V.N. authority through assassinations even within the Government's model settlements, known as agrovilles.

This leads to a discussion of the G.V.N.'s reply to the phased escalation of revolutionary guerrilla warfare. The agrovilles referred to

[1] *Threat to the Peace* op. cit.

above were established from 1959 onwards to provide the nuclei for pioneer settlement schemes; as the revolutionary war began to gain significant momentum—as always, the decision to meet the insurgency in a truly serious manner was made dangerously late—a plan was formed early in 1961 for the construction of 'strategic hamlets', the primary purpose of which was to protect the people from the increasing political and military activities of the Communists, though Diem and his brother counsellor, Ngo Dinh Nhu, also saw in them a way of changing public attitudes. Western advisers hoped that the strategic hamlets would provide a means of winning over the people through increasing their technical know-how and their living standards in general.

Though the strategic hamlets were based upon a false analogy with Malaya where they had been used to great effect during the Communist insurgency, they were in principle sound and caused the N.L.F. very great concern, as will be shown, but they depended for their ultimate success on precisely the same steady, cautious phasing which is the mark of a successful expansion of revolutionary guerrilla warfare. But this was just what Diem and Nhu were incapable of doing; they were men in a hurry. The success of the strategic hamlet complex also depended upon exercising intense control of movement, by road, track, and waterway; and this was never really attempted in South Vietnam until well after the arrival of the Americans *en masse*.

Even so, the strategic hamlet programme constituted a formidable response to the N.L.F. campaign. This is quite frankly admitted by the Australian Communist journalist, Wilfred Burchett, on the basis of talks with N.L.F. leaders in the field: 'If 1963 (the year of Diem's downfall) was a "(National Liberation) Front year", 1962 must be largely credited to Saigon. With U.S. aid in men and materials pouring in from the end of 1961, a major effort was made to destroy and isolate the Front's armed forces, to push Front influence back from the gates of Saigon and other provincial capitals and to re-install Diemist power in the countryside. The use of helicopters and amphibious tanks to increase rapidity of movement and to avoid the devastating ambushes that Diemist troops invariably fell into when they moved by road or river, caught the guerrillas off-balance at first. . . . The drive to set up 'strategic hamlets' was also a problem for N.L.F. organizers and additional hardship for the population.'[1]

It has been argued by Bernard Fall, a profound student of revolutionary warfare in Vietnam, that in time the N.F.L. began to work out

[1] *Vietnam: Inside Story of the Guerrilla War* op. cit.

effective counter-measures to the strategic hamlet programme; and by 1963 some American advisers (of whom there were about 12,000 by 1962), notably Colonel John Vann, came to the conclusion that, as it was then being fought, the struggle was being lost.[1] Colonel Vann still believed the war could be won but he considered that the South Vietnamese army was deficient in fighting morale and using technologically sophisticated methods inappropriate to the grass roots struggle in the vital delta area.

A quite different viewpoint was put forward by an anonymous member of the British advisory mission: 'In spite of all the mistakes that were made, the hamlets are working extremely well and proving their worth against the Communists. Of course the Americans have done wonders in providing arms to defend them and in supplying every hamlet with a radio transmitter for calling up help when it is attacked. They've brought in lots of helicopters, so that reinforcements can hop ambushes and get to where they're needed at top speed. . . .

'Areas of the countryside where the Vietcong had things pretty well their own way were covered with strategic hamlets once the programme got started. The results were remarkable. Peasant farmers felt more secure behind their barricades and when the Communists came for food they drove them off with gunfire. Information began to flow in, too, and soon the Vietcong found themselves in trouble. They concentrated their attacks on the hamlets and even destroyed some of them. But most of the time reinforcements would arrive and inflict heavy casualties on the attackers. More and more the Vietcong had to be withdrawn to the rear areas and put to work on growing their own food. Our chemical defoliants sprayed from aircraft killed what they grew and must have broken their hearts. Communist morale began to fall, and the number of surrenders climbed steeply. . . . If you want any confirmation about how well we were doing you have only to look at the North Vietnamese newspapers and read the propaganda attacks appearing daily against the strategic hamlets. . . .

'Yes, we have the Communists on the run all right. By last April I'd proved to my own satisfaction that the stragetic hamlets were the complete answer to Communist guerrilla tactics. We were over the top of the hill, and the end of the war was only a matter of time. Then in May (1963) the Buddhist troubles blew up and the political situation went to pieces. Since then it's got progressively worse. . . .'[2]

[1] *Street without Joy* op. cit.; David Halberstam op. cit.; and Denis Warner, The Last Confucian, Penguin, 1964.
[2] P. J. Honey, *Encounter*, December 1963.

The 'Buddhist troubles', which brought about Diem's downfall in 1963, were in part the result of Diem's policies and in part the result of a Press campaign that grew up in the West against him and his family from early 1962 onwards.[1] Diem's policies led to the G.V.N. becoming evermore like a replica in reverse of the kind of society the N.L.F. was trying to establish, including a quasi-covert political party, the Can-lao which was a mixture of counter-intelligence agency and coercive apparatus, and a vaguely defined, utterly inappropriate counter-ideology known as Personalism. As a corollary to this, the inner circle of the regime became evermore ingrown and incapable of relying even on its military commanders.

The intense, yet cloudy ideological formulations are nicely exemplified in a long speech by Ngo Dinh Nhu made just before the 'Buddhist troubles' flared up: 'New life is achieved within the framework of Personalism, struggle, community efforts and work from the lowest to the highest echelons and from top to bottom, so that as progress is being made the people may enjoy liberty and prosperity which they will have conquered themselves through their own effort and struggle. ... All our efforts were aimed at training a great number of cadres and at helping each cadre to acquire a sufficient intellectual and moral capital to successfully face the struggle. That includes among other things:

(a) ... A moral foundation with a personality endowed with the necessary virtues for struggle;

(b) ... An intellectual foundation which would enable a cadre to grasp a situation and to apply to it the dialectic of the struggle;

(c) ... A technical foundation with methods appropriate to mobilizing the people in the struggle.'[2]

It must of course always be remembered that the Diem regime was saddled from the beginning with the fact that it did not represent clearly observable legitimacy but instead had to try to *impose* it against an advancing armed totalitarian society; and that in conditions of civil war it is not simple to conciliate various nationalist groupings—it seems simpler to try to integrate society in the fashion adopted by the Ngos, along authoritarian and ideological lines. The strategic hamlets seemed to provide the opportunity for doing this. Ngo Dinh Diem saw the future of the strategic hamlets in terms that were noble but

---

[1] The campaign, as it *seemed* to be in Saigon, may be dated from the *Open Letter to President Kennedy*, New York Times, 11th April 1962.

[2] *Friendly Talk to the Militants*, Directorate of Information, Saigon, April 1963.

practically as cloudy as his brothers: 'A political, social and military revolution, such then is the triptych which our people, with our youth in the forefront, are now building in the strategic hamlets. Our solution of the double problem of the economic revolution and of the development of Man in his wellbeing, in freedom and justice, is inscribed in the most certain future, whatever communism, the enemy of mankind, may do.'[1]

Whatever may be said against this much defamed man, the Communists saw in him the most formidable adversary. One of them referred to the coups which brought him down and continued afterwards as 'gifts from heaven for us. . . . The military command has been turned upside down and weakened by purges . . . the coercive apparatus set up over the years with great care by Diem, is utterly shattered, *especially at the base*. The principal chiefs of security and secret police, on which mainly depended the protection of the regime and the repression of the revolutionary movement, have been eliminated, purged. Troops, officers and officials of the army and the administration are completely lost; they have no more confidence in their chiefs and have no idea to whom they should be loyal. . . . From the political viewpoint the weakening of our adversary is still clearer. Reactionary political organizations like the Labour and Personalism party, the National Revolutionary movement, the Young Republicans, the movement for Women's Solidarity and others which constituted an *appreciable support* for the regime have been dissolved and eliminated. . . .'[2]

Another member of the N.L.F. argued that '. . . they will search in vain for a more efficient horse than Diem. With all his faults and criminal stupidities, in nine years Diem did succeed in *setting up and maintaining* an army, an administration and some sort of political machine, with all the reins of power in his hands.' It may be thought that these testimonials offered by leaders of the N.L.F. are more convincing than the accounts of foreign observers.

However, while there is reason to believe that Diem's approach was in some ways formidable in the countryside, it contained within it the seeds of its own destruction elsewhere. In brief, Diem may be said to have thwarted all other expressions of nationalism and to have given the impression that he believed that only a chiefly Catholic group centred around his person was fit to shape the new South Vietnam

---

[1] *Vietnam's Strategic Hamlets*, Directorate of Information, Saigon, February 1963.
[2] Burchett op. cit. Italics added.

politically and socially. So long as he held the reins of power firmly in his hands—so long as he showed no signs of weakness *at all*—Diem could sustain his policy. But this was not to be. The repression of Buddhists in Hué who sought to present their own flag as superior to the national flag (as Diem's supporters saw it) ended in bloodshed; and the incident fired the energies of articulate Buddhist groups who drew attention to certain disabilities suffered by Buddhists under a Bao Dai ordinance which remained in force.

The harsh spotlight of the Western Press was by this time focused on the Diem regime and focused from such an angle that it illuminated all its shortcomings in urban matters—while leaving the desperate struggle in the countryside largely in the shadows. The cry of 'Persecution' went up in Western progressive and Protestant circles in the U.S.A.; totally misconceiving the situation, such circles evoked a picture of a medieval Catholic engaged in a crusade against the Albigensians rather than the reality of an authoritarian ruler, hated much more as the leader of a Northern élite in Saigon than as a Catholic, trying to hold together in his self-constructed 'iron frame' of administrative devices all anti-Communist activity.

He began to falter in a predicament compounded of local primitivism (monks immolating themselves) and outraged Western naïveté (when confronted by photographs of the monks burning). Never having really trusted the Americans, he found himself being publicly humiliated before Saigon's educated classes by 'progressive' Western propaganda. He hesitated: deputations of monks were received, conciliations were attempted, a U.N. Fact-Finding Mission was accepted.[1] Opposition from other groups, including students, the children of his own high administrators, began to manifest itself in mass demonstrations which the N.L.F. later claimed to have instigated.[2]

Hesitation was followed by a crack-down on the Buddhist leaders, which was carried out in a fashion that in those circumstances was fatal: 'If there was any hope (for the regime) it ended when security forces with guns and grenades forced their way into Saigon's Xa Loi pagoda last week', the very experienced Denis Warner reported at the time.[3] All the groups which had been disabled by Diem's authoritarian élite saw that their hour had at last struck. Mao's dictum to the

---

[1] Its report published on 7th December 1963, entitled *The Violation of Human Rights in South Viet-Nam*, contains no judgements; nor do its findings support the charge of persecution.
[2] Burchett op. cit.
[3] *The Herald*, Melbourne, 27th August 1963.

effect that it was the countryside which was important and that the cities would fall later like rotten fruit was proved incomplete in this instance. The aftermath of this essentially urban (Hué and Saigon) matter was very nearly catastrophic in the countryside, since a whole *regime* collapsed when Diem was assassinated and the suave politicians jockeying for positions in Saigon did not provide the alternative leadership that is necessary for the struggle against an expanding armed revolutionary society. The N.L.F. began to 'chew up' the formations of a demoralized South Vietnamese army. As it moved towards the phase of counter-offensive the N.L.F. came to rely more and more upon infiltrated specialists and arms from outside South Vietnam. The 47,000 or so who infiltrated from the north made a 'critical contribution to the Vietcong strength',[1] and Vietcong main-force units were coming to be Chinese-armed. Much has been made of the ability of the Vietcong to acquire their own arms from South Vietnamese forces but there is a strict, if not easily defined limit to this tactic once a general counter-offensive is planned. If it were not so, then the rate of acquiring enemy arms would be such as to suggest a rate of arms losses and desertions on the opposing side so great that it would disintegrate. Though the morale of the army of South Vietnam was low indeed in 1964, and early 1965, very heavy fighting continued.

By the time the Americans arrived in April 1965, the N.L.F. and the regular division infiltrated from North Vietnam were preparing to cut South Vietnam in half, moving out of the Central Highlands and aiming to attack provincial capitals. Here again a question of regionalism was to prove very important. For some time the N.L.F. enjoyed the advantage of handling the highland ethnic minorities with more political skill than the nationalists who were all too apt to regard them in traditional fashion as 'savages'. But they were the key to the control of the strategically important Central Highlands (the impending loss of control here significantly affected the French decision to terminate their Indo-China War). Though many of these montagnard tribes have taken to sedentary rice cultivation, unlike the more primitive slash-and-burn cultivators of the area, they in no sense feel they belong to South Vietnam. The tribes vary greatly in size. The Rhadé and Jarai, numbering over 100,000, while others number less than 10,000—do at least share one common characteristic: a loathing of Vietnamese of any political colour. Diem wished to use the Highlands for the resettlement of Vietnamese from the crowded coastal plain and to tame the montagnards by incorporating them into the econ-

[1] *New Zealand Assistance to the Republic of Vietnam.* State Paper, 1965.

omic and, to some extent, into the social fabric of South Vietnam. Here again there was a 'contradiction' for the Communists to exploit. The Diem scheme was 'aimed at raising the standard of living of those highlanders living in the villages bordering the lowland development centres. Using the latter as hubs, the Government's plan is to set up three outer rings in order to provide all the inhabitants with the most effective protection and guidance. Included within the scope of this plan are 200 highland villages with a total population of about 150,000.'[1]

But in fact the inevitable frictions between different races occurred and the N.L.F. very often using indoctrinated Rhadé tribesmen from North of the frontier, managed to secure in the highlands the bases and transport routes from Laos which they required. On the other hand the allegiance of the montagnards was all along a problematical factor, easily altered by relatively slight changes of circumstance and understanding; and American Special Forces operatives often proved themselves as able as the N.L.F. to recruit and effectively use the tribesmen.[2] Nevertheless when the Americans arrived in force they found a situation in Saigon and in the Delta and the Highlands that was rapidly deteriorating both politically and militarily. They wisely chose to leave the army of the G.V.N. to engage in holding operations in the Delta while they used their marvellous mobility and terrible firepower to destroy the N.L.F.'s capacity for an offensive based on the Highlands in Kontum-Pleikku area.

So far as the possible economic origins of the insurgency are concerned, it has been argued that Diem's failure to implement a large-scale land reform was an important causative factor. It is true that Diem's achievements (and even his aims) were modest in this respect. A legalistic sense of what was appropriate—a sense that did not always move him in judicial matters affecting individual rights—inhibited Diem from accepting land redistribution carried out under Vietminh occupation; the same kind of approach appears to have inhibited him from making significant efforts to establish peasant proprietorship.

At this point, the author is very much aware of his own over-optimism in the past about what Diem seemed to have achieved in this regard; for example, 'And yet it is to Diem's foresight and the expertise of his adviser, Wolf Ladejinsky, that Vietnam owes the greatest achievement of the regime: land reform. When the regime came to power about 40 per cent of the riceland areas was held by

---

[1] *The Highland Refugees*, Directorate of Information, Saigon. 1963
[2] Denis Warner, *The Last Confucian*, op. cit.

2,500 individuals—0·025 per cent of the rural population. Rent rates were commonly 50 per cent of the crop or more. The tenant had virtually no security at all.[1] The regime has been remarkably successful in reducing rents, granting security of tenure, and rehabilitating land; and also in establishing pioneer land development programmes in the uplands to absorb the overpopulation of the coastal plains. . . . There is no reason to doubt Ladejinsky's claim: 'The Vietminh's opposition to South Vietnam's reforms is violent precisely because they *are* successful. The regime has therefore laid the essential preliminary foundation for combatting peasant guerrilla warfare—land reform is a *sine qua non* in Asia—but it must be understood that it is still possible for the Vietcong to win simply through the application of military tactics, provided they are permitted virtually illimitable reinforcement and supply, as is the case today.'[2] In retrospect this view seems to have greatly over-rated Diem's land reform, which though more considerable than Magsaysay's as to redistribution of land, and theoretically fairly respectable so far as halving rents and securing tenures were concerned, was tardy in its implementation and was never backed up a true administrative effort to place peasant welfare at the very forefront of state activity.

Of course 'land reform' has become one of those privileged phrases which attract approval or disapproval very much according to the presumed nature of the regime carrying them out. Communist 'land reform' basically amounts to collectivization in the interests of Communist party state power and has everywhere proved agriculturally disastrous or at least seriously debilitating. Diem's land reform, though very incomplete, engendered no observable economic distress —and involved the settlement of hundreds of thousands of refugees from the North—and nor has it ever been demonstrated that significant sections of the N.L.F. insurgency can be attributed to failures of 'land reform' as such.

The pre-war rice production of South Vietnam was estimated at 3·1 million tons; it was over 5 million tons in 1960. During 1959–60 per capita food production rose by 2 per cent in the south while it declined by 10 per cent in the north; by 1960 South Vietnam's per capita gross national product was estimated at 110 dollars, North Vietnam's at 70 dollars.[3] Diem's regime achieved remarkable results

[1] J. P. Gittenger, *Land Tenure in Vietnam*, Terminal Report, December 1959, Division of Agricultural and National Resources, USOM.
[2] *Australia's Neighbours*, October 1962. Wolf Ladejinsky states his case in *Viet-Nam 1960*, Special Issue of *Viet-Nam in World Affairs*, Saigon 1960.
[3] *New Zealand Assistance to the Republic of Vietnam*, op. cit.

in other activities relevant to rural betterment, such as village dispensaries, primary schools, and malarial eradication.

The more obvious features of Diem's land reforms were judiciously described by Robert Scigliano: 'In response to awakened peasant aspirations for land (that is, as a result of Communist propaganda and interim policies during the anti-French war) the government in 1955 initiated a three-pronged land reform. Its aims were to settle peasants on abandoned land (some 400,000 acres), to safeguard tenants' rights by means of land contracts, and to transfer land (for which the peasant had to pay in instalments) from large holders to tenants and others with the aim of reducing land-holdings.'[1] By the middle of 1959 some three-quarters of tenant farmers had entered into contracts. The social realities underlying these formal arrangements were no doubt far from satisfactory for the peasant, since a real land reform must include the destruction of the middle-man's restrictive powers by the creation of peasant producers' co-operatives and offer government controlled rural credit, but there is no reason whatsoever to suppose that Diem fell because of his failure to solve the 'land problem', as has often been implied.

Diem's failure lay in his inability either to harness other nationalist groups to his nationally stated purpose or to keep these groups permanently down. 'Buddhism' became a rallying cry for all manner of dissident groups—none of which has ever consistently suggested accommodation with the N.L.F.—which represented, often in a misconceived or even incoherent fashion, certain genuine nationalist aspirations that Diem's approach could not satisfy. But here one touches upon complexly related particularities that cannot be included in a general study of revolutionary guerrilla warfare in South-East Asia.

It is not altogether difficult today to see the errors of understanding that led to Diem's downfall; it is very much more difficult to see how Diem, beginning as he did without widespread personal prestige, without a clearly viable form of government, and without being able to establish a generally acceptable syle of nationalist endeavour, could have acted, *before* he had won the struggle against the N.L.F., so as to fuse into a commonly acceptable national government the elements which in the event brought him down. Diem was a man not a natural dictator. Had the insurgency been put down, as it nearly was, then there is reason to suppose that he would have given play to other expressions of nationalism. . . . But he was a man called to power in

[1] *Nation under Stress*, Houghton Mifflin, 1963, op. cit.

quite extraordinary circumstances, which demanded a tremendous personal effort of will; and he never quite freed himself from the memories of those early days when he did, personally, subdue what appeared to be the forces of chaos; he thenceforth vastly over-estimated the potency of all divisive forces, even of the most definitely anti-Communist kinds, and permitted this over-estimation to undermine his traditional judiciousness and even, sometimes his natural humanity.

That he did this is attributable not only to himself and those around him; and not only to the circumstances of South Vietnamese politics. It is also attributable to the way in which he came to be treated by the Press in the West: his regime was subjected to the kind of moral criteria which is not applied to the government of Burma, for example. Again the double-standard of Western 'progressive' liberalism came into play; what was reported as 'preventive detention' in respect of Burma, Singapore, and Indonesia became concentration camps in South Vietnam; while students might be killed in Burma by the army without significant comment, the incarceration of student rioters in Saigon became a matter for international indignation. Other governments in South-East Asia could impose disabilities upon Christians, Hindus, and Muslims—or upon racial groups, such as the Chinese—without the Western Press becoming outraged; but the cry of religious *persecution* was quickly raised in the case of the Catholic leader of Vietnam.

This is said not in order to defend the man Diem—that is not to the author's purpose here—but to draw attention to the very great importance of international public opinion (a vague and formless thing, rather like a gas, which is necessarily engendered or magnified only by the Western Press with its enormous communicational power) in influencing events during an insurgency. It is of the utmost importance that no government faced by a Communist revolutionary insurgency should have applied to it criteria that no Western liberal would for a moment have accepted during the Spanish Civil War, for example.[1] Such a Press campaign as was launched against Diem could only have the effect of undermining the morale of the Government, causing it to lose face amongst its own intelligentsia, and if anything (in such conditions) exacerbate the very malpractices against which it was ostensibly directed, since in such a situation of Western 'moral dis-

---

[1] Preventive detention was not unknown in England during the Second World War, to cite another example; and in wholly unthreatened Australia wholly innocent men were incarcerated by Government *fiat*.

approbation' every move towards liberization could only be interpreted in South Vietnam as a sign of Government weakness. It can be predicted with some certainty that had South Vietnam been abandoned by the U.S.A. in 1965, then precisely the same kind of Western Press campaign would have been generated against the threatened government of Thailand, the least agreeable features of which could only have been exacerbated in conditions of violence and fear.

It is not for a moment being suggested that this increasingly important international component of revolutionary guerrilla warfare campaigns is the result of 'Communist conspiracy' in the West. Such a notion is quite absurd. What is at issue is the nature of Communist revolutionary guerrilla warfare itself. So long as this can be represented as basically a matter of spontaneous rural rising against specific injustices, a 'natural' response to social conditions, a thing marked primarily by the exploits of outraged peasants heroically using primitive devices against Western military might, then the raction against the earlier Western contempt for things 'Asian'—a clinically neurotic guilt-reaction—will predispose all those in the West who believe themselves to be personally uneasy about the colonial past (and today uneasy about the cosiness of their own affluent societies) to treat most unfairly any 'Asian' leader who is persistently dubbed 'reactionary', 'corrupt', and so on.

Diem was so treated in a moment of crisis. His downfall was quite naturally followed by a period in which contending factions, suddenly and severally possessed of a sense of representing the 'real' South Vietnam, schemed against each other; the very worst features of South Vietnamese factionalism came to the fore and were, quite obviously, far more corrupt than Diem's clique had ever been; and so a series of very ephemeral governments came to pass. These governments seemed to be dedicated to forms of political behaviour more acceptable to public opinion in the U.S.A. But they were, most of them, moved by sectional interests and ill-formed plans that, however unwittingly, were altogether subversive of the war effort. With the downfall of Diem, Saigonese politics began increasingly to resemble the welter of an Oriental bazaar. The Vietcong began to prepare for the general counter-offensive against a disintegrating regime. The first of the final Communist steps was to be the conquest of the Central Highlands or at least the cutting of South Vietnam in two. By the beginning of 1965 only intervention from outside could prevent the complete subjugation of non-Communist South Vietnam. At that point—so devastating had the consequences of Diem's downfall been

—even the political strait-jacket of a military junta could not be established in order to stop the deterioration of a society which had been under slowly increasing attack since mid-1957.

Chapter 11

RETROSPECT

It has not been the chief purpose of this book to justify American policy in Vietnam except in so far as the nature of revolutionary guerrilla warfare may have been shown to justify it. But since Vietnam has become the test case for this kind of warfare, a kind of warfare that is waged psychologically in the West just as hard as it is waged in rural Vietnam, it is inevitably that a book like this should be inextricably involved in that struggle.

Every available psychological weapon has been brought to bear upon Western public opinion, especially of course American public opinion, since the day the war began. The first psychological shots were fired in August 1945, when Vietnamese Communist aspirations were disguised as the language of Washington and the Rights of Man. Public opinion in the West has been *protractedly* conditioned by Communist psychological warfare; but since 1965 the campaign has been escalated.

However, it is necessary to make it quite clear that the growing efficacy of this campaign cannot be attributed only to the skills of Communist propaganda carried out by sympathizers in the West. The Communists needed the right kind of intellectual and emotional terrain on which to operate; the right kinds of 'contradictions' to exploit. It is desirable, therefore, to conclude by examining some of the kinds of propaganda which have dominated the protest movement against the Johnson policy.

At the beginning of the war two propaganda ideas in particular were cultivated by those concerned to work on liberal minds in the Communist interest. The first, which has by now become totally discredited, was the idea that the National Liberation Front was neither Hanoi-directed nor predominately Communist, but rather an organization of disgruntled democrats which included some Communists. This was the line which permitted Western support for Castro in the past. The second idea which was purposefully bruited about was this: President Johnson had wantonly injected unilateral violence into a situation in which the late President Kennedy had exercised diplomatic caution. But the fact was that the example of diplomatic caution cited was an example not only of a diplomatic failure but of a failure which made the war in South Vietnam inevitable if the U.S.A. were not to betray its whole alliance system. The failure was in Laos and its significance was spelt out by one of Kennedy's chief advisers: 'For Laos had an evident strategic importance. If the Communists gained possession of the Mekong valley they could materially intensify their pressure against South Vietnam and Thailand. If Laos was not precisely a dagger pointed at the heart of Kansas, it was very plainly a gateway to South-East Asia. . . .'[1]

The result of the diplomatic agreement on Laos, which in theory only permitted Hanoi to supply the Laotian Government with non-military aid, was the creation of the Ho Chi Minh network trails into South Vietnam and the strengthening of the Hanoi-directed Pathet Lao.[2] By the time President Johnson decided that the U.S.A. must intervene on a very large scale in South Vietnam, the situation that had resulted from the Laotian settlement and Diem's downfall was so critical for the anti-Communists that their defeat was probably only a matter of weeks.

The predicament in which President Johnson found himself was described indirectly by *The Economist* on 20th August 1966: 'Those who do not like the war in Vietnam, but equally do not want to see Mao Tse-tung's beliefs sweeping across Asia in a wave of guerrilla wars, have a duty to ask themselves where else they think the wave can be stopped? Thailand? But the non-Communist Thais are not going to call for help from a defeated American army, and in any case it is logistically much harder to get help into Thailand than into Vietnam. Burma? Not on the cards. India, then? But the mind swerves from the difficulty of doing anything to help that fragile country if the guerrillas once get to work in West Bengal or Kerala or wherever.'

The next idea that was canvassed in protest against the American commitment was the suggestion that the commitment would very seriously alienate 'Asian' opinion from sympathy for U.S. aims in the world at large. This has been proved to be grossly untrue. There is every reason to believe Mr. Richard Nixon's contention that, 'From Japan to India, Asian leaders know why we are in Vietnam and, pri-

[1] Arthur M. Schlesinger Jr., 'A Thousand Days', Quoted by Milton Sacks *The New Leader*, 8th May 1967.
[2] *North Vietnamese Interference in Laos*, Government White Paper, Vientiane, December 1964.

vately if not publicly, they urge us to see it through to a satisfactory conclusion.'¹

A number of leaders in Asia have publicly declared their support for the U.S. commitment in Vietnam, the most important of them being the Prime Minister of Japan during his visit to Australia in October, 1967. The significant aspect of such support has been the argument advanced by some of these leaders along the lines of President Eisenhower's so-called 'domino theory'. This unfortunate phrase has naturally been seized upon and used to good effect by protesters. It is therefore interesting to compare President Eisenhower's language in 1959 with the language of the left wing leader of Singapore, Mr. Lee Kuan Yew, in 1967. President Eisenhower argued in this fashion: 'Strategically, South Vietnam's capture by the Communists would bring their power several hundred miles into a hitherto free region. The remaining countries in South-East Asia would be menaced by a great flanking movement. The freedom of 12,000,000 people would be lost immediately, and that of 150,000,000 in adjacent areas would be seriously endangered. The loss of South Vietnam would set in motion a crumbling process that could, as it progressed, have grave consequences for us and for freedom. . . .'²

Compare Mr. Lee: 'Nothing would be more disastrous (for the rest of South-East Asia) than to see South Vietnam just erode away and become absorbed into the Communist group. It would telescope the time left to the rest of us. If people start believing that non-Communist Asia will be lost eventually to Communist Asia, then everybody will make his adjustment accordingly.'³ He was simply reiterating the language he had used to a group of Australian Labour Party politicians in September 1966 in Singapore. One of the politicians, Mr. Sam Benson, reported him as having said, '. . . if South Vietnam fell to the Communists, it would only be a matter of time before Singapore fell.'

The Prime Minister of Malaya, Tunku Abdul Rahman said in Parliament on 21st January 1967: 'Once South Vietnam is taken over by the Communists, it will only be a matter of time before Malaysia goes under. . . .'⁴ The President of the Philippines, Mr. Ferdinand E. Marcos, said on the radio on 19th February 1966: 'If the reds win

¹ *Foreign Affairs*, 1967.
² Lyndon B. Johnson's speech of 29th September 1967, in San Antonio, Texas.
³ *Sydney Morning Herald*, 20th October 1967.
⁴ *Viet-Nam, Australia, and Asia*, Department of External Affairs, Canberra, June 1967.

in Viet-Nam, that victory will signal the reactivation of Communist insurgency all over South-East Asia, including the Philippines. Almost certainly, it will mean renewed Communist activity in the Philippines. . . .'[1] His words have been echoed by the leaders of Thailand, Laos, Cambodia, and Korea in very much the same terms.

It is quite obvious that it cannot be proved in advance that a failure of American purpose in Vietnam will 'unscramble us all (in South-East Asia)', as Mr. Lee Kuan Yew expressed it; statesmen are never in any circumstances armed with such proof. They must act according to the balance of probabilities. No one realizes this better than the great Texan and consummate politician who is President of the U.S.A. at this grave time. In his speech at San Antonio, after quoting Mr. Lee Kuan Yew, 'I feel the fate of Asia—South and South-East Asia—will be decided in the next few years by what happens out in Vietnam,' said: 'I cannot tell you—with certainty—that a Communist conquest of South Vietnam would be followed by Communist conquest of South-East Asia. But I do know there are North Vietnamese troops in Laos; there are Vietnamese-trained guerrillas in North-East Thailand; there are Communist-supported guerrilla forces in Burma; a Communist coup was barely averted in Indonesia.

'I cannot tell you—with certainty—that a South-East Asia dominated by Communist power would bring a third world war much closer to reality. One could hope that it would not be so.

'But all that we have learnt in this tragic century strongly suggests it would be so. As President of the United States, I am not prepared to gamble on the chance that it is not so. I am not prepared to risk the security—indeed, the survival—of this nation on mere hope and wishful thinking. I am convinced that by seeing this struggle through now, in Vietnam, we are reducing the chances of a larger war—perhaps a nuclear war. I would rather stand in Vietnam, in our time, and by meeting this danger now, reduce the danger for our children and grandchildren.'

But of course the propaganda against the American commitment in Vietnam did not end with the ridiculing of the 'domino theory'. It has become more and more variegated as the months have passed; it has also become more and more emotional, a development that was vitally necessary if large numbers of Americans were to be involved in the protest movement. On the emotional plane what has been exploited has been the moral ambivalence of people who are psychologically and socially frustrated by liberal capitalist society; people who are

[1] ibid.

aware of their powerlessness in their own society and who therefore seek a vicarious revenge: the defeat of the representatives of 'the Establishment', the American soldiers in Vietnam. Such people make up the majority of the most vociferous protestors.

However, their lead has been increasingly followed by two other very large groups: those who have been constantly, and quite incorrectly, informed that this war is 'dirtier' than other wars so far as the American waging of it is concerned, and people who have been informed, equally incorrectly, that American power would impose a relatively quick solution upon South Vietnam's awful troubles. In fact, in no modern war has so much effort been made, even often enough at the risk of life or failure, to avoid unnecessary civilian casualties; but this has been obscured by important sections of the Western Press which have avidly exploited the atrociousness of the battlefield. The Press has also on the whole been much more concerned to dramatize every set-back rather than steadily survey the achievements.

The result of the protest campaign and the lack of a sense of proportion displayed by much of the Press has been a very serious decline in the popularity rating of President Johnson in the U.S.A.[1] The movement of supporters away from President Johnson includes members of both the groupings described above. This is the most dangerous development that could occur. On the one hand, President Johnson is being assailed by those who are eroding the staying-power of the U.S.A. in what must be fought as a protracted war; on the other hand, the number of opponents who would argue in favour of a possibly catastrophic escalation of the war are growing in numbers too.

This danger is being compounded by increasing demands, even from nations well disposed towards the American commitment in general, that the U.S.A. unilaterally cease its offensive against the North. Once again the debate has been successfully established on the emotional plane by the protesters: it has been successfully represented in many quarters that aerial bombing of North Vietnam is somehow impermissible. Altogether disproportionate weight has been placed in public discussion on the argument relating to the bombing of the north. Those who are obsessed by this argument do not appear

[1] From 65 per cent in March 1965 to less than 40 per cent in August 1967, according to the graph of Louis Harris and Associates published in the *New York Times* Weekly Review of 8th October 1967. Only 28 per cent of Americans at this latter date were prepared positively to approve of President Johnson's manner of waging the war in Vietnam. *The Canberra Times*, 19th October 1967.

to realize the very dangerous consequences of a bombing cessation which is unmatched by any *quid pro quo* by the Hanoi regime. If such a pause results only in a further movement of Communist troops southwards, as was the case in the past, then the argument of the 'super hawks' for the destruction of the Red River system of water control will be very difficult for President Johnson to resist. If it were not resisted, then something impermissible would indeed be set in train.

Another aspect of the war which has been exploited very successfully by the protesters has been the issue of diplomacy; in particular the suggestion that the U.S.A. has simply failed to put forward proposals for peace of a reasonable enough kind to find acceptance in Hanoi. This suggestion, in so far as it has been honestly made, is based upon a total misconception of what Communist revolutionary warfare is all about. American efforts to seek a basis for negotiations have gone to extreme lengths in trying to remove pre-conditions and prejudices.[1] Hanoi has throughout been altogether intransigent while seeking to use Western gullibility, through the agency of both fellow-travellers and other kinds of active dissenters, to keep the gleam of hope alive in the form of inspired 'leaks' and vague possibilities.[2] The real attitude of Hanoi was expressed by the Premier of North Vietnam, Mr. Pham Van Dong, when he declared: 'We shall not lift a finger to make initiatives or concessions. If the Americans want to talk peace, they may have *pourparlers* after a cessation of bombing and a pledge of total American withdrawal.'[3]

Here is the heart of the matter late in 1967 as it was in July 1965. This analysis of revolutionary guerrilla warfare began (p. 19) with a quotation from Hanoi which showed the basic assumption upon which the whole struggle would be waged by Hanoi: the assumption that the public of the U.S.A. would 'tear itself apart over the war'. This had been foreshadowed earlier by General Go Nguyen Giap. His argument and the late Bernard Fall's comments on it are so centrally important as to bear repetition at this point. Giap stated: 'The enemy will pass slowly from the offensive to the defensive. The blitzkrieg will transform itself into a war of long duration. Thus, the enemy will be caught in a dilemma: He has to drag out the war in

[1] Ambassador Arthur J. Goldberg, U.S. Representative to the United Nations, 21st September 1967.
[2] M. Monnerot's words should be recalled: 'Even during their most outrageous exploits the "gleam of hope" must be kept alive.' *The Sociology of Communism*, op. cit.
[3] *The Canberra Times*, 11th October 1967.

order to win it and does not possess, on the other hand, the psychological and political means to fight a long-drawn-out-war. . . .'

Bernard Fall commented as follows: 'In all likelihood, Giap concludes, public opinion in the democracy will demand an end to the "useless bloodshed", or its legislature will insist on knowing for how long it will have to vote astronomical credits without a clear-cut victory in sight. This is what eternally compels the military leaders of democratic armies to promise a quick end to the war—to "bring the boys home by Christmas"—or forces the democratic politicians to agree to almost any kind of humiliating compromise rather than to accept the idea of a semi-permanent anti-guerrilla operation. There is little indication in the 1960's that logical conclusions have been drawn from earlier lessons.'[1]

In late 1967 the appreciations of General Giap and Mr. Pham Van Dong are still based on this central assumption of a weakening of American resolve. Mr. Pham Van Dong remarked in the interview quoted above, his mind clearly fixed on the November 1968 Presidential elections, 'In any case, we trust neither President Johnson nor Rusk and will sign no agreement with the U.S. administration so long as they are there: we shall drag out the *pourparlers*.' In the same months, October 1967, an appreciation of the situation by General Giap also became available. He argued, as he had argued years before, that the Americans had unsuccessfully tried blitzkrieg methods but 'They could not fight quickly because they did not know their adversary and because they over-estimated their own strong points in the field of numerical strength and modern weapons. The fact that the U.S. imperialists have to fight a protracted war is a big defeat for them.'[2]

Neither of these Communist leaders talked in terms of military victory but simply in terms of an American incapacity to stay the distance. This was recognized by the ablest of the leaders of non-Communist South-East Asia, Mr. Lee Kuan Yew, when he said in Washington: 'The United States must show them that you can match them in sheer determination, and that you are prepared to go with them to the end of the road.'[3] Whether America and its allies will be prepared to go to the end of that terrible road depends upon their understanding the true nature of revolutionary guerrilla war and the great Peking-line Communist dream of catastrophically altering the

[1] *The Two Viet-Nams* op. cit.
[2] *The Canberra Times*, 12th October 1967.
[3] *Sydney Morning Herald*, 20th October 1967.

balance of world power which has been built upon its presumed efficacy throughout the whole under-developed world.

The enemy of the U.S.A. in Vietnam is the enemy of men everywhere who would wish to keep the future open; and who would support the denial of the declared right of totalitarianism to close the future on small nations—the shortcomings of whose governments are wholly disproportionate to the penalties inflicted by Communist conquest. The last words may safely be left to the U.S.A.'s formidable adversary, General Vo Nguyen Giap, and to the two most eloquent and informed opponents of the American commitments, M. Jean Lacouture and M. Philippe Devillers:

Giap: 'The People's Army is the instrument of the party and of the revolutionary State for the accomplishment, in armed form, of the tasks of the revolution . . . (The party) is the soul of the army. . . . If we win here, we shall win everywhere.'

Lacouture and Devillers: 'The best hope of one day renewing conversations with the greatest power in the Far East lies in reviving the spirit of the Geneva Agreements. On condition, however, that China renounces making her power, her grudges, her desires and her revolutionary faith the sole laws for Asia today.'[1]

---

[1] 'La fin d'une guerre' quoted and translated by Anthony Eden, Earl of Avon, *Towards Peace in Indo-China*, Chatham House Essays, O.U.P., 1966.

SELECT BIBLIOGRAPHY

1. General Works on or Relating to South-East Asia

D. G. E. Hall, *A History of South-East Asia*, Macmillan, 1958.
C. A. Fisher, *South-East Asia: A Social, Economic and Political Geography*, Methuen, 1965.
G. McT. Kahin (Editor), *Government and Politics of Southeast Asia*, Cornell University Press, 1959.
W. L. Holland (Editor), *Asian Nationalism and the West*, The Macmillan Company, 1953.
R. C. Bone, *Contemporary Southeast Asia*, Random House, 1962.
A. Vandenbosch and R. Butwell, *Southeast Asia among the World Powers*, University of Kentucky Press, 1957.
Saul Rose (Editor), *Politics in Southern Asia*, Macmillan, 1963.
P. Thayer, *Southeast Asia in the Coming World*, The Johns Hopkins Press, 1954.
L. Mills and Associates, *The New World of Southeast Asia*, The University of Minnesota Press, 1949.
Saul Rose, *Socialism in Southern Asia*, Oxford University Press, 1959.
Cultural Freedom in Asia, Charles E. Tuttle Company, 1956.
P. Thayer (Editor), *Nationalism and Progress in Free Asia*, The Johns Hopkins Press, 1956.
Denis Warner, *Reporting South-East Asia*, Angus and Robertson, 1966.
Russell H. Fifield, *Southeast Asia in United States Policy*, Praeger, 1963.
W. McMahon Ball, *Nationalism and Communism in East Asia*, Cheshires, 1952.
Guy Wint, *The British in Asia*, Faber and Faber, 1947.
Claude A. Buss, *Southeast Asia and the World Today*, Van Nostrand, 1958.
B. K. Sen Gupta, *South-East Asia's Challenge*, Oriental Agency, Calcutta, n.d.
Rupert E. Emerson, *Representative Government in Southeast Asia*, Harvard University Press, 1955.

BIBLIOGRAPHY

J. D. B. Miller, *The Politics of the Third World*, Oxford University Press, 1966.
John Bastin (Editor), *The Emergence of Southeast Asia, 1511-1957*, Prentice Hall, 1967.
I. R. Sinai, *The Challenge of Modernisation*, Chatto and Windus, 1964.
Michael Brecher, *The New States of Asia*, Oxford University Press, 1963.
R. L. Watts, *New Federations Experiments in the Commonwealth*, Oxford University Press, 1966.
T. B. Millar, *The Commonwealth and the United Nations*, Sydney University Press, 1967.
Erich H. Jacoby, *Agrarian Unrest in Southeast Asia*, Asia Publishing House, 1961.
M. Zinkin, *Development for Free Asia*, Chatto and Windus, 1963.
Virginia Thompson, *Labor Problems in Southeast Asia*, Yale University Press, 1947.
Eugene Staley, *The Future of Underdeveloped Countries*, Praeger, 1954.
John H. Kautsky, *Political Change in Underdeveloped Countries*, John Wiley, 1966.
Paul E. Sigmund, Jr., *The Ideologies of the Developing Countries*, Praeger, 1964.
B. Lasker, *Human Bondage in Southeast Asia*, University of North Carolina Press, 1950.
V. Thompson and R. Adloff, *Minority Problems in Southeast Asia*, Stanford University Press, 1955.

2. COMMUNISM IN SOUTH-EAST ASIA: GENERAL

J. H. Brimmell, *Communism in South-East Asia*, Oxford University Press, 1959.
D. E. Kennedy, *The Security of Southern Asia*, Chatto and Windus, 1965.
M. D. Kennedy, *A Short History of Communism in Asia*, Weidenfeld and Nicholson, 1957.
A. Doak Barnett (Editor), *Communist Strategies in Asia*, Frederick Praeger, 1963.
F. N. Trager (Editor), *Marxism in Southeast Asia*, Stanford University Press, 1960.
Denis Warner, *Out of the Gun*, Hutchinson, 1956.
V. Thompson and Richard Adloff, *The Left Wing in Southeast Asia*, William Sloane Associates, 1950.

Brian Crozier, *South-East Asia in Turmoil*, Penguin Special, 1965.
C. E. Black and T. P. Thornton, *Communism and Revolution*, Princeton University Press, 1964.

3. COMMUNIST THEORY AND PRACTICE

V. I. Lenin, *Selected Works*, Foreign Languages Publishing House, Moscow, 1950.
David Shub, *Lenin*, Mentor Books, 1948.
Alfred G. Mayer, *Leninism*, Frederick Praeger, 1957.
P. Selznick, *The Organizational Weapon*, Rand Corporation, 1952.
Jules Monnerot, *Sociology of Communism*, Allen and Unwin, 1953.
Gabriel A. Almond, *The Appeals of Communism*, Princeton University Press, 1954.
W. R. Kintner, *The Front is Everywhere*, University of Oklahoma Press, 1955.
G. Winfield, *The Threat of Soviet Imperialism*, The Johns Hopkins Press, 1954.
Hugh Seton-Watson, *Neither Peace Nor War*, Methuen, 1960.
G. F. Hudson, *Questions of East and West*, Odhams Press, 1953.
G. L. Arnold, *The Pattern of World Conflict*, Dial Press, 1955.
Brian Crozier, *The Rebels*, Chatto and Windus, 1960.
Mao Tse-Tung, *Selected Works*, Lawrence and Wishart, 1954.
Guy Wint, *Communist China's Crusade*, Praeger, 1965.
Stuart R. Schram, *The Political Thought of Mao Tse-Tung*, Praeger, 1963.

4. GUERRILLA WARFARE: GENERAL

Mao Tse-tung and Che Guevara, *Guerrilla Warfare*, Cassell, 1962.
Vo Nguyen Giap, *People's War, People's Army*, Foreign Languages Publishing House, 1961.
Truong Chinh, *Primer for Revolt*, Frederick Praeger, 1963.
Abdul H. Nasution, *Fundamentals of Guerrilla Warfare*, Pall Mall Press, 1965.
Peter Paret, *French Revolutionary Warfare from Indo-China to Algeria*, Pall Mall Press, 1964.
Bernard Fall, *The Two Vietnams*, Pall Mall Press, 1965.
Street Without Joy, Pall Mall Press, 1961.
Robert Thompson, *Defeating Communist Insurgency*, Chatto and Windus, 1966.
Franklin P. Osanka (Editor), *Modern Guerrilla Warfare*, Free Press of Glencoe, 1964.

BIBLIOGRAPHY

Peter Paret and John W. Shy, *Guerrillas in the 1960s*, Frederick Praeger, 1964.
David Galula, *Counterinsurgency Warfare*, Pall Mall Press, 1964.
C. W. Thayer, *Guerrilla*, Michael Joseph, 1965.
Lucien Pye, *Guerrilla Communism in Malaya*, Princeton University Press, 1956.
T. E. Lawrence, *The Seven Pillars of Wisdom*, Jonathan Cape, 1940.
B. H. Liddell-Hart, 'T. E. Lawrence', In *Arabia and After*, Jonathan Cape, 1934.
Otto Heilbrunn, *Partisan Warfare*, George Allen and Unwin, 1962.
J. S. Pustay, *Counterinsurgency Warfare*, The Free Press, 1965.
Harry Eckstein (Editor), *Internal War*, The Free Press of Glencoe, 1964.
T. N. Greene (Editor), *The Guerrilla—and how to fight him*, Frederick Praeger, 1962.
Roger Trinquier, *Modern Warfare—A French View of Counterinsurgency*, Pall Mall Press, 1964.
Denis Warner, *Out of the Gun*, Hutchinson, 1956.
F. O. Miksche, *Secret Forces*, Faber and Faber, 1950.
F. Spencer Chapman, *The Jungle is Neutral*, Corgi Books.
Colin Mason, *Dragon Army*, Horowitz, 1965.
Robin Moore, *The Green Berets*, Crown Publishers, 1965.
Malcolm Browne, *The New Face of War*, Cassell, 1965.

5. VIETNAM: COLLECTIONS OF DOCUMENTS

Harold R. Isaacs, *New Cycle in Asia*, The Macmillan Company, 1947.
Allan B. Cole, *Conflict in Indo-China and International Repercussions*, Cornell University Press, 1956.
Marcus G. Raskin and Bernard Fall, *The Viet-Nam Reader*, Random House, 1965.
Robin Murray, *Vietnam*, No. 1 in the Read-In Series, Eyre and Spottiswoode, 1965.
Marvin C. Gettleman, *Vietnam: History, Documents, and Opinions*, Penguin Special, 1965.
Rima Rathausky, *Documents of the August 1945 Revolution in Vietnam*, Department of International Relations, The Australian National University, 1963.

6. VIETNAM: BACKGROUND READING

Joseph Buttinger, *The Smaller Dragon, A Political History of Vietnam*, Frederick Praeger, 1958.

BIBLIOGRAPHY

Hoang Van Chi, *From Colonialism to Communism*, Popular Library, 1964.
T. E. Ennis, *French Policy and Development in Indo-China*, Chicago University Press, 1956.
John F. Cady, *The Roots of French Imperialism in Eastern Asia*, Cornell University Press, 1954.
Donald Lancaster, *The Emancipation of French Indochina*, Oxford University Press, 1961.
Charles Robequain, *The Economic Development of French Indo-china*, Oxford University Press, 1944.
Ellen Hammer, *Vietnam Yesterday and Today*, Holt, Rhinehart and Winston, 1966.
Roger Levy, Guy Lacam, and Andrew Roth, *French Interests and Policies in the Far East*, Institute of Pacific Relations, 1941.

7. VIETNAM: THE FRENCH WAR

Bernard Fall, *The Viet-Minh Regime*, Institute of Pacific Relations, 1956.
Donald Lancaster, *The Emancipation of French Indo-china*, op. cit.
Ellen Hammer, *The Struggle for Indochina*, Stanford University Press, 1954.
Edgar O'Ballance, *The Indochina War, 1945-54*, Faber and Faber, 1966.
Jules Roy. *The Battle of Dienbienphu*, Faber and Faber, 1965.
Bernard Fall, *Street Without Joy*, Pall Mall Press, 1964.
George K. Tanham, *Communist Revolutionary Warfare: The Vietminh in Indochina*, Praeger, 1961.

Note. This select bibliography is confined to books in English. Donald Lancaster and Ellen Hammer, amongst others, contain bibliographies of the most important works in French. The writings of Philippe Devillers, Paul Mus, and Jean Lacouture are particularly important; so of course are the works of the French military.

8. VIETNAM: THE DIEM REGIME AND REVOLUTIONARY WARFARE

Denis Warner, *The Last Confucian*, Penguin Special, 1964.
Robert Shaplen, *The Lost Revolution*, André Deutsch, 1966.
Jean Lacouture, *Vietnam between Two Truces*, Secker and Warburg, 1966.
David Halberstam, *The Making of a Quagmire*, The Bodley Head, 1965.

BIBLIOGRAPHY

Wilfred G. Burchett, *Inside Story of a Guerrilla War*, International Publishers, 1965.
Bernard Fall, *Viet-Nam Witness*, Frederick Praeger, 1966.
Robert Scigliano, *South Vietnam: Nation under Stress*, Houghton Mifflin, 1963.
Weshley R. Fishel (Editor), *Problems of Freedom*, Free Press of Glencoe, 1961.
Douglas Pike, *The Vietcong*, M. I. T. Press, 1966.
Michael Field, *The Prevailing Wind*, Methuen, 1965.
Government of South Vietnam, *Violations of the Geneva Agreement*, Saigon, July 1960.
Communist Aggressive Policy, Saigon, July 1960.
Communist Aggression Against Vietnam, Saigon, July 1964.
Report of the United Nations Fact Finding Mission to South Viet-Nam, 7th December, 1963.

9. VIETNAM: THE DISPUTE IN THE WEST AND THE AMERICAN WAR

U.S. State Department, *A Threat To The Peace*, Washington, December, 1961.
Aggression from the North, Washington, February, 1965.
U.S. Information Service, *20 Questions and Answers*, 1966.
Australian Department of External Affairs, *Questions and Answers*, Canberra, May 1966.
Studies on Vietnam, August 1965.
Vietnam First Half of 1965, Canberra 1965.
New Zealand Department of External Affairs, *New Zealand Assistance to the Republic of Vietnam*, Wellington 1965.
George Carver, *The Faceless Vietcong*, Foreign Affairs, 1960.
American Friends Service Committee, *Peace in Vietnam*, Hill and Wang, 1966.
University Study Group on Vietnam, *Vietnam and Australia*, University Study Group, 1966.
Arthur M. Schlesinger, Jr., *The Bitter Heritage*, Sphere Books, 1966.
Thich Nhat Hanh, *Vietnam The Lotus in the Sea of Fire*, SCM Press, 1967.
Gerald Stone, *War without Honour*, The Jacaranda Press, 1966.
Walter Cronkite, *Vietnam Perspective*, Pocket Book Special, 1965.
Anthony Syme (Compiler), *Vietnam The Cruel War*, Horowitz, 1966.
Sibnarayan Ray (Editor), *Vietnam Seen from East and West*, Thomas Nelson, 1966.

BIBLIOGRAPHY

M. Sivaram, *The Vietnam War: Why?*, Charles E. Tuttle, 1966.
Jay Mallin, *Terror in Vietnam*, D. Van Nostrand Company, 1966.
George K. Tanham and others, *War Without Guns*, Praeger, 1966.
William Warbey, *Vietnam The Truth*, The Merlin Press, 1965.
J. F. Cairns, *Living with Asia*, Lansdowne Press, 1965.
Bernard Fall, *Vietnam*, Foreign Affairs, October 1966.
Anthony Eden Earl of Avon, *Towards Peace in Indo-China*, Oxford University Press, 1966.
Quentin L. Quade, *Vietnam—Is the Price Too High?*, Twentieth Century (Melbourne), Spring 1967.
Chester A. Bain, *Vietnam The Roots of the Conflict*, Prentice Hall, 1967.
Milton E. Osborne, *Strategic Hamlets in South Vietnam*, Cornell University Data Paper, 1965.
Victor Bator, *Vietnam, A Diplomatic Tragedy*, Dobbs Ferry, 1965.
Frank N. Trager, *Why Vietnam?*, New York, 1966.
Hans J. Morgenthau, *Vietnam and the United States*, Washington, 1965.

10. LAOS

Arthur J. Dommen, *Conflict in Laos*, Pall Mall Press, 1964.
George Modelski, *International Settlement of the Laotian Question, 1961–62*, Department of International Relations, The Australian National University, 1962.
Government of Laos, *North Vietnamese Interference in Laos*, Vientiane, December 1964.

CAMBODIA

Michael Leifer, *Cambodia and Neutrality*, Department of International Relations, The Australian National University, 1962.

THE PHILIPPINES

N. D. Valeriano and C. T. R. Bohannan, *Counterguerrilla Operations: The Philippines Experience*, Praeger, 1962.
Alvin Scarf, *The Philippine Answer to Communism*, Stanford University Press, n.d.
Luiz Taruc, *Born of the People*, International Publishers, 1953.

MALAYA

Robert Thompson, *Defeating Communist Insurgency*, Chatto and Windus, 1966.

Lucian Pye, *Guerrilla Communism in Malaya*, Princeton University Press, 1956.

BURMA

Government of Burma, *Burma and the Insurrections*, Rangoon, September, 1949.
Ministry of Information, *Insurgent Atrocities in Burma*, Rangoon, 1952.
Frank N. Trager, *Burma From Kingdom to Republic*, Pall Mall Press, 1966.
Hugh Tinker, *The Union of Burma*, Oxford University Press, 1957.

INDONESIA

Robert A. Scalapino (Editor), *The Communist Revolution in Asia*, Englewood Cliffs, N.J., 1965.
Justus M. Van der Kroef, *The Communist Party of Indonesia*, Vancouver, 1965.
Donald Hindley, *The Communist Party of Indonesia, 1951–63*, Berkeley, 1964.

INDEX

Afro-Asian nationalism and neutralism, 15
Akyat, 198
Alexander of Rhodes, 218
Algeria, 19, 158, 206
All-Burma Peasants' Organization, 108
Anglo-Burmese Treaty, 96
Annam, 220, 222
Anti-Fascist People's Freedom League (Burma), 94–6, 105, 109
Arakan, 79, 104, 194
Arnott, Professor Heinz, 43
August Revolution, 1945, 224–9, 234
Australia, 39–40, 45, 48–9, 54–5, 57–8, 69, 91, 137, 189, 266
Australian Communist Party, 39–42, 53–5, 58, 91, 93n., 144
Australian Council of Trade Unions, 53
Australian Labour Party, 53, 56, 266
Australia, strength of Trade Union movement in, 55

Baker, 'Doc', 202–3
Ban Methuet, 180–1
Bangkok, 80, 82–4, 87, 125, 167, 170–3, 197
Bao Dai, 185, 224, 231, 256
Barnett, Doak A., 40–1
Beazeley, Kim, 54
Bell, Miss Cora, 26n., 100
Bernanos, Georges, 49
Binh Dinh, 190
Boden, Scout, 195–6
Borneo, 85, 120, 194
Boxer Rebellion, 65

Brimmell, J. H., 91n., 93
Brogan, Professor Sir Denis, 28n., 71–2
'Brushfire Wars', 16–17
Buddhism, 216, 254, 256
Bulgaria, 90
Burchett, Wilfred G., 245n., 252, 255n., 256n.
Burma, 27, 70–2, 79–81, 83–7, 89, 91–100, 103–8, 122, 128–9, 136, 149, 194, 198, 201, 218, 232, 261, 265, 267
Burma Communist Party, 94–9, 104–5, 108–9, 118
Butterfield, Professor Herbert, 26–7

Cadres, 32–4, 50, 81, 108, 118, 163, 174, 179, 192, 223, 242, 245, 248
Cairns, Dr. J. F., 74: Works, *Living with Asia*, 74q.
Calcutta Conference, 91–3, 95, 109, 111, 138, 232
Cambodia, 18, 71, 81–5, 87, 123, 153, 181–3, 190, 214–15, 232, 245, 267
Canada, 91
Cao-Dai sect, 242
Carver, George, 165n., 264n.: Works, *The Faceless Victory*, 249q.
Castro, Fidel, 38, 148, 202, 264
'Causes', 49–51, 53, 58, 60, 82, 128, 149–50, 162, 174, 178, 187
Celebes, 86, 118
Chang, Sergeant, 196
'Chauvinists', 81, 85–6
Chekhov, Anton, 63
Chesterton, G. K., 63

281

INDEX

Chiang Kai-shek, Generalissimo, 229
China, 22, 26, 48, 65–6, 71–3, 75, 80, 88, 91–3, 102, 107, 126–7, 130–1, 134, 141, 145, 157–8, 162, 167, 213–14, 217, 222, 226, 248
China, Communist Party of, 53, 134–5, 225
Chinese Clandestine Communist Organization, 119
Chu-teh, 151
Clausewitz, Karl von, 132, 151, 160
'Cold War', 91, 94
Cominform, 91
Communist Review, 54
Communist Terrorists, 111–12
Corral, Señor Luiz Diez del, 66
Crosthwaite, Sir Charles, 99, 150, 201
Crypto-Communists, 42–3, 46, 131
Czechoslovakia, 91, 116, 157

Dai Viet, 230
Danang, 190, 192–3, 197
D'Argenlieu, 230–1
Darwee, Air Chief Marshal, 171
DePuy, General William, 205, 207
Devillers, Philippe, 165n., 224n., 230, 244, 248, 271
Dickinson, Goldsworthy Lowes, 64
Dien-Bien-Phu, 82, 124, 153, 161, 205, 233–4, 241
Dimitrov, George, 33
Djakarta, 57, 117, 119
'Domino Theory', 57, 83, 266
'Double standard', 48
Dulles, John Foster, 241
Dutt, Rajani Palme, 92

Economist, The, 140–1, 265
Eisenhower, President Dwight D., 266
Engels, Friedrich, 26, 35, 148, 218

Fall, Bernard, 20–1, 61, 89n., 97, 99–100, 120n., 128n., 155n., 156, 161n., 162n., 215, 222n., 228n., 233n., 237n., 249, 252–3, 269–70: Works, *The Two Vietnams*, 99–100q.
Feudalism, 63, 80, 235
France, 19, 59, 91, 219, 225, 230–3, 240
'Front' Organizations, 170–1, 179–80, 227, 235
Furnivall, J. S., 51

Galula, Colonel David, 167n., 186
Geneva Conference, 236–7, 241, 244
Giap, General Vo Nguyen, 19–20, 37, 61, 87, 120–1, 131, 141, 144, 155n., 156, 159, 169, 180, 204, 228, 230–2, 235, 238, 246, 249, 269–71
Giau, 101–2
Gibson, Ralph, 56
Goëlkhieux, Claude, 154
Goshal, H. N., 94–5
Gottwald, Klementi, 116
Gourou, Pierre, 220
Great Britain, 40
Great Britain, Communist Party of, 54, 92
Greece, 17
Guevara, Che, 148, 173

Haiphone, 230
Halberstam, David, 248, 253n.
Hanoi, 20, 22, 24, 29–30, 46, 54, 56–7, 61, 82, 126, 141–2, 158, 172, 214, 224, 226, 229–30, 232, 244–9, 265, 269
Hawaii, 58
Higgins, Benjamin, 86
Hinsley, F. H., 16, 76n.
Hoa-Hao sect, 230, 242
Hoang Van Chi, 213, 215, 222n., 229n., 230n., 239–40, 246n.: Works, *From Colonialism to Communism*, 213q.
Ho-Chi-Minh, 23, 29, 123, 190–1, 217, 222, 224–5, 238, 246, 265
Hoffman, Stanley, 17–18
Honey, P. J., 213, 217–18, 238n., 244n., 249, 253n.
Hudson, Geoffrey, 69

INDEX

Hué, 169, 192, 240, 256–7
Hukbalahaps, 50, 102, 126–9, 187
Hungary, 41, 90

I. F. Stone's Weekly, 40
India, 17, 65, 71, 74, 87–8, 91, 93, 137, 146, 265
Indian Communist Party, 95
Indian Mutiny, 65
Indo-China, 91, 113
Indo-China, Communist Party of, 59, 96, 123, 126, 178, 218, 222–4, 226–7
Indonesia, 27, 39, 52, 57, 65, 70–1, 74, 85–6, 88–9, 91, 117–18, 122, 218, 232, 261, 267
Indonesian Communist Party (PKI), 51, 57, 116–18
Industrialization, 68–9
International Control Commission, 208, 245
Iran, 23
Isaacs, Harold, 225
Israel, 17

Japan, 17, 50, 217, 221, 226, 265–6
Java, 78, 86, 116–17, 150
Johnson, President Lyndon B., 29, 40n., 264–5, 266n., 268–70
Jones, James, 194: Works, *From Here to Eternity*, 194q.
Josey, Alex, 111: Works, *Trade Unionism in Malaya*, 111q.

Kachins, 79–80, 104, 107–8, 149
Karens, 79–80, 104, 107
Kennedy, Dr. D. E., 81
Kennedy, President John F., 264–5
Khrushchev, Nikita, 131–3, 135, 139–40, 238
Kissinger, Henry, 18
Kittikachorn, Thanom, 172–3
Knopfelmacher, Dr. Frank, 43–7, 54n.
Ko Yin Gyi, 103–4
Konfrontasi, 117, 119, 121
Korea, 38, 61, 91, 116, 130, 189–90, 267
Kovacs, Bela, 90

Kuomintang, 53, 80, 91, 157, 168, 223, 229

Lacoutre, M. Jean, 99n., 150, 201, 271
Ladejinsky, Wolf, 258–9
Lamannais, Abbé, 64
Land Reform, 235, 237, 259–60
Lansdale, General, 127
Laos, 57, 71, 82–3, 85, 122–5, 142, 153, 171, 181–2, 190, 214–15, 232, 248, 258, 265, 267
Lartéguy, Jean, 154, 205
Lawrence, D. H., 64
Lawrence, T. E., 46, 143–4, 151–4, 155n., 201: Works, *Seven Pillars of Wisdom*, 46q.
Le Loi, Emperor, 219
Lee Kuan Yew, 266–7, 270
Lenin, Vladimir Ilyich, 31–2, 35n., 36–8, 53, 71, 88, 97, 100, 131–3, 137, 139, 151, 155, 166, 173, 175n., 187n., 224, 237
Les Temps Modernes, 156, 159
Lin Piao, Marshal, 139–40
Liu Shao-chi, 137–9, 237–8
Lloyd, Captain, 201–3
Lodge, Cabot, 209
Luzon, 126

Macaulay, T. B., 65
Maduin, 116–17
Magsaysay, Ramon, 64n., 113, 127–8, 168, 187, 243, 259
Malaya, 21, 27, 38, 71, 74, 81, 85, 88, 91–3, 110, 112–16, 119, 122, 127, 194, 198–9, 218, 232–3, 247, 252, 266
Malayan Chinese Association, 85
Malayan Communist Party, 49, 57, 93, 110–12, 114, 118, 187
Malaysia, 51, 266
Malraux, M. André, 20, 46n., 194, 221n.
Mao-Tse-Tung, 29–30, 32, 36, 50, 77, 98, 131, 137, 139–41, 144–5, 151–2, 153n., 155n., 156–7, 159–60, 162–3, 168, 171, 174, 179, 181, 238, 265

INDEX

Ma Paw Sein, 103-4
Marcos, Ferdinand E., 266-7
Marx, Karl, 26-7, 35, 37, 50, 73, 146, 166, 196, 218
Marxism, 56
Marxist Leninist ideology, 55-6, 134-5, 155, 239-40
McNamara, Robert S., 25
Miller, Harry, 187: Works, *Menace in Malaya*, 187q.
Mischke, F. O., 38n., 148, 158
Mitrany, Professor David, 167
Mobile Development Units, 172
Mongolia, 91
Monnerot, M. Jules, 20, 31n., 41n.
Mons, 104
Moscow, 39-42, 72, 88, 90, 96, 109, 138, 145, 247
'Movements', 221-2
Mus, M. Paul, 44, 68, 161, 215n., 235n.
Muso, 116

Narayan, Jayaprakash, 77
Nasution, General Abdul Haris, 18n., 119-21
National Liberation Front, 31, 83, 157, 217, 242, 244-6, 249, 252, 254-5
National Party of Vietnam, 222
Navarre, General Henri, 154
Neo-Colonialism, 70, 209
Neo Lao Haksat, 124, 126
Nepal, 91
Ne Win, General, 69n., 80-1, 100, 108, 128
New York Times, 91, 241n.
Nghe-An-Soviet, 171, 238
Ngo Dinh Diem, 49, 123, 197, 216, 231, 239-48, 252, 254-9, 260-2, 265
Ngo Dinh Nhu, 206, 241, 252, 254
Nguyen-Cong-Tru, 218
Nguyen van Sam, 230
Nguyen van Long, 232
Nguyen van Tay, 232
Nixon, Richard, 265-6
Norodom, Prince, 84

Pakistan, 16-17, 70-1, 79, 91, 137
Paret, Professor Peter, 19, 50, 179, 206
Pathet Lao, 82, 123-4, 126, 171, 232, 265
'Peace in Vietnam' campaign, 57
Peking, 15, 24, 29-30, 39, 56, 58, 72, 87-8, 90, 117, 129, 132, 135-8, 145, 158, 170, 172, 174, 233, 247
Peking Review, 134-5, 139
People's Courts, 97
People's Liberation Army, 162, 193, 238
People's Volunteer Organisation, 105
Perrior, Sergeant, 221
Personalism, 254
Pham Van Dong, 269-70
Philippines, 88, 91, 102, 126-8, 146, 168, 187, 243, 266-7
Philippines Communist Party, 52
Phong, Mai Xuan, 120
Pirey, Philippe de, 153, 154n.
Poland, 90
Police Field Force, 203-4
Polycentrism, 38-9
Popular Army, 159-61, 169
Pracheakorn Party, 123
Prapas, General, 170
Pridi Pahnomyang, 233
Prome, 97-9
Purcell, Victor, 113
Pye, Lucien, 116n., 129n., 146-7

Quang Ngai campaign, 245

Rahman, Tungku Abdul, 85, 266
Rangoon, 79-80, 105, 197
Rangoon Nation, 105-6, 109
Red Flag (Trotskyites), 105, 107
Republican Youth Movement, 101
Rhineland, German occupation of, 47
Rostow, Walt, 89, 168
Roumania, 90
Roy, Colonel Jules, 102, 234n., 235n.: Works, *The Battle of Dienbienphu*, 102-3q.

284

INDEX

Roy, M. N., 70-1
Russell, Lord, 48

Sabandrio, Dr., 51
Saigon, 84, 169, 181, 184, 197, 200, 212, 214, 220-2, 240, 254n., 255n., 256-8
Sandbank, Corporal, 195-6, 202
Sarawak, 119
Sawbwas, 105
Scigliano, Robert, 244n., 260
Selznick, Philip, 30n., 31n., 32n., 33, 41n., 52n., 57n., 60n., 61n., 158, 166
Seton-Watson, Professor Hugh, 53n., 90
Shans, 79-80, 104-8, 149, 194, 198
Sharkey, Lance, 91, 93
Shy, John W., 50, 179
Sihanouk, Prince, 124
Sinai, I. R., 15-16, 76n.
Singapore, 71, 85, 87, 111, 197, 261, 266
Sino-Soviet split, 39, 41, 131, 134-5, 138
Soviet Union, 22-5, 35, 67, 69, 75, 88, 117, 130-4, 139, 144-5, 156, 167, 221
Spear, Dr. Perceval, 76
Staley, Eugene, 75-6
Stalin, Joseph, 39, 88, 91, 117, 131, 133, 145, 150, 237
Stone, Gerald, 248
Subversion, 89
Sukarno, President, 51, 70, 86, 117, 119-20
Sumatra, 86, 118
Sumitro, Dr., 119
Suophanouvong, Prince, 123, 232

Taiwan, 17
Tanzania, 27
Taoism, 216
Taruc, Luiz, 102, 126, 127n., 150
Taylor, General Maxwell, 125
Taylor, James, 110-11
Technology, 68
Templer, General Sir Gerald, 113, 127

Thailand, 17-18, 27, 66, 70-2, 75, 81-3, 85, 107, 112, 142, 167-8, 170-1, 173, 177, 189, 194, 209, 232, 262, 265, 267
Thinh, Dr., 231
Thompson, Sir Robert, 21, 44n., 114n., 147, 165, 176n., 206n., 247n.
Tin Pe, Brigadier, 108
Tonking, 99, 167, 212, 220, 223, 229, 233
Toynbee, Professor Arnold, 66-7
Tran Van Dinh, 123
Tran Van Giau, 225
Trinquier, Colonel Roger, 154, 205
Trotsky, Leon, 60n., 167
Truong Chinh, 184, 186, 188-9, 222-4, 226, 228n., 230-1, 239, 244, 246
Truong, Dinh Tri, 230
Truong Tu Anh, 230
Tun, Thakin Than, 94-5
Turkey, 17

U Nu, Premier, 70, 98
United Malays' National Organization, 85
United Nations, 16, 23, 208, 236
United States of America, 16-20, 22-4, 28-30, 40, 47-8, 54, 56-8, 61, 69, 83-4, 87, 93, 127, 131, 135, 138-42, 145, 147, 157-8, 170, 182, 184, 189, 191, 202, 204, 206, 209-10, 221, 223, 225, 233-4, 241, 247-8, 253, 256, 258, 262, 264-71

Vann, Colonel John, 253
Vietcong, 18, 31, 46, 53, 55, 61-2, 68, 98, 101, 120, 124, 147, 153, 158, 162, 182-3, 189-91, 193, 195-7, 199-200, 202-5, 218, 242, 245, 247
Vietminh, 39, 43, 58, 99, 123-4, 126, 153-4, 161, 164, 171, 173n., 223-35, 241-2, 244-6, 258-9
Vietnam, North, 18, 22, 59, 61, 67, 73-4, 98-9, 101, 120-1, 124-5, 128, 141, 164, 171, 181, 189, 211,

INDEX

Vietnam, North—cont.
    213, 229, 234, 237–8, 240, 246, 248, 253, 257, 267–8
Vietnam, South, 15, 18, 22–3, 27, 29–30, 34, 37, 44–5, 47–9, 56–8, 61, 73–4, 83–4, 96–8, 100–2, 109, 115, 118, 120, 123–5, 128, 130–1, 135, 141–2, 144, 157–9, 162, 164, 168, 173n., 177, 184–5, 187, 189–90, 197, 207–15, 217, 234, 236, 240–2, 244, 247–9, 255, 257–9, 261–2, 265–8
Vongvichit Phoumi, 123

Warner, Denis, 92, 93n., 137, 153n., 248n., 253n., 256, 258n.
Wyndham, Cyril, 55–6

Yebaw Nyunt Aung, 109
Yugoslavia, 91

Zaehner, Professor, 26
Zaw, Brigadier Kyaw, 107
Zhdanov, Andrei Alexandrovitch, 91, 116
Zinkin, Maurice, 75